MY ARMY LIFE

FRANCES COURTNEY GRUMMOND CARRINGTON OF FRANKLIN, TENNESSEE
As she appeared in 1864, shortly before her marriage to Lieutenant George W. Grummond
(American Heritage Center, University of Wyoming)

MY ARMY LIFE

A SOLDIER'S WIFE AT FORT PHIL KEARNY

WITH

AN ACCOUNT OF THE CELEBRATION
of "WYOMING OPENED"

BY

FRANCES C. CARRINGTON

Introduction by John D. McDermott

Originally Published as

MY ARMY LIFE
AND THE
FORT PHIL. KEARNEY MASSACRE

PRUETT PUBLISHING COMPANY
BOULDER, COLORADO

FIRST EDITION

1 2 3 4 5 6 7 8 9

Jacket/Cover Design by Jody Chapel

Originally Published in 1910
BY J.B. LIPPINCOTT COMPANY

In Memory

OF THE

EIGHTEENTH REGIMENT UNITED STATES INFANTRY
ITS CIVIL WAR SERVICE
FROM 1861 TO 1865

AND

ITS FRONTIER INDIAN SERVICE
FROM 1865 TO 1867

PREFACE

AFTER the passing of many years, at the suggestion of interested friends, the setting down for permanent record of the narrative of my life on the Plains in 1866 was assumed and completed, though not published, but laid away for a "more convenient season."

There it has remained for two years.

Eighteen months ago, on revisiting the scenes of forty-two years past, the later experiences so supplemented the former that both are joined to complete the whole.

My visit recalled, intensified, the life in 1866. Bridging the years I seem to see again the plodding of weary but hopeful travellers journeying over a broad, desert waste, the isolation of a small defenseless caravan, and the green spots here and there like angel dwelling places.

The arrival at our destination after the dangers and risks of our journey, the completion of the strong stockade,—our temporary home,—the raising of the flag at its completion, the rehabilitation of the kaleidoscopic scenes of that long ago with the forms that were companions in that tragic experience, are even now more like the fantasies of a fearful dream than matters of personal experience.

That transient dwelling place, so strong and apparently impregnable if sufficiently defended, was deliberately abandoned by our Government through lack of soldiers sufficient for its defense, and burned by the victorious tribes.

Strangest of all is the fact that at present scarcely twenty-three miles distant from that very spot is the County Seat of Sheridan County, most intensely the reverse of every condition of life that marked the experience of the earlier narrative, and teeming with life, peace, and prosperity.

And yet all is epitomized in a simple monument, which stands on Massacre Hill, to mark the battle-field of December 21, 1866, with an explanatory tablet in memory of those who gave their lives to uphold the authority of the Government.

F. C. C.

CONTENTS

PART I.

OUTWARD BOUND.

FROM GOVERNOR S ISLAND TO FORT PHIL. KEARNEY, DAKOTA.

PART II.

OUR FRONTIER HOME.

GARRISON LIFE ENCIRCLED BY SAVAGE LIFE.

CONTENTS

PART III.
HOMEWARD BOUND.
FROM FORT PHIL. KEARNEY, DAKOTA, TO TENNESSEE.

PART IV.
AFTER MANY DAYS.
THE TRIUMPH OF PEACE.

INTRODUCTION

by John D. McDermott

TODAY, Fort Phil Kearny State Historic Site preserves
the setting and subsurface remains of what one U.S.
Army inspector reported in 1867 as the best stockaded
military post he had ever seen.* A small visitor center
hosts 20,000 travelers annually. Nearby, the state of
Wyoming also owns sections of Fetterman Battlefield
and the Wagon Box Fight Site, scenes of two of the
most dramatic encounters with the Sioux and their allies during Red Cloud's War of 1866–1868. One mile
away, automobiles rush by on Interstate 90 south to
Buffalo or north to Sheridan, and the greatly expanded
waters of Lake DeSmet serve boaters and fishermen,
while the rising Big Horn Mountains lure campers and
climbers to their heights.

In 1991, Fort Phil Kearny will celebrate its 125th anniversary. In most cases, commemorations of this kind
pass by with little more than a salute to events dimly
remembered from slight acquaintance in school his-

---

* The reader will notice that the spelling of this post is now
"Kearny," which contrasts with the "Kearney" found in *My Army
Life*. Although the post was named for Brig. Gen. Philip Kearny,
killed on September 1, 1862, during the Battle of Chantilly, Virginia,
those who lived there during its short life generally used an "e"
spelling. When queried early in the twentieth century, the army
ruled that the correct spelling should be "Kearny," which supports
the present usage. Fort Kearny, Nebraska, named for Stephen Watts
Kearny, predates the establishment of Fort Phil Kearny by eighteen
years and is the reason for the addition of the given name in reference to the Wyoming post.

tories. But because of two women, the anniversary of the establishment of Fort Phil Kearny and the fortification of the Bozeman Trail will be different. They have left us with books that bring back memories of long-dead hopes and fears and reacquaint us with the rivalries and camaraderie that made life at a military post in the mid-nineteenth century a bittersweet experience.

Unlike the standard practice in other wars, families came to share in the lives of the soldiers who fought the Indian wars, and while it may be true that army officers left us with detailed descriptions of the events of battle, their wives turned out to be the true chroniclers of life on the Indian frontier. When Lieut. Gen. William Sherman visited Fort Kearny, Nebraska, in the spring of 1866 to discuss with Col. Henry Carrington the impending march to the north, he encouraged officers' wives in the command to keep diaries so that the adventure might be recorded.

Carrington's first wife, Margaret, responded to Sherman's urging. The result was *Absaraka, Home of the Crows*, published in 1868 by J.B. Lippincott and Company of Philadelphia, leading indirectly to this volume, which makes use of Margaret's work indiscriminately. The central character in both books is Henry Beebee Carrington, husband in turn to both Margaret and Frances, and who no doubt had much to do with the writing of both volumes.

Born on March 24, 1824, in Wallingford, Connecticut, Henry Beebee Carrington came from an old New England family that included a grandfather who was for twenty-five years a partner of Eli Whitney. Graduating from Yale in 1845, Carrington taught for a year and a half at Irving Institute, founded by Washington Irving, in Tarrytown, New York. In addition to his teaching duties, he served as amanuensis for Irving in his work the *Life of Washington,* an experience that later turned him to writing his own histories of the early days of the republic. Graduating from Yale Law School in 1848, Carrington settled in Columbus, Ohio, becoming in 1850 the law partner of William Dennison, later governor of the state.

In 1851, Carrington married Margaret Irvin McDowell Sullivant. Born on May 10, 1831, in Danville, Kentucky, Margaret belonged to a family whose members had achieved state, national, and international distinction. Her grandfather was the founder of what is now Columbus, Ohio; her grand uncle and her father were noted scientists; and her second cousin was Gen. Irvin McDowell of Civil War fame. The Carringtons produced six children, only two of whom, Henry, born in 1857, and James, born in 1860, reached adulthood.

In 1857, Carrington was appointed adjutant general of the Ohio militia. Four years later, when Lincoln issued his first call for troops, Carrington hurried nine regiments across the Ohio River to save West Virginia for the Union. Shortly afterward, on May 14, he received an unsolicited appointment as colonel of the Eighteenth Infantry. However, Carrington did not join his command, remaining on special service for the duration of the war. On the other hand, his regiment was continually in combat, suffering more casualties than any other regular army unit during four years of conflict.

Carrington moved to Indianapolis, Indiana, in August 1862, where he organized the soldiery of the state, enlisting more than 100,000 men. On November 29, he was promoted to brigadier general. While he saw no service on the front lines, Carrington continued to play an important role in recruiting and supplying troops to the army and in maintaining the internal security of Indiana. In May 1865 he rejoined his regiment in Louisville, Kentucky. His instructions were to fill the ranks of the Eighteenth for service on the frontier, to replace volunteer regiments in the West. Winter found him at Fort Kearny, Nebraska, and on March 10, 1866, he received his orders to move northwest into Dakota Territory to fortify the Bozeman Trail, the shortcut to the Montana gold fields through the heartland of the Teton Sioux, the Northern Cheyennes, and their allies.

When Carrington left Fort Kearny on May 19, he became a principal player in a drama that had begun in the 1940s. One can view the history of the Rocky Mountain West between the years 1843 and 1868 as a period of initial contact and conflict between the nomads of the plains and the vanguards of white settlement. Significant overland migration began in 1843, and in the succeeding quarter-century, covered wagons were a familiar sight following the Great Platte River Road across Nebraska and Wyoming, eventually to diverge on trails to Oregon, Utah, and California.

The trails traversed land roamed by the Northern Plains Indians, and as emigration increased, conflict occurred. Travelers depleted the Indians' game, and soon hunting became difficult in regions near the emigrant road, firing resentment. In the late 1840s, the federal government ordered three posts garrisoned to guard the Oregon-California Trail—Fort Kearny in Nebraska, Fort Laramie in Wyoming, and Fort Hall in Idaho. In September 1851, Indian commissioners D.D. Mitchell and Thomas Fitzpatrick met with the Sioux, Cheyenne, Arapaho, Shoshoni, and Crow at Fort Laramie to reach some formal agreement concerning travel through the area. In return for an annual payment of $50,000 in trade goods, the Indians guaranteed whites safe passage and acknowledged the permanence of military posts in their homeland.

The first real trouble occurred in 1854, eight miles east of Fort Laramie, when Lt. John L. Grattan, twenty-nine enlisted men, and a drunken interpreter attempted to arrest a Miniconjou brave who had killed and butchered a stray cow from a Mormon caravan. When the warrior refused to give himself up, a fight ensued in which Grattan and his command perished. That battle marked the beginning of an intermittent struggle between the United States Army and the Northern Plains Indians that did not end until Lt. Col. George Armstrong Custer had made his last stand, Sitting Bull had surrendered to U.S. Army troops at Fort Buford, North Dakota, and Big Foot and his followers lay dead in the snow at Wounded Knee.

Hostilities in the north began in the early 1860s when goldseekers headed for Montana began to cut through the last, best hunting grounds of the Sioux along the eastern edge of the Big Horn Mountains. Blazed by John Bozeman in 1863, the trail struck north from the Oregon-California Trail near present-day Douglas, Wyoming, and ended in Virginia City, Montana, in the center of the gold fields.

As Carrington marched west to Fort Laramie, Indian

commissioners were attempting to convince the Sioux to sign a treaty condoning fortification of the trail. The untimely arrival of the Eighteenth Infantry led to the departure of Red Cloud and other bands, who claimed treachery and vowed to resist military intrusion. And resist they did. While Carrington garrisoned three posts, Fort Reno, Fort Phil Kearny, and Fort C.F. Smith, the troops who occupied them were virtual prisoners. One report claimed that 51 hostile demonstrations occurred in front of Fort Phil Kearny from July 26 to December 21. During the same period, 96 officers and soldiers and 58 civilians lost their lives. Ultimate disaster came near Fort Phil Kearny on December 21, 1866, when Bvt. Lt. Col. William Judd Fetterman disobeyed orders and led 80 men across Lodge Trail Ridge, where 1,500 Sioux and their allies cut them down to the last man.

When Department of the Platte Commander Philip St. George Cooke learned of the disaster, he sent Carrington packing in subzero weather to Fort Caspar and oblivion. While the press portrayed Carrington as either a milksop or a fiend, Congress called for an investigation. First to repond was President Andrew Johnson, who on February 18, 1867, appointed a Special Indian Commission to investigate the Fetterman disaster and determine how to avoid a full-scale Sioux war. Members were Gens. Alfred Sully, John B. Sanborn, and N.B. Buford; Col. Ely S. Parker; the experienced Missouri trader G.P. Beauvais; and former Fort Phil Kearny post sutler's agent, Judge John Fitz Kinney. The latter was an interesting choice, since Carrington had earned the sutler's displeasure by denying one of his claims against the government, and the two held opposing political views.

The commission convened in Omaha on March 4 and then moved west, spending thirty days at Fort McPherson taking the testimonies of Carrington and others before moving on to Fort Sedgwick and Fort Laramie. The group split up on May 8, with Sully and Parker going to the Upper Missouri to visit various bands of Sioux and Kinney returning to Fort Phil Kearny to meet with the Crows. While at Fort Phil Kearny, Kinney took the testimony of Capt. James Powell, who had been at the post on December 21. In a most remarkable statement, dated July 24, 1867, Powell claimed that he had managed the entire defense of Fort Phil Kearny, taking charge at Carrington's request, and it was he who had armed citizen employees and sent Capt. Ten Eyck out to see what had happened to Fetterman. Why Powell's testimony was so blatant a lie, "a stupendous tissue of falsehoods," one fellow officer called it, is hard to determine. One writer has suggested that Powell, who was later judged insane, was already mentally ill. Whatever the case, Kinney used it to discredit Carrington, sending the testimony directly and privately to Gen. Grant.

None of the commissioners in their official reports found Carrington culpable. Sanborn was perhaps the most articulate in stating the problem when he wrote in his report of July 8, 1867: "The difficulty in a nutshell was that the commanding officer of the district was furnished no more troops or supplies for this state of war than had been provided and furnished in a state of profound peace. In regions where all was peace, as at Laramie in November, twelve companies were stationed, while in regions where all was war, as at Phil

Kearny, there were only five companies allowed."

The army conducted its own investigation, convening a military court of inquiry by Special Order 128, Headquarters U.S. Army, March 13, 1867. The court heard testimony at Fort McPherson and forwarded the document without findings. Grant reviewed the record and recommended that a court-martial convene, but Judge Advocate General Joseph Holt decided not to pursue the matter because of certain procedural technicalities.

After completing his testimony, on May 27, 1867, Carrington applied for six months leave. Carrington gave as his reason the need to recuperate from a wound received on February 6, 1867, when his pistol discharged while he was riding rapidly to close up a wagon train. The ball had entered the left thigh, injuring the sciatic nerves, and he could only walk with the aid of a cane. At the same time, he also needed to plead his case in Washington. He had learned of Powell's testimony through his friend, Secretary of the Interior Orville Browning, and accusations against him were growing in the Congress, where some anonymous letters condemning him had been published as part of a report of the Indian Bureau in Senate Executive Document No. 13, 40th Congress, 1st session. His plan was to obtain permission to publish his official report of the Fetterman Fight, in which he had noted the lack of reinforcements and other extenuating circumstances.

Upon his arrival in the nation's capital, Carrington went to see Secretary of War Stanton. Declaring that he had nothing to do with such matters, Stanton referred him to the General of the Army. In his conversation with Grant, Carrington offered to prefer charges against

Powell, but Grant simply referred him back to Stanton, saying that the latter had the authority to settle the matter. The colonel was not aware that Grant had just recommended Powell for a brevet as the commander of the Wagon Box Fight of August 2, 1867, a resounding victory over the Sioux by a small detachment armed with the breech-loading weapons Carrington had repeatedly requested. In the end, Carrington recognized the futility of his position and looked for other ways to get his story before the public. The vehicle for apologia was *Absaraka*.

Carrington later wrote to a friend that Margaret had written the book at the suggestion of Governor Dennison of Ohio, but obviously the publication of a history of service at Fort Phil Kearny would give the much-maligned colonel an opportunity to present his side of the story. Wisely, Carrington requested and received Sherman's imprimatur. Dedicating the book to the general provided the opportunity for publicly indicating his approval. Sherman's correspondence following the Fetterman disaster shows him to be of mixed feelings concerning Carrington and his abilities, and it maybe that by this time he had tempered his views to the extent that he believed Carrington deserved a hearing.

No doubt exists that Henry Carrington assisted in the writing of *Absaraka*. As to how much he contributed, it is difficult to surmise. One of Carrington's subordinates and perhaps his worst enemy, William Bisbee, wrote in a reminiscence that the book, "under the alleged authorship of Mrs. Carrington," revealed "much evidence of the Colonel's style in diction and larger knowledge of the subject matter than a woman could ordinarily possess."

Whatever the degree of authorship by Carrington, the book is a full defense of his actions and repeatedly makes the point that he had been left dangling without promised support. For example, Margaret writes:

> It was a matter of notoriety and fact that, while the officers were anxious for repeating arms or breach-loaders, only old styles of rifles were on the way, and also that ammunition, not more than four or five months previously started from Leavenworth was resting itself at some place not disclosed to the white warriors of Absaraka. Then the reinforcements had not come. . .

In the second edition of *Absaraka*, published in 1869, Carrington included, with Sherman's permission, his January 3, 1867, report of the Fetterman disaster, the report that the Congress had twice requested from the War Department but had not yet received. The report, in fact, did not appear in an official document until 1887, when Carrington's political friends were able to get it published as Senate Executive Document No. 33 of the 50th Congress, 1st session. Issued in 1878, the third edition of Margaret's book was entitled *Absaraka, Land of Massacre; being the Experience of an Officer's Wife on the Plains. With an Outline of Indian Operations and Conferences from 1865–1878. By Colonel Carrington, Revised, Enlarged and Illustrated with Maps, Cuts, Indian Portraits, etc.* Lippincott and Company produced seven editions in all, the last appearing in 1896. Each varied somewhat in title and supplementary material provided by Carrington.

It is quite interesting in retrospect that the most appealing person in *Absaraka* is Frances Grummond, within three years to become the second Mrs. Carrington. Born on January 14, 1845, Frances Courtney Grummond was a dark, Southern beauty, the youngest daughter of Robert and Eliza J. (Haynes) Courtney, a Virginia family relocated in Franklin, Tennessee. Steadfastly loyal to the Union, the family earned commendation from the United States Army by nursing 200 wounded soldiers following the Battle of Franklin on November 30, 1864, until federal troops reoccupied the city eighteen days later. During George Washington Grummond's military service in Tennessee, he and Frances became acquainted, and on August 3, 1865, they were married at Frances' home. We learn in *Absaraka* that Grummond had joined the Eighteenth Infantry as a second lieutenant on May 7, 1866. Reaching Fort Phil Kearny in mid-September, Grummond eventually commanded the Mounted Infantry, and it was in that role that he went to his death three months later, on December 21, 1866.

At one point in *Absaraka*, Margaret writes of Frances, "the Christian fortitude and holy calmness with which Mrs. Grummond looked upward to her Heavenly Father for wisdom and strength, inspired all with something of her same patience to know the worst and meet its issues." Pregnant, plucky, devout, considerate of the feelings of others, Frances seemed to embody all the desired qualities of Victorian America. For Phil Kearny courier John "Portugee" Phillips loved her, and so do we. His volunteering to ride to Fort Laramie with word of the Fetterman disaster was prompted by his desire to save her from harm. By association we like her husband, George Washington Grummond, a dashing hotblood, anxious for combat, who died with his boots on with Fetterman's command.

The publication of *Absaraka*, while important to Carrington's peace of mind, was too late to affect his military career. The whole episode had passed into history. While troops were successful in fights near Fort C.F. Smith (the Hayfield Fight) and Fort Phil Kearny (the Wagon Box Fight) on August 1 and 2, 1867, the army decided to abandon the Bozeman Trail, giving priority to the protection of the Union Pacific Railroad across southern Wyoming. In August 1868, the last troops left, and Red Cloud's will had prevailed.

Never one to sit still for long, Carrington found new channels for his creative energy. On Christmas Day 1869, he stepped off the train at Crawfordsville, Indiana, to begin a career as professor of military science at Wabash College. He was commandant of cadets, gymnastic instructor, and lecturer on subjects ranging from military science to architecture to temperance. Before he became settled in his work, however, tragedy struck. Margaret died on May 11, 1870. Burial was in the Green Lawn Cemetery in Columbus, beside four of her children. In November, a retirement board found Carrington unfit for active service, ending whatever hope he may have had of rejuvenating his career.

Margaret's death prompted a letter from an old acquaintance—Frances Grummond. Frances had returned to Franklin, Tennessee, in March 1867 with her husband's remains. On a visit to Cincinnati in 1868, she had discovered and read *Absaraka*, learning that Carrington taught at Wabash College. Seeing the announcement of the death of a Mrs. Carrington, she wrote to learn if it was, indeed, the wife of the former Fort Phil Kearny commander. As Frances described it, "correspondence ensued that resulted in our marriage," which occurred on April 3, 1871. Frances now had a son, William Wands, born four months after Grummond's death, on April 15, 1866. Later adopted by Carrington, William died at age thirty-one.

One of the things that Frances had learned upon her return to Franklin was that her first husband had been previously married. On February 22, 1855, Grummond had married Delia Elizabeth Shannon in Buffalo, New York. Born of the union were two children, George Welnot (1859) and May Evangeline Amelia (1863). The first wife upon reading of the Fetterman disaster in the newspapers had put in a claim for the body.

Further investigation proved that not only was Grummond previously married, his divorce was not final when he wed Frances. The first union officially ended August 23, 1865, twenty days after he had married wife number two, thus George Washington Grummond was a bigamist. The whole story came out when both wives applied for pensions for their children by him. W.B. Bailey, attorney for the Pension Bureau, resolved the predicament when he ruled that both marriages were legitimate. The second was valid because the laws of Dakota Territory recognized cohabitation for twelve months as a binding union, and George and Frances had lived together for a year following August 23.

Henry and Frances Carrington had a good life in Crawfordsville. The colonel kept busy. Besides his teaching duties, he exercised his skills as an architect, designing the Polytechnic Gymnasium, city hall, and other buildings. Active in the affairs of town and county, he appeared on patriotic programs in every section of the state. Frances was a great favorite in Crawfordsville musical circles as a soprano soloist. The couple's three children were born during this period: Robert Chase (1872), Henrietta (1874), and Eliza Jane (1875).

Beginning in 1873, the Wabash trustees repeatedly refused to appropriate college funds to support the chair of military science, and the government would not grant extra pay for the assignment. Consequently, in 1878, the military ordnance was withdrawn, and Carrington's job was quietly ended. From then on, Carrington devoted himself solely to writing. In 1875 D. Appleton & Company of New York published his *Battles of the American Revolution, 1775–1781*, probably his chief literary accomplishment, still in print today.

In 1882, the family moved to Boston, where Carrington was in charge of the educational works of A.S. Barnes & Co. Three years later, the Carringtons moved to Hyde Park, where they lived in a big, roomy house with a library on the ground floor and a big attic study. Late in life, Carrington served the federal government in work with Indian tribes. In 1889, he negotiated a treaty with the Flathead Indians of Montana for the sale of their lands in the Bitterroot Valley, and two years later personally conducted their removal to their new home in the Jocko Valley. In 1890, he visited the 1,009 families of the Six Nations of New York, surveying and mapping their reservations.

Forty years after the abandonment of Fort Phil

Kearny, the citizens of Sheridan and Buffalo, Wyoming, planned a dedication for a monument marking Fetterman Battlefield and invited the Carringtons to attend. They accepted. During the celebration on July 3–4, 1908, both husband and wife had the opportunity to speak of those early days. Henry had his chance to defend himself in public, and at the Sheridan Library he left a typewritten manuscript in which he excerpted documents and stated his case in full.

The reunion in Sheridan had inspired Frances to work on her memoirs, and she had nearly finished the manuscript at the time of the celebration. In 1910, she saw it published by J.B. Lippincott Company. Carrington later revealed that funding for the project had come from William Daley, who as a young man had helped to construct the flagstaff for Fort Phil Kearny. Within a year, Frances was dead, apparently succumbing to cancer. Confined at least once in a sanitorium during her last nine months, she died on October 17, 1911, and now lies by her husband in Hyde Park Cemetery. Henry died on October 26, 1912.

Entitled *My Army Life and the Fort Phil Kearney Massacre. With an account of the Celebration of "Wyoming Opened,"* the first 217 pages of the book covers the story of life at Fort Phil Kearny until Frances and the Carringtons left for Fort Caspar on January 23, 1867, thus duplicating the material covered in *Absaraka*. In fact, the first two-thirds of the book are in part a shameless job of copying, with some rewriting and some new material inserted. The last third of the book, 97 pages, treats the Carringtons' return to Sheridan and the 1908 celebration.

If *Absaraka* is an apologia for Henry Carrington, *My Army Life* is his vindication. Here the whole story as he saw it is revealed: the suppression of his report and testimony, the role of Grant in determining his fate, and the confrontations with Cooke and Powell. Here too one finds much self-congratulation on the part of those who survived the ordeal and see their former wilderness a community of thriving farms and ranches.

Knowing about her initial marital problem, the reader will be interested to see how Frances treats her first husband. We know now that bigamy was only one of Grummond's transgressions; he was, in fact, a man who continually broke the rules of convention and his calling. It is difficult to tell how much Frances knew of Grummond's previous life. In any event, she chooses to tell us nothing.

In many respects, George Washington Grummond was the most willful of the officers who served at Fort Phil Kearny, and his disregard of common sense made him perhaps its most dangerous defender. Born in Marine City, Michigan, in 1834 to one of the state's oldest families, Grummond was destined for a life of controversy, violence, and tragedy. In society, he was considered genial, and those who knew him casually held him in high esteem, but Grummond proved to have an uncontrollable temper, brought to the fore when drinking, and on occasion his rages threatened his own life and those with whom he came in contact.

Apparently he was the younger brother of Stephen B. Grummond, who became the owner of a steamship line and operator of one of the largest lines of tugs on the Great Lakes and mayor of Detroit in his eighties.

George Grummond appears in Detroit directories from 1857 on as a sailor. When the Civil War broke out in April 1861, he was serving as first sergeant of the Light Guard Company, the city's most notable military organization. On April 16, 1861, the unit offered itself in a body to become Company A of the First Michigan Regiment of three-month troops, and, as first sergeant, Grummond, then aged twenty-seven, was the fourth man to sign the roll. The three-month troops disbanded on August 7, and upon reorganization of the regiment on September 12, he earned commission as a captain. In 1862, while serving with his command in the Pennisular Campaign, he contracted a severe illness, causing him to resign his commission at Harrison's Landing on July 14. Eight months later, on March 9, 1863, he joined the reorganized Fourteenth Michigan as a major and in six weeks earned promotion to lieutenant colonel.

As a combat officer during the Civil War, Grummond led the troops in several bloody conflicts, including the Battle of Bentonville, North Carolina, on March 19, 1865, where the Fourteenth particularly distinguished itself. Leaping out of its breastworks, the regiment made a gallant charge against superior numbers, taking many prisoners and capturing one general officer and the colors of the Fortieth North Carolina Infantry. When the commander of the Fourteenth received orders to join his regiment in the Regular Army on June 23, 1865, Grummond took charge. He was mustered out on July 18.

On the surface, Grummond's record appeared noteworthy. In writing a recommendation for him, his commander, Col. Henry Mizner, stated that the veteran campaigner was the most proficient officer in his command, leading his men into action rather than driving them, and displaying conspicuous gallantry during the Battle of Bentonville. However, a closer look reveals a series of transgressions that prophesied a stormy future. A series of brutal acts while intoxicated earned Grummond the hatred of his junior officers. On August 17, 1864, eight of them petitioned the assistant adjutant general of the Department of the Cumberland, requesting an investigation to determine whether Grummond was fit to command. The letter detailed numerous offenses committed between August 22, 1863, and July 6, 1864. Among them were repeated drunkenness on duty in the presence of the enemy, shooting at a fellow officer who was in the process of complying with an order, pistol whipping a sergeant, brutally beating a private, and shooting in the breast an unarmed, aged civilian of Columbus, Tennessee, whom he then denied medical attention. At midnight on June 26, 1864, in a drunken rage, he had ordered his men to storm the heights at Kenesaw Mountain, Georgia. Only a ruse by Cpl. Patrick Walsh of Company B deterred him from this suicidal act. Climbing above him, Walsh pelted the officer with gravel, convincing his, by this time, not-too-perceptive commander that the little stones were enemy bullets.

As a result of the petition, Grummond appeared before a general court-martial, which found him guilty of threatening to shoot a junior officer and of shooting an unarmed civilian. His punishment was a public reprimand, the written form of which was read at dress parade to every regiment and detachment of the Second Division of the Army of the Cumberland.

Another who was unappreciative of Grummond's behavior during the Civil War was his wife, Delia, who sued him for divorce in Wayne County Court, Detroit. The grounds were that he had "grossly, wantonly, and cruelly refused and neglected to provide" suitable maintenance for his family *in absentia*. In the divorce decree, the court ordered him to pay two thousand dollars alimony within one year, a staggering sum in those times, which may help to explain the fact that while at Fort Phil Kearny Grummond was borrowing money from the enlisted men in his company. This practice, which violates an officer's principal taboo, was discovered when Pvts. John Burke and John Murphy petitioned the Adjutant General of the Army on January 10, 1867, to secure payment of the money owed them by Grummond from his estate. In retrospect, Grummond's erratic behavior in a skirmish with Sioux on December 6 and his final reckoning were simply concluding episodes in a life of recklessness that could only end in tragedy.

How does *My Army Life* stand the test of time? Research in recent decades has corrected the record in some respects. For example, Portugee Philips was not the only messenger sent to Fort Laramie, being accompanied by Daniel Dixon and others at various points. And we know a great deal more about some of the characters in the drama and their motivation, Grummond being a good example. In the end, the volume remains an important account of the life of an officer's wife on the western frontier and an embodiment of values held by those who comprised the greater family of the United States Army in the nineteenth century.

PART I
OUTWARD BOUND
FROM GOVERNOR'S ISLAND TO FORT PHIL. KEARNEY, DAKOTA

CHAPTER I.

AT the close of the Civil War all volunteer regiments that had been employed on the Plains against Indian aggression, including the Minnesota Territory, which had been a theatre of active war, were ordered to be mustered out, and pending the reorganization of the regular army the frontier was but feebly guarded.

The Eighteenth Infantry, having three battalions but depleted by active service, was ordered from the Army of the Cumberland to be recruited to its maximum and sent beyond the Missouri River.

Upon reaching Fort Leavenworth, Kansas, the First Battalion was detached for service on the lower line westward. Headquarters were established at Fort Kearney, Nebraska, its commander having jurisdiction along the Platte and Republican Rivers. In the month of December, 1865, the command reached Fort Kearney in a great snow-storm.

The winter was spent in frequent minor operations against the Indians of that section while having the cordial support of Pe-ta-la-sha-ra (Chowee Band), a noted chief of the Pawnee Tribe, which at that time occupied the reservation near the growing town of Columbus, in Nebraska, then a territory. Four companies from his tribe were organized and

15

mustered into service as scouts, then known as "Pawnee Scouts," and placed under command of Major North.

Major North, after the muster out of his battalion, became universally known as the drill-master of many of his old command who afterward formed a part of the great travelling show under the general charge of William Cody, who at that time was in army service as a guide and scout at the moderate pay of $5.00 per day.

With the approaching spring of 1866 plans had matured for building the Union Pacific Railroad from Omaha westward, and General Carrington was charged with the special duty of making careful surveys of the Platte River as far eastward as Grand Island, with a view to the possibility of a safe crossing of the river at that point, so that the railroad might go westward along the south side.

In May, 1866, the expedition left Fort Kearney, fully equipped for opening a wagon route for future peaceful settlement of the new country beyond; the entire force, including recruits, to be largely distributed at western posts to replace mustered out volunteers. Nineteen hundred recruits were added to less than three hundred veterans; all but eight companies of the Second Battalion being ordered to occupy forts from Fort Sedgwick westward to Salt Lake and Fort Bridger, leaving the Second Battalion of eight companies as the sole force with which to open the proposed wagon route around the Big Horn Mountains to Montana, through a country most fruitful in game but occupied chiefly by Indians who were as hostile as Red Cloud himself to the military movement, and who defied the proposed peace arrangements at Fort Laramie in the following June and actually went on the war-path.

Careful abstract of public document No. 33, of the First Session of the Fiftieth American Congress gives abundant proof that the expedition itself, while not in harmony with treaties made with the Indians by Generals Harney and Sanborn in 1865, was systematically conducted in accordance with written instructions from Lieutenant General Sherman to "avoid a general Indian war if possible," and methods of conciliation were carried to the utmost possible extent, while the courage and zeal of officers and men never wavered in duty to the flag, however powerful the assailants, when life itself became the price of its successful defense.

The expedition took up its tedious march to that country, a country originally owned by the Crow Indians,—always friendly to the whites,—who had long resisted its despoilment by the hostile Sioux, marching onward over alkaline waste, through numberless buffalo herds, with dried sage bush and buffalo chips for fuel, and passing the carcasses of cattle, called Mormon milestones from the cattle lost in their western migration, and halting at Laramie in June while the great Conference between the assembled tribes was in session, as will be noticed later in the progress of the narrative.

When hostilities between the North and South had ceased many officers of high rank, brevet or otherwise, secured commissions in the Regular Army, although of much lower grade than those held by them in the Volunteer Service. Attracted by the life of the soldier, these men, after years of service for their country, were reluctant to return to purely civil life and thereby practically begin life anew. Captains, majors, and even generals, were commissioned as lieutenants in the Regular Service, it being a life appointment, somewhat reversing the process at the beginning of the war when officers were gradually advanced from the lowest grades to regimental and even brigade commands.

My husband was one of these. Responding to the first call upon his native State, he became a captain of infantry and was later promoted and transferred to another regiment as lieutenant-colonel. Eventually he not only served through the Atlanta Campaign but marched with Sherman to the sea. After the Battle of Bentonville, North Carolina, he was recommended by his superior officers to a brevet as brigadier-general "for gallant and meritorious services in that action."

When the war actually closed, renewed acquaintance led to my marriage with Colonel Grummond, who a few months later was commissioned as lieutenant in the Eighteenth U. S. Infantry, under the command of Colonel Henry B. Carrington, who was already on the march for the Plains.

While awaiting orders to report for duty, at my home in Tennessee, preliminary preparations were made by the packing of trunks to be ready for departure westward at a moment's notice.

When orders actually reached us, it was found that our first destination was Governor's Island, New York Harbor, and my first introduction to army life, in time of peace, began there in 1866.

I knew instinctively that if I were to emulate the devotion and self denials of other army women I had much to learn, and I began its alphabet without dissent, if not with enthusiastic assent.

My first experience, common to soldiers' wives, was to understand distinctly that upon reaching a given place there was no certainty of protracted rest, but that successive orders might almost immediately require change, so that army women must learn to make the necessary adjustments in an incredibly short time.

It is the purpose of this narrative to give facts that may be more or less suggestive to those who read between the lines, rather than to pause and enlighten the reader by philosophising upon the incidents of such life experiences.

In this instance I had no sooner become initiated in my boarding-house arrangements, with trunks unpacked and necessaries, as well as nicknacks, disposed in the most favorable places suggestive of home enjoyment, than orders came to proceed to Vicksburg, Mississippi, as my husband and several other officers were placed in charge of detachments of recruits for distribution from that station.

The transit from New York was uneventful, except for the intense heat, while the cars, crowded as they were by the compactness of the men and their equipments, brought only discomfort and remediless fatigue. Still, the prospect of changing from these cars to a Mississippi steamer was cheering, and we could almost imagine the white craft at anchor, or at the landing, awaiting our approach with the promise of a sail down the Mississippi where grateful breezes would temper the heated atmosphere. The very thought of it was refreshing!

The trip to the steam-boat, however, may be illustrated by the story of a threatened ferry disaster, where pandemonium reigned supreme for a short season, and unmanageable horses, intensified by the cries of nervous women passengers, were parts of the scene incident to the occasion. There was one quiet woman who sat apparently unmoved by imminent danger from the heels of a horse. The bit was held with a firm grip by the driver who was swearing as if he had served apprenticeship with the army mule. When he was remonstrated with for swearing in the presence of ladies we were surprised to hear this particular lady remark, ''Don't stop him, he is the only one doing justice to the occasion.'' One may not approve of swearing, but when we finally reached the wharf, our starting point, and took in the situaticn, the real one, with scarcely a breath of air stirring on land or river, on a hot, dazzling July morning, if there were emphatic expressions from any of our company at the prospect I do not recall making any protest against them. Certainly the river did not suggest ''Minnehaha,'' ''laughing water,'' in its midsummer condition as I stood upon the landing watching the embarkation of our detachment, ordered to Vicksburg in time of peace. The steamer, which had been utilized for the transportation of troops, had been recently disinfected and painted, so that though ours was not a fancied pleasure trip, might it not prove after all more comfortable than the immediate outlook indicated?

"All aboard!"

The gang-plank once withdrawn, we were soon mid-stream, and I retired to my stateroom to make myself more comfortable for the journey. The first discovery was that the transom, as well as the outer door, stuck fast. Vain was the endeavor to counteract the effect of that paint. No human power could alleviate its stickiness, and the problem of enduring, without curing, was left for future solution. No other stateroom was available, as I had choice of the best at the start, being the only woman passenger on board. My discomfort was only beginning, as other discoveries quickly disclosed. The nettings around the berths were like a cloudy drapery, charged with intense heat, and the mosquitoes swarmed in countless numbers, ready to begin their nightly attack. Though the river had been poetically styled "The Father of Waters" from time immemorial, it was more literally interpreted, by experience, as the prolific "Mother of Mosquitoes." If they had possessed the qualifications for business that others of a later date were credited with, I doubt if I should now be recording their ravages on my defenseless body. The sole

relief was to sit for a few brief moments at a time
at the bow of the steamer where occasionally a slight
breeze was felt, but even this was so conducive to
sleep that the very effort to keep awake made one
positively miserable. It was simply existence, with
no joy to anticipate the dawn, for that heralded
another day of intense heat, with no welcome for
the setting sun and no suggestion of repose or relief
from this persistent mosquito pest.

I confess to utter lack of patriotic impulse or
fervor, when the morning of the Fourth of July
dawned, as we slowly sailed down the sluggish river.
The pen cannot adequately describe this journey in
all its details. The brush would be equally ineffective. There was not life or energy sufficient for
posing, if such a medium for delineation had been
offered. Perhaps Mark Twain might give a humorous turn to the situation from familiarity with river
travel in his earlier years, and yet, more consonant
with my own feelings, Dante might prove equal to
the task and add another circle to his "Inferno,"
with the description of a real rather than an "imaginary journey."

The historical siege of Vicksburg itself counted
for naught at that time in comparison with our
siege on the journey thither. General Grant could
not have been more anxious to terminate hostilities,
nor indeed that devoted city itself, than were we
when the city "set on a hill" loomed up before us.

"Every lane has its turning," "every journey
has its ending," every steam-boat has its landing,
and so did ours, and at last we disembarked to enter

the garrison in various mental moods and stages of physical suffering, *hors de combat,* every soul of us.

Being tired, hungry, and thirsty is the probable reason why the first object of interest that greeted my eye on entering the post was a fig-tree, a novelty surely, as my knowledge hitherto had included only the packed variety. The development of *this* specimen had passed beyond the leafy stage, and I partook of some of its unpalatable fruit, an arrested development probably, and for all practical purposes the tree might well have been withered leaves, branch, and root with no great loss.

Compensation was, however, in store for us in the gracious reception accorded by General Nathan A. M. Dudley and his charming wife, who made our sojourn delightful, seconded as it was by the other officers and their wives, who contributed to the pleasant social amenities of garrison life and made us forget, for the time being, our misery, as "waters that have passed away."

All bore part in restoring the mental equilibrium, however tardy the process might be from a purely bodily point of view. Recovering so much of former elasticity of spirits as possible under this pleasant environment, with the aid of headquarters friends, I felt equal to the pleasant task of singing some of the old songs I had sung in the long ago, with a conscious reciprocal pleasure on the part of those who so kindly ministered to my comfort.

Mrs. Dudley was the possessor of some beautiful white pigeons of which she was very proud, and they were an unfailing source of pleasure. Their proximity, as they fed from her hand, produced far different sensations than did those winged things that had so recently occupied my entire attention.

Reluctantly we parted with our genial hosts and retraced our steps to the landing, where we found a much more comfortable steamer for our return to St. Louis, there to await orders for further movement. These reached us without delay, and we exchanged both steamers and rivers, continuing our journey up the Missouri to Fort Leavenworth, Kansas.

CHAPTER II.

IT was my good fortune during our sojourn at Fort Leavenworth to be domesticated temporarily in the house of an officer of General Hancock's staff. His wife was a charming little German woman who could not speak a word of English, and, being unacquainted with German myself, our conversation was carried on mainly by a sort of sign language in quite a primitive manner. It was sufficient, however, to indicate our mutual kindly feeling and interest, as she, in social hours, drank her mild beer and kept industriously at work at her knitting, while I, for want of a beer taste and inclination, was relegated to lemonade and fancy work.

This respite doubtless strengthened me in a measure, at least, for future activities immediately at hand.

When the hour arrived for my departure, this sympathetic, considerate friend, on bidding good-by, handed me two "Prayer Books," a "Life of Benjamin Franklin," and one of "Thaddeus of Warsaw" for my diversion along the way. Possibly she did not know the Prayer Books as such, and that they might prove otherwise than a diversion on the journey. And then, on the turbid Missouri, my husband and myself were bound for Omaha, not the Omaha of to-day with its teeming population and commercial importance, but an

ordinary river town ambitious to become the gateway to a future magnificent State.

We Americans already treat as a matter of
course the union of the two oceans by the construction of the Panama Canal, and cease to wonder at
such a mighty project, but at the close of the Civil
War the idea of uniting the Atlantic slope to the
Pacific slope by rail had not been conceived, but its
execution was put in hand, through the construction
of the Union Pacific Railroad from Omaha as its
initial point, conceded by all concerned to be a
great step in national expansion and a colossal event
in the history of American railroad enterprise.
That wizard of practical science, the civil engineer,
had faith, ability, and the backing of patriotic citizens with ample money at their command, so that
if he did not remove the Rocky Mountains he went
over them and through them, until he constructed
a steel railway to transport a resistless tide of
humanity westward, such as never before had been
deemed within the reach of many coming generations. And if, as has been stated, there lingered in
the public mind at the close of the Civil War the
possibility of the far west being dissatisfied with a
Union of States so entirely cut off from compen-
satory advantages by high mountain barriers and
broad barren plains that it would also secede from
the old Union and form an independent government
of its own, it remains a fact that to the patriotism
of a few rich men who furnished the capital, and not
alone to the Government, we are largely indebted for
this gigantic enterprise.

The Government did indeed vote a subsidy in land, and issued bonds to the company at the rate of $16,000.00 per mile across the plains and $45,000.00 per mile across the mountains; and now, instead of one road, as then anticipated, we have three transcontinental lines, all built within the memory of the writer, who had the unique experience of being the only woman passenger on the first passenger train that went over the newly-laid track, nearly one hundred miles west from Omaha.

And so, upon leaving Fort Leavenworth, we embarked for the untried future, whatever that might prove to be, and any calculations, based upon former experiences, were of no avail whatever. Our initiation, however, was not long delayed. Even before we reached the terminus of the new track, to exchange our means of conveyance, a wrecked construction train impeded further progress and we were forced to halt, high, and very dry, for one entire day, "waiting for things to come to pass," and, "more than twenty miles from a lemon." I felt, perhaps not unworthily, the experience and attitude of "patience on a monument," so I endured the ordeal, while patient hands extricated us from our dilemma.

One can imagine the physical discomfort to a lone woman stranded on the broad open plain, minus the present every-day conveniences of tank and toilet, so indispensable to comfort in travel.

The monotony of our first ambulance ride, after leaving the railroad, was absolutely barren of interest, and in view of our later experience with the

27

Platte River, of which we had no previous warning, I have never understood exactly how we actually crossed it in company with several emigrant wagons, wholly oblivious of its hidden mysteries and manifold dangers, unless the very change from the other modes of travel made the ambulance ride a consoling hint that we were actually on the way to our destined goal.

We passed through, or rather by, old Fort Kearney, once a famous frontier post, which had been left in the charge of an Ordnance Sergeant soon after the Eighteenth Infantry had left its barracks early in the summer for their western expedition to Montana, which we were about to join, and began to realize that "thus far" we were still within the limits of civilized occupation, but practically on its very frontier. Little "Dobey Town," dignified by the ambitious *sobriquet* of Kearney City, only three miles west from the fort and long known as an Overland Stage Station, was left behind without regret, and with eager anticipations we hastened toward Fort McPherson, the first army post along the great stretch of land that separated us from our journey's end.

CHAPTER III.

" Thus far" had chiefly embraced river travel,
with very little railroad experience, and the import
of these laconic words is more or less familiar to
the soldier enlisted for war, but what imagination
can adequately convey their meaning to a young
woman just celebrating her first marriage anniversary and starting on her first sentimental and sensational journey across the trackless plains, with
her husband, to join his command, more than a
thousand miles distant, and through the heart of a
hostile Indian country with a mail party made up of
an escort of six men, with two ambulances and one
wagon for baggage!

With this small personal outfit, gradually augmented from ranches along the roadway, we began
our real journey across the Plains to "Absaraka,"
now called Wyoming, the old "Home of the
Crows." *

Some ranchmen were sufficiently hospitable to
give us a night's lodging, but at other times the
ambulance proved to us a bed indeed. With straw
pillows and army blankets as accessories to the
necessary outfit we had to make ourselves comfort-

---

* The ancestral abode of the Crow Indian tribe.

able. Our camp was invariably along the river side
and possessed its novel but uninteresting features.
The air was salubrious and conducive to sleep after
each day's march, but the fear of rattlesnakes caused
disturbance in sleep, as well as vigilance by the
camp-fire.

The purchase of supplies at ranches for variety
of *menu* consisted of canned goods and bread and
greatly simplified the preparation of meals, fortunately for me, in the absence of knowledge in the
culinary art. Our fuel consisted of whatever we
could find of a combustible nature, and at times we
utilized buffalo chips as well as dried sage-brush
of the last year's growth.

At one of the ranches where we were accorded
entertainment for a night or more, near the point
where the stage struck off on the overland route to
Denver, we found several travellers quite diverse in
character, dress, and manners.

An Indian, "Wild Bill" by name, first elicited
my attention as the first Indian I had seen, and he
was in full Indian trappings. His appearance was
alarming, as his very dress suggested the war-path,
although for the time being a friendly specimen.
Whether as prophet or seer, or merely conscious of
the present impression he was making, he did make
certain statements as to the movements of Indians
which indicated that in his opinion all the north-
western tribes were going on the war-path immediately. All this was subsequently verified, and indeed
even then far to the north and west Red Cloud had
inaugurated his fatal campaign. Fortunately for

my peace of mind the facts were not then known to us. This name, "Wild Bill," I suppose had some significance in Indian usage, as they, like the ancient Hebrews, gave names to indicate some particular characteristic or change of circumstances. It may have been adopted from the celebrated American "Wild Bill" of earlier days, as he was a man of such courage and daring that others of his own race adopted it, and as one has observed, "it was the palmy days of our Wild Bills." The original of the name seemed to have been a gentleman with long hair and long mustache, with the usual characteristics of the plainsmen. Our visitor, to me a hero, could not imitate the original in every particular, as Indians have neither beards nor mustaches. His dress was probably donned for the time being through vanity or for effect, and it certainly impressed me with foreboding no less than his talk. In reality he was a scout then and afterwards, and it was a mere ruse when he left his pony and rode off with the stage driver in friendly chat. My information was received from another traveller, a little boy of fourteen years of age, whose name was Charles Sylvester, belonging to Quincy, Illinois. He had been stolen by the Indians when but seven years of age and spent his early years among his captors. One day he was out hunting with a party of Indian boys and accidentally killed a comrade. He dared not return to the village so he escaped on his pony to the white people. After a time, becoming discontented with his own people and civilization in general, he returned to his adopted friends on the North

Platte and became an interpreter. It was at this time that I met him and he divulged, or interpreted, what he understood from Wild Bill.

He appeared to have an eye upon business as well, and offered his services to me in the capacity of a servant for $40.00 per month, and "no bacon to eat," as he expressed it. He seemed attracted to me, for some unknown cause, and dogged my footsteps, perhaps hoping that I might relent and make a contract; barring that, he eventually followed the business of interpreter and became in time an Indian trader with enlarged possibilities, as I afterwards learned from one who knew him well.

The third character was a woman of unique personality and dress, as typical of her craft, in those days, as was Wild Bill himself. Of swarthy skin, with keen black eyes, with black curling hair, and casting furtive glances when conscious of particular notice, her appearance as well as her professions suggested gypsy antecedents. Decided and varied colors marked her dress. Her hands and ears were lavishly jewelled, whether with real or imitation gems my proximity did not disclose, though if real, certainly not of the first water. Her self-conscious importance and my lack of inclination precluded judgment on this point. She was a fortune-teller, with clairvoyant powers, so said, en route to the little settlement of Denver to ply her vocation there. I did not know of her reputation as possessing occult powers until after her departure, otherwise I might have lengthened my story. I had the misfortune to lose a diamond brooch at or near our rendezvous, a

matter of great concern on account of its sentimental as well as real value, and had I suspected her
ability in her boasted powers I might possibly have
invoked her aid for its recovery, and might have
been tempted even to take a peep into the future at
her behest.

These wayside ranch stories, limited in their
range, and minus the Canterbury features, are typical in a small way of the old life of the times.

The Plains, at that season, were barren of green-
ness, as everything of a vegetable nature was sere
and brown, possessing no beauty worthy of description. The level prairies had nothing to break the
monotony of this sea of waste. Trees and patches
of grass were to be found along the water courses
and justified the wisdom of previous travellers in
choosing, so far as possible, their camping places
near them. We were certainly travelling across the
"Great American Desert."

And yet the soil was afterwards found to be rich,
and only needed modern irrigation to make it won-
derfully productive. Once, when General Sherman
was serving in that region, some one remarked to
him that "it was a fine country and all that it needed
was plenty of water and good society." To this
the General is reported to have replied very
brusquely, "That is all hell needs." As with the
soil, so the wild cactus was waiting for modern
science to transform and evolve it into food fit for
beasts. Then, contact with it had to be avoided
with scrupulous care, and no one dreamed that it
could serve any good purpose to justify its exist-

ence and the evil function it seemed to serve. A thousand needles in a single plant were so adjusted as to prick and pierce both the hands and feet of the unwary traveller as she descended from her ambulance for a short respite from cramped limbs and bodily weariness incident to the day's travel. How painfully we afterwards understood its character will develop later in our story.

It is said that one of the favorite tortures of some tribes of Indians was to strip their unfortunate captives and bind them tightly to a large cactus of the country, and it was a common saying in regard to a bright boy, "He will make a fine boy if the Apaches don't tie him to a cactus."

CHAPTER IV.

FORT McPherson, Nebraska, afterwards a well built Post constructed of the red cedar which there abounded and gave beauty, when varnished, to all interior wood-work, consisted of only shabby log and adobe quarters upon our arrival, and we were not loath to leave it behind, though each halting place where we could commune with others than our own little party proved a welcome relief. If I could have ridden on horseback for even a brief spell, what a relief it would have been. I had been quite an expert in the saddle from childhood, and had not entirely lost the art. It did seem but fair, if Uncle Sam could only see things that way and consider the personal comfort of women travellers bound to follow their husbands at whatever cost; but the Government carriage, called "ambulance," was always at command upon transition from rail or steam-boat conveyance to the limited methods of transportation on the frontier.

After another hundred miles of travel, and three hundred and ninety miles from Omaha, we reached Fort Sedgwick with but little to interrupt the continuity of brown grass and sand hills along our immediate route.

Fort Sedgwick, in the northeast corner of Colorado, was the old site of Julesburg, now across the Platte River, and had been burned by the son of

35

old "Little Dog," but had been rebuilt and contained a dozen houses and stores. According to the nomenclature of town designation in those days in the West, the tradition is as follows: In the days of the overland stage service, and during the early Mormon migration to Salt Lake, one Jules, a Cherokee exile, kept the so-called "hotel" there for passing travel, and in the cheerful frankness of western life the place was known as "Dirty Jules Ranch" thence to Jules, finally, Julesburg. Here it was my good fortune to meet Captain J. P. W. Neil, belonging to the same regiment as my husband, the Eighteenth U. S. Infantry; his company had been left to garrison the post when the regiment went westward the previous May. To this day I feel indebted to Mrs. Neil for ministering to my necessities and giving valuable suggestions for enhancing my comfort during the wearisome days to follow. And what a blessing to sit at her hospitable board and eat good square meals, if only for a few days.

The best preserver of kindnesses is the remembrance of them and perpetual thanksgiving for them. It was said of a Kentucky soldier during the Civil War that often in the camp, far from home, he would stir an invisible beverage with an imaginary spoon. Perhaps I experienced a kindred sensation afterwards, when I recalled the taste and aroma of Mrs. Neil's coffee as contrasted with our own made over a camp fire of "buffalo chips," the only fuel obtainable at times, and if sorrow's crowning sorrow be the remembering of happier days and events, surely there was nothing left for me to do but fortify myself for and not against the decoction of the camp-fire article.

We had followed the course of the South Platte but now were to cross that strange river, thus described by one who had made the experiment: "The River Platte is a broad, but dirty, uninviting stream, differing from a slough in having a swift current, often a mile wide, but with no more water than would fill an ordinary canal; three inches of fluid running on the top of several feet of moving quicksand; too deep for safe fording; too yellow to wash in; and too pale to paint with, it is the most useless and disappointing river in America."

Such was the Platte River in 1866. To-day the river and its tributaries irrigate one million nine hundred and twenty-five thousand four hundred and sixty-two acres of land, which fifty years ago, or even less, were regarded as worthless. Measurements of water once used and then returned to the river bed bring out the fact that a large percentage of the water diverted to a particular canal is not wholly lost but returns to the stream and is used over again. Some of the measurements show that in low water the return seepage tends to increase the flow of the stream rather than to diminish that flow. Such is the statement of the Superintendent of Irrigation Affairs.

The very anticipation of crossing, or seeming to cross, this strange river at any given point was at least disconcerting, as we had to expect new eddies, more spiteful currents, more desperate quicksands, and constantly varying depths of water, with no

competent guide to direct our course. But we had
to risk it at Fort Sedgwick, braced up for the
ordeal, and entered the stream. I had the uncom-
fortable feeling, at times, that we were gliding down-
ward, while to the optical vision our mules were
certainly headed for the opposite shore. Several
long poles were noticed in one place stuck down deep
into the water and sand, and upon anxious inquiry,
"What it all meant as a sign," the information was
lucidly returned that "they were a warning to travellers to avoid that particular place, as once upon a
time, wagons, mules, and men had disappeared
beyond recovery." This was not a comforting
assurance at that moment to the lone woman in the
ambulance, with every nerve on tension, watching
progress, hoping, and praying too, for a safe landing on the other side.

I might have felt safer on horseback, as I recalled one occasion during the Civil War when in an
emergency I crossed the swollen Harpeth River in
Tennessee on the back of a blind mare, guiding by
a rope bridle, with the current so swift that the
swimming of the beast, with my arms clinging tena-
ciously to her neck to keep from drowning, produced
a mental fear and physical discomfort that lingered
in the memory with special distinctness at this later
experience.

But the Platte River was crossed!

How I felt the lack of womanly sympathy at such
an hour was known only to Him who "marks the
sparrows' fall," so much I had to endure in silence.
I seemed all along the journey to be possessed of

dual mental states, one voiced through outward expression and not the same that held me subconsciously to serious duty from beginning to end. It was anything but a pleasure trip, except so far as loyalty to that duty and obedience to orders brought their compensations in doing things because "they can be done," "they must be done," "they will be done." We did not set up a monumental stone after crossing the Platte River. We had no visible ark to lead us as did the Israelites of old, but an over-ruling Providence, our guide, though invisible to mortal sight, then, as ever after in the days to come, was my comfort and my strength.

CHAPTER V.

A MARCH of seventeen miles brought our small cavalcade in sight of a ranch, like a beacon to a sailor when he sings out "Land, Ho!" In our case the expletive, spontaneous and joyous, was "Ranch, Ho!" With kindred emotion of joy, and as if to herald our coming as we approached nearer, we were greeted by the vociferous crowing of a rooster, which, interpreted into its natural significance, meant the presence of chickens. An imaginary *menu* for supper was quickly formulated, with chicken heading the list. The ranchman, for reasons of his own and without due appreciation of what a chicken supper would really mean to the travellers, declined to part with any, but compromised on the rooster and made the evening sacrifice. It seemed a pity afterwards, as the rooster was so disappointing, and like the possum of the childhood game he was "rough and very tough, and more than all could eat."

It was said of Parson Williams, one of the most celebrated characters of the Rocky Mountains at an early date, that he told of himself when a Circuit Rider in Missouri that he was so well known that even the chickens recognized him as he came riding past the farm-houses. The old chanticleers would crow, "Here comes Parson Williams! Here comes Parson Williams! One of us must be ready for

40

dinner!" Our rooster's crowing unconsciously to himself may have been prophetic. At all events there was nothing else to do after our disappointment but to become readjusted to our usual fare and experimental inevitable camp-fire cooking, if not reconciled, in a more subdued state of mind, and retire for the night, not on a downy couch but with grass pillows and army blankets to seek the repose of the ambulance bed with another day behind us.

The next day's march brought us to Pumpkin Creek, which flows past Court House Rock, not rock indeed, but sand, hard pan and clay, rising six hundred feet above the water of the creek. After partaking of supper, and the tin cups and pans had been washed in the clear waters of the creek, and camp-fires were burning low, I proposed to take a saunter to the great rock. The idea was at once ridiculed as it was actually five miles distant, so deceptive was the clear atmosphere of the plains. "Chimney Rock," with its singular proportions, loomed up miles further to the northwest. Both of these sand mountains were noted landmarks to travellers. Though undergoing change through frequent blizzard and waste, they retained the natural proportions which gave to each its characteristic name. The gathering of débris about their base will in time efface the bold outline and fair symmetry of their present proportions.

The pass through Scott's Bluff was reached by a deep gorge in which wagons could pass each other only at a few places, and which was so tortuous that the first wagon of a train making a turn, if you were near the centre, would appear to be retracing the journey instead of leading you in its pursuit.

The legend of this strange formation is of interest. Captain B. L. Bonneville relates that "a number of years ago a party were descending the upper part of the river in canoes when their frail barks were overturned and all their powder spoiled. Their rifles being thus rendered useless they were unable to procure food by hunting and had to depend upon roots and wild fruits for subsistence. After suffering extremely from hunger they arrived at Laramie's Fork, a small tributary of the north branch of the Nebraska River, about sixty miles from the cliffs just mentioned. Here one of the party by the name of Scott was taken ill, and his companions came to a halt until he might recover sufficient breath and strength to proceed. While they were searching after edible roots they discovered the trail of white men who had evidently preceded them. What was to be done? By a forced march they might be able to overtake this party and thus reach the settlements in safety. Should they linger, all might die from famine and exhaustion. Scott, however, was incapable of moving, and his companions were too feeble to aid him forward. They dreaded that if they attempted to do so he would be such a clog upon their way that they never would come up with the advance party and determined to abandon him to his fate. Accordingly, under pretense of seeking food and such simple things as might be efficacious in his malady they deserted him and hastened forward upon the trail.

" They succeeded in overtaking the party of
which they were in quest, but concealed their faith-
less desertion of Scott, alleging that he died of
disease.

"During the ensuing summer the same party,
visiting that region with others, came suddenly
upon the bleached bones and grinning skull of a
human skeleton, which by certain signs indicated
that they were the remains of Scott. This was sixty
miles from the place where he was abandoned, so
that the wretched man had crawled that immense
distance before death put an end to his miseries.
The wild and picturesque bluffs in the neighbor-
hood of his lonely grave have ever since borne his
name."

At the very foot of the bluffs, as we passed
through, we reached the peculiar and compact little
Fort Mitchell, unlike any fort I have ever seen. The
external log walls of the quarters, which were in
the form of a rectangle, were loopholed and formed
the line of defence, with a small parade ground in
the centre, and here were the quarters of officers,
soldiers, horses, and warehouse supplies. Here we
were accorded hospitable entertainment by the commandant of the little garrison, Brevet-Major Robert
Hughes, who had long served upon the staff of
General Terry, as he did also at a later date, but
was a captain in our own regiment, the Eighteenth,
at the time of our visit. Here at last we realized
that sense of security never experienced while sleeping in an ambulance on the broad open prairie. But
those intercalary words, "Forward March," still

sounded in our ears like a bugle-call and we must onward to Fort Laramie.

"Thus far," in this partial itinerary, army fashion, and in chronological order, must be interpreted by the reader, if placed under similar conditions to those so feebly outlined. There are always vivid soul experiences during such ordeals that only eternity can explain and recompense. Imagination may catch glimpses of strain and endurance that words cannot express, and the very effort would afford no satisfaction to myself or benefit the reader.

" Thus far " the country, to my observation, had seemed like a "no man's land." The former centres of Indian life along the route had been deserted for the hunt or chase, or more likely for change of their uncertain domiciles to regions farther north, as the call of the Government for all the northwest tribes to assemble at Laramie in the June preceding had directed them in that quarter.

The purpose of the Government was to open a new wagon road through the Powder River Country, around the Big Horn Mountains, greatly shortening the travel to Montana; but all hinged upon the possibility of peace negotiations at the Laramie Council proving satisfactory to the Indians themselves, the very Indians whose security in the possession of the coveted new roadway route had been guaranteed to them by the Harney-Sanborn Treaty of 1865, at the end of the Minnesota war. Hence, to the Indian it meant the surrender of a fair portion of his favorite hunting-grounds, almost the last upon which his living depended, for in the region of the proposed road the country abounded with game. Mountain sheep, elk, deer, and buffalo ranged through it in vast numbers, and it is small wonder that they were reluctant to part with it. They were quick to perceive that such a proposition involved the practical and permanent advent of the white man, the presence of soldiers and the building of military posts in the very heart of their best hunting-grounds. Quite a number who did not occupy that particular portion of the country under consideration were anxious to make a treaty and remain at peace. Some of this class had long resided near Fort Laramie and were still there when we reached the Fort in September, 1866. Many of these retained their residence there for a long time, keeping their own treaty obligations, until at a later period all the Indians of that country were gathered in large reservations, one under the general control of Red Cloud and the other under the similar leadership of Spotted Tail.

At the time of my arrival it had become apparent to any sensible observer that the Indians of that country would fight to the death for home and native land, with spirit akin to that of the American soldier of our early history, and who could say that their spirit was not commendable and to be respected?

While negotiations were under consideration at Laramie in June to induce Red Cloud, a leader of the young warriors of the Northern Sioux, and the principal chiefs themselves to yield the privilege of peaceably establishing the new road with military posts along the route, Colonel H. B. Carrington, of the Eighteenth U. S. Infantry, with the Second Battalion of his regiment, about seven hundred strong, arrived at Fort Laramie under peremptory orders of Major General Pope, commanding the Department of Missouri, to immediately occupy and build forts along the route, which was still under consideration by the special Indian Commission and the Indians who had met with them for conference.

The destination and orders of Colonel Carrington were communicated to the assembled chiefs, and they at once recognized the fact that the occupation of the country then in debate was to be forcibly effected in advance of any agreement as to the terms. They immediately gave unequivocal demonstrations of their disapproval. The leading chiefs withdrew from the council with their adherents, refused to accept any presents from the Commission, returned to their own country, and with a strong force of warriors commenced a vigorous and relentless war against all whites, citizens as well as soldiers, who attempted to occupy the route in question. One intimation then given was this, that "in two moons the command would not have a hoof left."

Red Cloud himself, it is officially reported, when he saw Colonel Carrington at his visit to the council, upon his arrival threw his blanket around himself, refused an introduction, and left with this announcement of his views, pointing to the officer who had just arrived, "The Great Father sends us presents and wants us to sell him the road, but White Chief goes with soldiers to steal the road before the Indians say Yes or No.''

These events occurred in June, 1866, before our arrival, but were communicated to us when in September the proceedings were fully made known as they now appear in the Government Official Records of ''The History of Indian Operations on the Plains during the Campaign of 1866.'' *

---

* Executive Senate Document, No. 33, 1st Session, 50th Congress.

CHAPTER VI.

FORT Laramie, next in size after Fort Leavenworth, and the first post garrisoned in the section now constituting the State of Wyoming, is full of romantic and tragic interest, possessing more historic incidents than any other military post at the West. Built by Robert Campbell, its first commander, in 1834, for a trading-post, it was destined in the succeeding fifty years to become an important fur-trade centre, and the theatre of great military events. Laramie was named for James Laramie, a Canadian, who also gave his name to Laramie River, Laramie Plains, Laramie Peak, Laramie County, and Laramie City. Laramie himself was well worthy to have his name commemorated, and is described as a man of resolute character, manly in conduct and kindly in disposition. His associates regarded him as absolutely honest, and his courage was never questioned. His conduct toward the Indians was such as to command both their respect and good will. Every act of his life commended him as worthy the friendship of both white men and red men. And yet he met his death at the hands of Indians. A sketch of his life is told in story by Mr. Coutant, the Wyoming Historian,* if not in song.

Francis Parkman visited Fort Laramie in 1846,

---

* Coutant's History of Wyoming, vol. i, chap. xxiii.

accompanied by the Honorable Quincy Shaw of Boston, and remained several months, hunting buffalo with the Indians, and meeting many traders and trappers, among others three grandsons of Daniel Boone. It seems to me that when the trapper changed the canoe for a horse one might begin the material for a great American epic, and very possibly have for its theme "Winning the West," so felicitously chosen by President Roosevelt for his volume with that title.

Suggestive of the theme is the expedition of Fremont, who, when upon the summit of a lofty, snow-clad mountain, forced a ramrod into the crevice of a rock, and unfurled our national banner to wave in the breeze where the flag never waved before; and on Independence Rock placed the cross, the symbol of the Christian Faith. He says of that occasion, "Not unmindful of the custom of early travellers and explorers in our country, I engraved the symbol of the Christian Faith. Among the thickly inscribed names I made on the hard granite the impression of a large cross, which I covered with a preparation of India rubber, well calculated to resist the influence of wind and rain." It stands amidst the names of many who have long since found their way to the grave, and for whom the huge rock is a giant gravestone. And with the heroes of canal, foot, and wave, we recall also those of discovery, those of the fur-trade, and the heroes of missions, that host of worthies who formed the vanguard of civilization and religion, of Ashley and Parkman, of Whitman, the Christian doctor, none the less a patriot, a very Nestor among men, who carried within his own devoted soul the destiny of an empire for his mission, and made it the outpost of Oregon, now an American State.

Almost one hundred and twenty years before his day, Bishop Berkley had sung with prophetic soul:

"There shall be another golden age,
    The first four acts already past;
  A fifth shall close the drama with her days,
    Time's noblest offering is the last.

"Not such as Europe breeds in her decay,
    Such as she had when fresh and young,
  When Heavenly flame did animate her clay,
    By poet shall be sung.

"Westward the course of empire takes its way,
    The first four acts already past,
  A fifth shall close the drama with the day,
    Time's noblest offering is the last."

Whitman travelled with his little party up the North Platte on July 3, 1836, and paused long enough to celebrate American Independence Day. Taking from his wagon a national flag and a Bible, spreading a blanket upon the ground, placing a Bible upon it, and taking the flag-staff in his hand, he said "Let us pray." Then and there he took possession of the territory, not unlike the Patriarch Noah of old, and fervently prayed for his country and the cause of Christ, Mrs. Whitman leading in a patriotic hymn.

The recent attempts to cast doubt upon the historical accuracy of the generally accepted words and deeds of Whitman in the settlement of the Oregon dispute, reminds one of the famous Bacon-Shakespeare controversy.

One author, writing upon Indian characteristics, says, "There are plenty of well-authenticated instances of Indian chivalry. The romance of war and the chase has always been theirs. If you want the romance of love, a thousand elopements in the face of deadly peril will supply you with Lochinvars! If you want the romance of friendship, you may find it in the companion warriors of the prairie rivals for Damon and Pythias! If you want the romance of grief, take that magnificent Mandan Wah-ta-ta-pa (Four Bears), who starved himself to death because of the ravages of small-pox in his tribe, or Har-won-ge-ta, the Minneconjou Chief (One Horn), who was so maddened by the death of his son that he swore to kill the first living thing that crossed his path. Armed with only a knife, he attacked a buffalo bull and perished on the horns of the infuriated animal. If you seek pure knight-errantry, I commend you to the young Pawnee hero, Pe-ta-la-sha-ra, who at the risk of his life freed a Comanche girl from the stake, and returned unharmed to his people, and who afterwards saved a Spanish boy from a similar fate by offering a ransom, and interposed his own life to force the release. If you desire the grander chivalry of strength of mind and nobility of soul, I will put Chief Joseph (the Nez Perces Chief) against any barbarian that ever lived.

"Perchance some Indian may arise to the height

of this great argument and invoke the poetic muse to adventurous song, but as an untamed, or wild Indian, he has had no speech or literature through which he might appeal.

"There may yet be found among the Six Nations the famous 'Iroquois Confederacy,' which, according to Parkman, would have controlled the American continent if the white man had a little longer delayed his advent, either in the descendants of Cornplanter, the personal friend of Washington, or of Handsome Lake, and Red Jacket, the coming type of the Epic poet, since in their devotion to the Great Father of American Liberty, ever a friend of the Red Man, and up to the date of the Eleventh United States Census, they cherish the tradition that Washington still occupies a palace at the entrance to the Happy Hunting Grounds of the Indian Paradise, to receive and welcome the Senecas, and that he will abide there to receive their salutes as they enter so long as man shall have his earthly existence prolonged. Although they have children named from every American President from Adams down to Cleveland, and later, they have held the name of Washington as too sacred for adoption in their own households."

CHAPTER VII.

But I must retrace my footsteps from this tempting excursion into the past to the realities of the very present. With all deference to its historic character, Fort Laramie, in my observation and experience, did not impress me as particularly interesting. We crossed the clear, beautiful stream as we approached the Fort, but at that season its glory had departed. The parade ground was bare of sod, but in its centre "the flag was still there." The adobe houses of gray appearance imparted their sombre hue to the whole surroundings. The scenery, however, beautiful or otherwise, affected me but little, except in a general depression, so great was my concern to escape the ambulance and plant my feet on any kind of earth whatever.

The attempt to adjust myself to the surroundings began at once, although I knew perfectly well that our stay would be transient. I was learning the army habit, and this was but another step in the process of development into a full-fledged army woman, unless that development were diverted in some unforeseen experience. Quarters were assigned us, and with alacrity, if not delight, I took possession of my first adobe ("dobey") residence. The first duty after a survey of the rooms was to unpack trunks, for the first time since leaving Fort Leavenworth, as the most needful articles for the journey had been stored in the ambulance. Two small rooms and a kitchen of like proportions, which seemed, however, like spacious apartments, were to be our own for the present. Gray army blankets were tacked upon the floors to the extent of their capacity. Hospital cots were utilized for beds, and we began, as the children say, "to keep house." And now for my nick-nacks and such belongings to reproduce home environment, as I attempted once before on Governor's Island, where my initial army experience began! The thought was ever recurrent that my stay would not be long, as my husband was under orders to join his regiment at Fort Phil. Kearney, two hundred and forty miles beyond.

Even while at Omaha there appeared to be an indefinite idea at headquarters that Indian operations had begun; but few, even at Laramie, so far west, realized that a real war of extermination prevailed about Fort Phil. Kearney, and that this war was being waged for the extermination of the white man and not of the Indian. And yet, at that very time, the advantage was on the side of the redman in every particular, firearms included, as we learned later to our sorrow. There was no telegraphic communication between the two posts, and practically no travel, except with an occasional mail party which the colonel commanding persisted in sending over the trail at great risk of life, as we viewed it. There were plenty of Indians of the friendly sort visible at any hour of the day, but there was a feeling of perfect security at Fort Laramie itself.

All was vague, uninviting, and apparently almost

impracticable, for the transportation of trunks in army wagons for a long distance was certainly a hazardous undertaking, as I found when the task of unpacking began. As I lifted the trunk trays every article was permeated with dust, and some of them unrecognizable. Garments immediately beneath had been so cut that the trays seemed to have been converted into chopping knives, or saws would better describe them and their work.

The long drawn out process of mending and darning was, to say the least, inopportune and unanticipated. In my dilemma the servant question confronted me at once. In slavery days it was no question at all, for my father was a slave owner, though an ideal one, and I had no occasion to give this subject thought. Few lieutenants in active service on the Plains took the responsibility of securing servants, as transportation was limited and accommodations very circumscribed. During all my married life, however, the same question has from time to time arisen, ghost-like, and will not down. It was finally settled, or half settled, in this instance by securing the services of a squaw to do laundry work and extricate me from the accumulated dust of travel. I simply had to make a beginning somewhere, and this was easier of accomplishment than the risk involved in cooking. My new-found helper was in total ignorance of the use of the wash-boiler, in lieu of which she rubbed the clothing into holes to remove refractory stains, so that I reluctantly settled down to the conviction that *chawed* clothing I was fated to wear.

Calico could be obtained at the sutler's store, and in a measure retrieved my loss, though I was very forcibly reminded of war prices paid for similar goods at my Southern home not so very long before. When my squaw had completed her task, as I supposed, I sat waiting for a signal to that effect by her reappearance. Instead of that I found her just outside my quarters sitting down in the dirt, but fast asleep, by no means suggesting a "Madonna of the Tub," although she wore two pairs of earrings and chains depended from her neck. As I confronted her for settlement the Atlantic Ocean might as well have rolled between us so far as any communication we were able to make could help the situation. Someone was needed to break the spell and bring about an understanding. Finally a soldier appeared who knew some words of her language and offered to act as interpreter, so that between his efforts and a combination of signs and grunts I was relieved of all responsibility.

The water used at Laramie was at that time hauled from the river for all purposes and was abundant and clear, and yet there was a consciousness that you were limited in its use, perhaps on account of the process of conveyance. I had not then the experience which came later in Texas of buying water that had been transported sixty miles by railroad and was peddled in the streets by wagons at exorbitant prices. In that case the only alternative was a choice between the strong alkaline water of the Rio Grande, which seemed no barrier to

Mexican taste, or the purchase of melted manu-
factured ice at its great cost.

We had, of course, our mess-chest with its limited
supply of cooking utensils and the inevitable camp-
kettle for the journey, and when these were augmented by stock from the sutler's store and the
stove set up in the kitchen the puzzle in this domestic
experience was, "Where is the cook?"

For a consideration we were invited to join the
"Mess," composed of a dozen or more officers at the
post, who were most courteous and obliging to the
only woman at their board. Fortunately there were
quite comfortable chairs in the quarters. We also
had our own two small camp chairs, an important
portion of our worldly goods, or it might have de-
volved upon us to sit on the hospital cots, a position
beyond endurance. I am conscious that I made great
effort to be comfortable upon very little, and simply
had to do it, not of choice but of necessity. A small
mirror was discovered on a shelf one day, probably
left by a former occupant of the quarters, but its
surface so much resembled tin and was so discourag-
ing in its reflections that I resorted to my little hand
mirror to be reassured of my own identity.

I made another discovery a little later, greatly
to my surprise and gratification, that my squaw was
not the only representative of my sex at Laramie.
The other was a school teacher sent out to teach the
young Indian idea "how to shoot." They could
shoot well enough in other directions, if opportunity
offered, and this was an innovation surely, though
it absorbed so much of her time as to leave scant

57

leisure for social visiting; but her very presence was a pleasant thought.

I grew somewhat interested in the little Indians. Children intuitively recognize their friends and these Indian children were no exception to the rule. Their eyes would follow me curiously and earnestly as I strolled about the garrison. I was sitting near my window one day, occupied with some work, when a dark cloud seemed to obscure my vision. Looking up I found the window space covered by little brown faces, to which I gave a smile of recognition, and with a friendly word, which, of course, they could not understand, though my manner was easily interpreted, I beckoned them to the door and dispensed with generous hand some ginger-snaps obtained from the sutler's store.

Indian children, like other children, have ways of conveying information readily, and very soon both windows would be crowded. This continued for several days, and my first experiment was in danger of getting beyond control, so that I had to change my "Infantry Tactics" and bribe them with other ginger-snaps to cease their visitations. My experience must have been like that of Mark Twain in the Swiss mountain "yodling." The novel sound so pleased him at first that he paid the boys generously to keep it up for his entertainment. Thus encouraged, their number was so augmented that the sound became monotonous, and, in fact, such a bore that in self-defence he bribed them to desist.

One day during the first week of my sojourn I went with my husband and several of the other

officers on a hunting excursion and as it was the only
time I left the fort it was quite a diversion. We did
not go sufficiently far, however, to require us to be
mounted. Hunting and shooting were no novelty to
me, except that the conditions were quite different.
Hitherto I had accompanied my husband several
times on horseback and he had taught me to lay
my small gun between the animal's ears and fire
without fear, so gentle was the little mare he had
given me, but I think without ever having brought
down any game for my venture. On this occasion
Indian boys, who formed a part of the company,
were very agile in finding any game that dropped in
obscure places and quite adept, true to their natural
instinct, in such exercise. These little boys had
adopted the American boy's dress, with some difference of adjustment, minus the seats of their trousers.

On our return I visited the small Indian cemetery. A burying-ground, in the ordinary sense,
would literally mean nothing to one of these Indians.
I came upon what had been the burial *place* of a
chief's daughter. The receptacle for the body was
a platform erected on four poles and the tails of her
favorite ponies that had been slain were tacked to
the posts. This was all that remained to tell the
story. Their idea is that ponies would be ridden
after reaching the Happy Hunting Grounds.
Articles used by the dead during life, or furnished
by the generosity of friends, are considered necessary to the comfort or appearance of the dweller in
the future life. It is said that Indians near some
of the agencies frequently used the boxes in which

Government or other stores came to them, so that inscriptions which at a distance look like an elaborate epitaph on a closer inspection may be found to read "Best Soap," or "Star Crackers," and otherwise.

And so the days at Laramie passed by, always with strange apprehensions not suggested by the immediate environment of the Post. With the courage of youth, and an abiding sense of the presence of Him who leads by cloud or fiery pillar, I felt sustained through dark hours, but there are times when human nature is self assertive. The prospect of a long tedious journey to Fort Phil. Kearney, in another ambulance, and the possibilities of disaster to myself over the rough way through a hostile Indian country, would almost paralyze me with fear and foreboding. My mind would be filled with such desperation that at times I would close my doors and windows and pace the floor from agony at the situation. The officers at the Fort would not admit that there was any danger for even a small party following the established trail, but the apprehension, long maturing, and from signs and portents that only can be appreciated on the frontier, never left me.

And yet after a storm the calm and the still small voice of comfort and consolation were so real to my soul that I could write cheering letters to my far away home while under the grateful spell, and live to-day to chronicle my safe deliverance *then,* and *through subsequent times of peril and disaster.*

CHAPTER VIII.

LEAVING LARAMIE—ALARMS OF WAR
DISCREDITED.

How did the authorities at Washington, or
Omaha, from whence orders emanated, know what
the execution of these orders involved or would
entail upon individual officers here and there distributed over the country but imperatively needed
with their regiments on the frontier, where, without
reason, all conditions were assumed to be those of
absolute peace? Certainly any provision for women
to accompany their husbands westward was farthest
from thought. Officers' wives thus travelling, risking all trials and exposures for that purpose, have
certain advantages thereby, rather than to follow
after by themselves, and all these trials and exposures have been set forth by abler pens than mine.
My own experience was at least unique, and not
realized fully at the time, for we only lived day by
day—"Sufficient unto the day is the evil thereof."
It certainly was enough for us, when we had the day
to live in, and the thought of remaining behind
never had consideration. Even General Sherman
himself, in 1866, when he left his headquarters at
St. Louis to assist in the organization of the Montana expedition of that year, urged all army officers'
wives to accompany their husbands and to take with
them all needed comforts for a pleasant garrison
life in the newly opened country, where all would

be healthful, with pleasant service and absolute peace.

The day of packing once more rolled around, and with mixed mental activities, which I cannot even at this late day exactly crystallize into a fully recognized expression. Which is the more agreeable task —packing or unpacking? So the converse springs to mind; which is the more disagreeable—unpacking or packing? It may seem a trivial question. Much depends upon the object in view from either standpoint. Thus far physical activities involved both, and life seemed narrowed to just this kind of exercise. We surrendered our "dobey" house, our hospital cots, our sombre blankets, even our tin mirror, unmolested, and with packed mess-chest boarded the everlasting ambulance. Two young "contract surgeons," Mr. Van Volzah, one of Colonel Carrington's most trusty mail carriers, and an escort of only six men, and our baggage-wagon, are all in readiness for the last good-by to the pleasant group of officers and friends who bade us God speed on our journey, and we take up our march northward, one of the little party never to return again. . . .

We kept steadily along our trail to Nine Mile Ranch for several miles with nothing to relieve the dull monotony of the journey. There was no temptation to diversion, as it began to dawn upon us in some degree that we were advancing directly in the face of hostilities, while their full import could not be felt then as later on. Some of the officers who had previously traversed the same route, as we learned later, had fired pistols in the cañon, then named after our Regimental Adjutant, "Phisterer Cañon," to awaken the echoes which were startling and many times repeated, and upon subsequently reaching our destination and meeting the famous guide of the expedition, the noted James Bridger, we could appreciate the warning he gave to that party, when, checking their careless amusement, he quaintly told them, "Better not go fur, there's Injuns enough lying under wolf skins, or skulking in them cliffs. I warrant ye, they's seen ye every day, and when ye don't see eny of 'em about is just the time they'se thickest, and just the time to look for their devilment." We saw no Indians that day, but I had an experience with cactus that, in the expressive term of a later day was "the limit."

I had occasion to leave the ambulance at one stage of the journey, and my driver, with no special instructions to wait for my reappearance, drove slowly along in the track of the other team, while our escort and other drivers, having no occasion of their own for halting, moved tranquilly along oblivious of transactions in their rear.

When I returned to the road I found to my dismay that they had covered quite a·distance. It was my custom to wear cloth slippers in travelling, sleeping in them also, ready for any emergency that might arise, and this had hitherto proven a wise use of them, particularly on the over-land journey when cramped space in the ambulance was the inevitable. In my haste to reach the road, or trail, I had the dreadful misfortune to run into a cactus clump. My slippers were instantly punctured with innumerable needles. There was no time to stop even for an initial attempt to extricate them, as fear of some unseen enemy possessed my mind as cactus needles possessed my feet. A realizing sense of the distance between myself and my escort was one of torture, if not by Indians, none the less real. With limping step, increasing the pain every moment, and without sufficient voice left to be heard, I ran nearly a mile. . . . The team stopped as I neared it. Thoroughly exhausted, I fell prostrate. On being lifted into the ambulance, I was unable to stir or explain my dilemma, for sensations are felt not expressed at the actual time of their occurrence. My head was not crowned with a "victor's wreath," but my feet were filled with the "trophies of the race."

On recovering strength, with intermitted effort and perseverance I spent much of two days' journeying, so far as tearful eyes would permit, in extricating the cactus needles, a novel employment indeed, but one that demanded thoroughness as the price of future comfort.

Certainly, whatever else I might reasonably have expected as incidental to the journey, this particular trial was not catalogued as a contingent adversary in my path. Of all the trials that I heard or read as confronting my sex in travelling the Plains, this was to me the most trying episode, up to that date.

CHAPTER IX.

THE journey of forty miles from Fort Laramie
brought us to Bridger's Ferry, where the North
Platte was crossed, and with the exception of at
Fort Reno and Fort Phil. Kearney there was not at
that time a resident white man between the ferry and
Bozeman, afterwards known as Bozeman City,
Montana. At the date of our march John Bozeman
owned the little semi-fortified ranch occupied by him
and had realized much success in the cultivation of
vegetables. He also furnished many supplies to the
few emigrants that had tried the old Bozeman trail
prior to the attempt to establish a permanent road
for emigrants to Montana by that route.

What was most necessary and always important
was to find wood and water for camping purposes.
It was almost impossible to detach oneself from
present dreary surroundings, even in thought. Con-
templation of beautiful mountains, even though one
had to but lift the eyes to behold them apparently
so near in the clear blue sky, brought no corresponding uplift of spirit, for mountains, hills, cañons
and ridges suggested a hidden foe, and yet the fact
remained, topographically, that from the South Fork
of the Cheyenne River we had a fine view of Laramie Peak five thousand nine hundred feet above
sea level.

In some places where we found the river dry only a slight digging was necessary to start the water to the surface and secure the needed supply. Lack of fuel along this portion of the route as elsewhere, already noted, compelled us to use the dry sage-brush and buffalo chips.

When the Dry Branch of Powder River was reached we obtained our first view of the Big Horn Mountains, eighty miles distant. Cloud Peak, which we knew to be just behind Fort Phil. Kearney, rose thirteen thousand feet above the sea. With but semi-consciousness one could not but feel in some degree the grandeur of the scene that unfolded constantly, like a great panorama, appealing to the sense as both picturesque and sublime. But I honestly confess that the most appealing sense at that time was that we had reached Fort Reno and would find something to eat, when once at the officers' mess-table, different from the contents of a mess-chest, our only source of supply during the long days of dusty travel.

The two officers stationed there, Captain Proctor and Adjutant Thaddeus P. Kirtland, a cousin of our Colonel, were most hospitable and kind, surrendering their own quarters for my accommodation, and especially considerate in many ways to a lone woman who chanced to be their temporary guest. Two companies of the Eighteenth constituted the garrison, and this was a source of special confidence.

Fort Reno, formerly Fort Connor, was sufficiently safe at that time, except from marauding bands of hostile Indians who would drive off stock at every available opportunity. These Indians were willing to pledge themselves not to disturb Reno, if the soldiers would simply occupy that Post and neither go nor build additional forts beyond that point. But Colonel Carrington, commanding the expedition of the summer just past and the entire Mountain District, had peremptory orders not only to garrison and repair Fort Reno, but to build two forts beyond, in the very face of intensely hostile protests. Our safety from molestation on the last day's march to Reno was wholly due to the fact that the tribes further north were preparing a great rally, to go upon the war path in great force against Fort Phil. Kearney and its vicinity. Hence it was that the farther we advanced only brought us nearer to the scene of greatest danger, and how great that was I did not then realize; otherwise, the journey might have terminated fatally for me before I reached there.

I can say with the Psalmist, most truly, "He sheltered me from the terror by night, and from the arrow that flieth by noonday." In great mercy the veil was not drawn. The actual conditions at Phil. Kearney were not known fully even at Reno, or were considerately kept from our knowledge. The little travelling was done by occasional mail parties under imperative orders from Omaha, impossible of execution, "to forward a mail weekly at the rate of fifty miles per day, or stand a court martial for failure so to do." Of course, under my peculiar circumstances, the officers at Reno withheld all uncertain rumors to hasten our safe progress before any more violent demonstrations were made by the Indians between Reno and Phil. Kearney. My husband was a soldier reporting for duty and had no hesitation in implicity obeying orders, so that as soon as rested we bade good-by to our kind hosts, never dreaming, thank God, that we should ever visit Fort Reno so differently, as proved to be our destiny.

CHAPTER X.

AFTER a march of twenty-six miles we reached Crazy Woman's Fork of the Powder River in safety. Just at the crossing, the stream makes a sharp turn, giving two separate fords, and having a steep bank on the east side as the traveller enters its basin, but on the west side rising gradually to the summit of the divide that separates its waters from those of Clear Creek.

The only episode connected with this camp was the discovery of a lone stray white cow, that suggested to myself an apparition, at first, in the distance. Not so to the men of the party, who made a precipitate movement toward her in the hope of securing fresh beef. After considerable effort the cow was captured. She must have had a history, but she kept it all to herself, for if there had been any adequate endowment of her use of the English language, in place of her limited vocal range, I doubt not that she would have given us an interesting narrative, for record here. It certainly did seem strange to us to see this isolated specimen of civilized association so completely astray from all suitable guardianship or care. Was she lost from some emigrant train, or had she been run off by Indians and managed to subsist upon buffalo grass in lieu of better provender? We wondered in vain, but afterwards learned that several estrays from a large herd that accompanied the expedition in the summer were lost on the way. At any rate she was our captive, and after improvised methods of the speediest style we made a sacrifice of her person. In previous travels in Arkansas I had eaten bear steak, and it was not very uncommon to eat warm chicken in my Southern home; but this was the first instance in my experience of practical lessons in the culinary art, and that of cooking warm beef, awaited demonstration. I remembered how the deft hand of the colored cook unceremoniously wrung the neck of a chicken, dipped it in hot water to remove its feathers quickly, dismembered it, rolled the parts in batter, and transferred all to the frying pan; but warm beef, never! Our frying pans were soon in evidence and the experiment began. It reminded me of the days of my childhood when I often witnessed my grandfather's darkies cooking turtles of their own capture. The piece of turtle would tremble during the process of cooking, and even after they were pronounced "dun" and placed upon the cabin table before them. Children could never be prevailed upon to touch them. They seemed so uncanny to our eyes that we could not banish the thought that, after all, they must be alive.

I essayed to partake of my portion of cow at the auspicious moment, for the thought sprang up that meat at the stage of fresh, *very fresh,* must be preferable to the canned or salt meat of which one grows weary when limited to its nourishment during a long journey. I made progress, possibly too rapid progress, with my experiment, for I soon lost it.

with all else in the shape of food, and promptly
banished the thought of ever again being successfully tempted to eat any *very fresh* meat. This
mental resolve did not end my discomfort, for I had
to go to bed, and in an ambulance too, as if I had
been naughty, and at a time when I had put forth
my very best efforts to do the thing that seemed
right, and in which all concerned had concurred. I
had accordingly to munch crackers when the internal
equilibrium was restored, and with intermittent
sleep patiently await the morning camp-fire for my
next refreshment.

"Only two more camp-fires to build" before
reaching our final destination, "and nothing of incident worthy of notice."

The poet's words, "to live and move and have
our being," were translated into the most literal
prose, and reduced, mathematically, to its "lowest
terms," and its narrowest limits, *"one* road, *one*
object to attain, and *one* small party on the way."

To reach our goal in safety was the single desire
of our hearts and the concentrated thought of our
minds, and so we dragged along until we reached the
beautiful Lake De Smedt, on the last day of the
journey. This lake * was named for the celebrated
Catholic missionary priest first sent to the Flathead,
Crow, and other Indians of the northwest, and whose

* Captain Palmer says (see page 515, vol. 1, " Coutant's
History of Wyoming"), "Lake Smedt is so strongly impreg-
nated with alkali that an egg or potato will not sink if thrown
in the water. Not many miles from the lake is a flowing oil
well. A scheme might be inaugurated to tunnel under the lake,

successful and honored labors eventually took him to the country now known as Wyoming. He visited the Powder River country, and if he had no other monument than that erected at St. Louis in 1873, this lake will be a perpetual reminder of his useful life among the Indians more than twenty years before the period of which I am writing. He published two volumes, "Letters and Sketches" and "Oregon Missions," which contain most valuable information of western occupation and his efforts to Christianize the savages of the far west. There still remain in Wyoming a few old residents who remember his beneficent work and testify to the personal merit of "Black Robe," as he was called by the Indians upon his first arrival to labor in their behalf.

There are two traditions regarding the name of "Crazy Woman's Fork." One is that a poor demented squaw once lived near this branch of Powder River, in a miserable hut, and died there. Another is, that a party once travelling in that locality, following as they supposed the footsteps of Father De Smedt, were attacked by Indians and one of the men was killed and mutilated in their characteristic

---

set the tunnel on fire and boil the whole body of alkali water and oil into soap."

But, more seriously, we were informed after reaching our destination that the officers of the fort, soon after their arrival, found the north shore of the lake a mass of excoriæ, as from an iron furnace, and that the water was so intensely alkaline that no fishes could live in it, and that they could not force their horses into its waters when trying to collect some brant which fell on the surface during a hunting trip.

manner, and that his wife became insane, wandered away, and was never heard from. The latter tradition is most readily credited by people now living in that vicinity as the more reasonable one, from the fact, as I was recently informed, that such a condition as insanity is unknown among squaws, and if insanity is sometimes attributed to the red man, it is due to the white man's firewater.

But other associations connected with the place are of a historical and authentic nature.

On July 20, 1866, about two months before we encamped on the same spot, there occurred a desperate fight with a band of Indians, which, beyond official report, has never been in print until now, after the lapse of forty-two years, when the story is given me in detail by the only survivor of that day's fight, Mr. S. S. Peters, of Omaha. It reads as follows:

" Our detachment had left Fort Laramie about the 10th of July, and after an exhausting march of eight or nine days reached Fort Reno, on Powder River, and went into camp just outside the stockade. Lieutenant A. H. Wands was in command of the party, and with him were Lieutenants James H. Bradley, P. M. Skinner, George H. Templeton, and Napoleon H. Daniels. All of these officers and men had seen stirring service during the Civil War in various volunteer regiments, and some of the officers had been promoted to the regular army for gallantry during the war. There was with the detachment also an ex-Captain Marr, of a Missouri Regiment, and two civilians. Chaplain David Wright and Assistant Surgeon Heintz joined the party at Fort Reno, and were to proceed with it to the new post at the forks of the Pineys in the Big Horn Mountain country, which was then known as Fort Carrington, in honor of the Colonel commanding the Eighteenth Infantry. The name of Fort Phil. Kearney was given to the post afterward.

73

"The detachment remained in camp a day at Fort Reno, and even then it was with considerable reluctance that Captain Joseph L. Proctor, commanding the post, consented for the party to proceed on to Fort Carrington, with so few numbers, as the Indians were known to be very bad, and it was extremely dangerous for small parties to venture away from the immediate protection of the fort, especially toward the west. Red Cloud was the leader of the hostile Indians and had given out the word that he would massacre every party of white soldiers that dared cross Crazy Woman. He and his Minneconjou Sioux felt that they had been driven to bay by the encroachments of the whites into that country, and with their hereditary enemies on the further west, the Crows, the rapid encroachment of the white soldiers from the east and south had driven him and his band of Sioux to desperation.

"Lieutenant Wands was determined, however, to proceed, and orders were given to prepare for a very early start in the morning of July 20, 1866, from Fort Reno. The outfit consisted all told of twenty-six individuals, including two women, one the wife of Lieutenant Wands and the other the wife of an enlisted man. Five wagons, two ambulances, and four riding horses, one a handsome stallion belonging to Captain Marr, completed the cavalcade.

"The following night was excessively warm and sleep was almost out of the question, and, with all night howling of the great drove of timber wolves and coyotes hovering about the camp, very few of the detachment got any sleep at all.

"Lieutenant Daniels, an Indianian, was especially restless and came over to where I was on guard and walked the beat with me. He said that he had a presentiment that something was going to happen to him very soon and he did not know how to account for it. All efforts to discourage him from entertaining the gloomy phantasy were unavailing, and he seemed determined to dwell upon it, and remained with me until the signal for calling in the guard was given and preparations were ordered made for the start before daylight.

"The purpose of the early start was to get over as much ground as possible before the heat of the day had got in its work. We were advised to take as little water with us as possible, because there was a pool and spring at a place about sixteen miles from Reno, known as Dry Creek, and the water was much better than the Powder River water, which was warm and insipid.

"The march to Dry Creek was made without incident and we reached it just as the sun was rising. To our dismay and grievous disappointment, the spring and pool were found to be about dry, and the dead, scalped and naked body of a white man was found lying in the dry basin of the pool. The body was filled with arrows and had suffered numerous and unmentionable indignities. The fragment of a gray shirt still hanging about the shoulders of the dead man indicated that he was in all probability a soldier. He was evidently a courier from Fort Carrington, and had been waylaid and shot the night before while trying to scoop out the sand in the little basin to find a drink of water.

"We buried the body near the road, and proceeded on toward Crazy Woman Creek, still fifteen or twenty miles away, by the route we must take.

"The finding of the dead body at the pool had a very depressing effect on the entire command, and with the ascending sun the heat became intense. Our water supply, which was meagre at the best, had now given completely out and the animals began showing signs of severe suffering.

"By urging the tired brutes we managed about nine o'clock to reach the crest of the divide that led down into Crazy Woman Valley. A mile or two further and the thin fringe of trees bordering the creek came into view, probably five miles away to the west. Beyond the belt of trees were observed numerous objects which were at once pronounced to be buffalo. The field glasses were brought into requisition and it was agreed that a couple of officers should ride on ahead, cross the creek somewhat above the buffalo, and getting on the other side of them turn the herd in toward the creek, so that about the time the wagon train and command got down into the valley near the timber all could join in a big chase, and several hundred weight of fresh buffalo meat be added to the larder of the command.

"As the train descended the hill toward the creek, the

timber gradually obscured the view beyond, so that neither the two officers nor the buffalo could possibly be seen until they had crossed through the timber toward us. The command was all on the alert for the chase, and thirst and heat were forgotten in the promised excitement that was sure to greet us when we reached the valley near the creek.

" The trail led across a dry timbered branch that joined with Crazy Woman Creek probably an eighth of a mile below the road. This dry creek was a veritable sand pit, and it was extremely heavy pulling through it. We had to follow down this sandy bed about a hundred yards before getting out on to the rise between the two creeks.

" The entire detachment was in this dry bed urging the teams through the sand, when to our complete astonishment a volley of arrows and rifle-shots were poured into us. The shots were accompanied with a chorus of savage yells, and the timber and brush above and about us was fairly alive with Indians. Fortunately no one was hurt by the first onslaught and a detail of ten men under Lieutenant Bradley hurriedly charged up the bank ahead of the lead team and drove a gang of painted devils back toward the Crazy Woman Creek. By almost superhuman exertions the wagons and ambulances were brought up out of the dry sandy bed and hurriedly corraled on the little rise between the creeks.

" The corral was under a hot fire from the Indians, and really before it had been completed, Lieutenant Daniels' horse came tearing into the corral, with the saddle turned under him and a couple of arrows sticking in his neck and two more in his flank. The horse was of course riderless. A second later, Lieutenant Templeton appeared riding up out of the dry bed of the creek hatless, two or three arrows in his horse's withers and flanks, and an arrow in his own back. Templeton was bleeding profusely from a wound in the face, and his whole visage was one of extreme terror, and as soon as he reached the corral he reeled and partly fell from his horse. He was lifted from the saddle in a state of complete collapse. He merely uttered, "Daniels! My God, Indians! They wasn't buffalo." Poor Templeton was quickly laid in one of the wagons for protection, as the Indians were fast closing in around the corral. Already two of the mules had been killed and had to be cut out of the teams. We stood the red devils off as well as we could, but it very soon became evident that we must get out of that hole or every last one of us would be massacred in a very few minutes.

"It was thereupon decided that we should bunch the wagons, two in front with the two ambulances next, and the other three to follow behind, and in this way retreat to a high knoll south of us about a half mile away between the two creeks. We would thus get away from the timber that was sheltering the Indians and would stand some show of giving them as good as they sent. The two dead mules belonged to the cook wagon team, and consequently this somewhat disarranged affairs. We had not more than got started when another of the mules was disabled by a bullet, and it had to be cut out. The rear guard of seven men under Lieutenant Bradley held the Indians off until the mule was cut out. There being no time to lose, as the Indians were constantly being reinforced, we determined to abandon the cook wagon and make our retreat as rapidly as possible. This was done and then it was a fight for life.

"A party of Indians seeing what we were up to undertook to cut off our retreat and to take possession of the hill we were aiming for.

"The advance guard held their ground like heroes and fought every foot of the way. The teams were kept on the run and then came the charge of twelve men under Lieutenant Wands and Lieutenant Skinner up the hill for its possession. The Indians were poor shooters, and wounded only one man in the charge, and then, the cowards they were, broke and ran from the hill. Captain Marr, who had a Henry rifle, a sixteen shooter, used it with wholesome effect on the running Indians, and stopped two of them permanently. They were gathered up, however, by a bunch of Indian horsemen and carried away.

"In the meanwhile the rear guard was holding the Indians in check from the creek side, and the wagons and ambulances were safely brought to the hill. A corral was immediately made, with the mules inside the corral. The ambulances were protected by the wagons, and all the stock in fact were sheltered inside the corral.

"From the hill it could be seen that the Indians were receiving constant reinforcements, and we were fairly surrounded by between two and three hundred of them.

"Rifle pits were dug just outside the corral, and we lay there in the scorching sun, famishing for water. But the Indians were between us and the much desired water, and in fact it seemed as if Indians were everywhere. Off to our left three or four hundred yards was a high sandy ridge, that terminated in a knoll down at the creek. Between the corral and this ridge was a deep narrow cleft in the earth, that led in a crooked course down toward the creek. We did not know of the existence of this ravine until a shower of arrows flew from it toward the corral, which succeeded in wounding three of the men.

"Chaplain Wright was one of the men slightly wounded by the fusilade of arrows from the ravine, and he and a gallant young soldier named Fuller volunteered to charge the ravine and drive the Indians out of it. Wright was armed with but an old-fashioned "pepper box" seven shooter pistol, but undaunted and furiously mad he and Fuller started on the run for the ravine. A moment later we heard a strange volley of shots, something like the modern rapid fire guns, and several Indians were observed climbing up out of the ravine and making hot haste for the ridge to the west. We hurried their departure with a volley from the rifle pits and saw one of them tumble and roll back down the hill and disappear into the ravine. Fuller and Wright appeared again from a point fifty or more yards down the ravine and shouted that they had got two of the devils and that the ravine was clear down as far as the creek. Wright had killed an Indian in the ravine with the "pepper box," it having gone off altogether, thus accounting for the strange volley we had heard.

"The Indians began to get very cautious and were not disposed to take any more chances in the ravine. However, parties of them would mount their ponies, and swinging themselves to the off side of them would make a ferocious dash close to the corral, and fire at us from under their horses' necks. Two more men were wounded by these charges and matters began to look very serious for us. Over half of the detachment were now wounded, several of them seriously, and they were making piteous calls for water.

" The middle of the afternoon wore away, and finally it was determined that a heroic effort should be made to secure water from the creek by way of the ravine at our left. A detail of gallant fellows loaded themselves down with canteens and a couple of buckets and started for the creek. They were covered by a detachment of like number, and further protection was guaranteed them from the wagons.

" The Indians did not seem to catch on to the move, and instead of following the water detail, renewed their attack on the wagons with great vigor. The two ladies were angels of mercy and tenderness and looked after the wounded most hero-ically and bravely. During the absence of the water detail we suffered no casualities, and the detail returned, having met with unbounded success. The water tremendously refreshed all of us, and the poor thirsty animals were also given a portion.

" The Indians by this time discovered that something had happened to revive our spirits and they determined on a con-certed attack to finish us. They made two charges on the corral but were repulsed. We lost, however, one man killed, Sergeant Terrel, and three more wounded. The Indians again withdrew out of range for conference and our own condition was now becoming so desperate that a council of war was held. It was solemnly decided, that in case it came to the worst that we would mercifully kill all the wounded and the two women and then our-selves. The thought then occurred to Chaplain Wright that the attempt might be made for one or two of the command to cut through the Indians, and make the ride back to Fort Reno for reinforcements.

" Captain Marr offered his fine stallion as one of the horses for the ride and Lieutenant Wands tendered his horse for the same purpose. Chaplain Wright and Private William Wallace volunteered to make the heroic attempt.

" They were properly mounted and furnished with a revolver each, and heroically rode out from the corral amid the prayers and God speeds of the little band. They succeeded in reaching the dry creek bed before they were apparently discovered by the Indians. As they rode out of the creek bed up toward the hill, a body of Indians were seen to hurriedly ride out from the forks of the two creeks up the hill toward the two couriers. The ride was a magnificent one. Wright and Wallace saw the Indians coming and put their spurs to their horses and soon reached the crest of the hill far in advance of their pursuers. A moment or two later, pursued and pursuers were lost to view in the gathering twilight, for the sun was already going down beyond the Big Horn Mountains to the west of us.

" Scarcely had Wallace and Wright disappeared in the east, when a cloud of dust was to be observed across the creek to the northwest of us. We divined it to be reinforcements for the Indians. The Indians saw the dust, and they began to rally together and shortly thereafter disappeared in groups down in the timber northward. This movement was unaccountable for some time. The sun had now set and it was growing perceptibly darker.

" Finally a solitary horseman was observed coming over the little ridge to our left. Before he reached the ravine he was ordered to halt. He did so and shouted back that he was a friend.

" ' What's your name? '

" ' Jim Bridger.'

" And so it was. He was shown a crossing through the ravine and came on up to the corral.

" ' I knew there was hell to pay here to-day at Crazy Woman,' said he to a group of officers. ' I could see it from the signs the Indians made on the buffalo skulls. But cheer up, boys, Captain Burroughs and two hundred soldiers are coming down the road there about two miles away.'

" After further inquiry it was learned that Captain Burroughs with a detachment of two hundred men of the Eighteenth were on the road from Fort Carrington to Fort Reno for supplies. The command had intended to make the usual camp that night at Clear Fork, but Jim Bridger, the famous scout who was with the party, reported that he had discovered several signs by markings made by Indians on buffalo skulls that a battle was to be fought at Crazy Woman to-day, and advising all Indians who saw the sign to be on hand. Burroughs rather derided the story, and expressed his serious doubts about there being any party at Crazy Woman to-day at all. Bridger was insistent, however, and so the Burroughs command decided to make the Crazy Woman camp by a forced march.

" So our little command was saved from annihilation.

" The body of Lieutenant Daniels was found the next morning over near the road across Crazy Woman. The entire scalp had been cut from his head and his body was frightfully mutilated. His fingers had been cut off to get a couple of rings from them, and he was subjected to other nameless indignities.

" One of the Indians killed in the ravine was found to have Daniels' shirt on, as well as a large portion of his bleeding scalp.

" The body of Sergeant Terrel was buried on the knoll where we fought, and the body of Lieutenant Daniels was taken to Fort Reno, where it was buried with suitable military honors.

" The wounded were carefully looked after, and on our road back to Fort Reno we met a detachment of the Second United States Cavalry, under Lieutenant H. F. Bingham, coming to our rescue.

" Wright and Wallace had made the ride to Fort Reno successfully, but both horses died from the exertion.

" After a day or two of rest we started again on the march to Fort Carrington and arrived there without incident. We carried with us the order changing the name of the post to Fort Phil. Kearney, and thus it was ever afterwards known.

" S. S. PETERS,
" Company F, Eighteenth United States Infantry.

OMAHA, NEBRASKA, July 6, 1908."

PART II
OUR FRONTIER HOME
GARRISON LIFE ENCIRCLED BY SAVAGE LIFE

CHAPTER XI.

THE long-sought fort was in sight. I could have clapped my hands for joy, but that would not have adequately expressed my experience, which was that of a far deeper current of emotion beyond the province of mere words to express. That fort was even more to me than "the shadow of a rock in a weary land." That metaphor embodies comfort, quiet, peace. It was all that indeed, but more, as a place of refuge from fatigue and danger in the most literal sense, and none the less did I feel to be under the shadow of the Almighty.

We came in sight of Pilot Hill and could see the picket guard waving a signal, a double signal, if we could have interpreted it, and it was well that we did not. The first signal indicated that the wood train had been attacked by Indians just west of the fort, and the second signal gave notice of the appearance of a small party from the eastward, approaching the fort. Detachments had been sent in fevered haste in both directions.

The small party was ours, and we did not quite comprehend the meaning of our tardy welcome from without the gates. Presently the escort fell in line and we moved toward the stockade, but just before entering a halt was made, and I looked eagerly for the occasion of the delay. It almost took my breath away, for a strange feeling of apprehension came over me. We had halted to give passage to a wagon, escorted by a guard from the wood train, coming from the opposite direction. In that wagon was the scalped and naked body of one of their comrades, scarcely cold, who had been murdered so near the fort that the signals by the picket, given almost simultaneously, were now fully understood. My whole being seemed to be absorbed in the one desire,—an agonized but un-uttered cry, "Let me get within the gate!"

Our arrival was hailed with manifestations of great pleasure. We had come through safely, were an addition, though a very small one, to their numbers, and we brought the mail! Commingled feelings possessed all hearts as our ambulance drove up to headquarters, and the wagon containing the dead turned off to the extemporized hospital.

That strange feeling of apprehension never left me, enhanced as it was by my delicate condition; yet once safely within the garrison I gradually adjusted myself so far as possible to the duties and social pleasures that army people avail themselves of, whatever their environment, Indian or otherwise. Here we were again among women, four of them, and officers' wives, too, who extended their kindly and sisterly greetings. Hope sprang up! Might we not indeed realize some compensation for the tiresome ordeal of the previous months!

For the present, at least, our "forward march" had ended. At this new post, so excellently built, we found houses for the officers and soldiers' quarters instead of tents. Here also were warehouses, sutler's store, band-quarters, and a guard-house, either completed or under construction, a fine parade ground, which imparted form, comeliness, and system to the whole, without a flag-staff planted as yet, but one prone on the ground where busy workers were preparing for that event. The presence of mountain howitzers in proper position was a more assuring feature, bearing, in case of need, their own distinctive message.

The incessant labor of chopping, hauling, and hewing wood, with saw-mills in full operation, with ditching and such other varied duty that claimed attention day by day, was the execution of plans and drawings of Colonel Carrington, matured at old Fort Kearney in the early spring. Some of the officers' quarters were not finished, and ours were not completed until November, so that for the time tents were substituted for the ambulance, quite an advance for comfort, in comparison.

While sitting with Mrs. Carrington in the office of her husband waiting for luncheon and also for our tents to be erected, conversation quite naturally turned upon the current incidents of their garrison life, as suggested by the painful episode of the murdered soldier attendant upon our arrival. With interjected expressions of gratitude for our safety, the fate of another comrade of the wood party guard was spoken of which had occurred but recently; how "he had been badly wounded with arrows and scalped, but managed to break off the shafts so as not to be impeded in crawling through the thicket, dragging himself nearly half a mile to the block-house, where he lived but a short time; and of the artist Grover, correspondent of Frank Leslie's Weekly, who had been scalped one Sunday afternoon while only a few minutes' walk from the post. As they were surrounded by Indians, these incidents were matters of almost daily occurrence. Not a stick of timber could be cut, nor a load of hay secured for the garrison without conflict. Listening unavoidably to the conversation might have been part of my initiation, but it did not tend to produce a comfortable or quieting state of mind; needless to say, quite the reverse!

The presence of other women, however, was reassuring and certainly comforting after I had been for so many weary days and nights exiled from their companionship. Besides Mrs. Carrington were Mrs. Wands, Mrs. Bisbee, and Mrs. Horton, wife of Surgeon Horton, Surgeon in Chief of the Mountain District, on the Colonel's staff, charming ladies all, each of whom in her own way gave tokens of friendship; and their kindly, considerate acts come up fresh to mind when the chord is touched. Even the mention of their names brings up pleasant memories of the past. "I was sick and ye visited me," I trust may be their reward, for "their works do follow them."

Through a gap of forty-two years, the friendship of Mrs. Horton still abides, and we have only to look into each other's faces to reread the story. Surely one of the greatest joys of heaven will be a resuscitated memory.

"Lulled in the countless chambers of the brain,
Our thoughts are linked by many a golden chain,
Awake but one, and lo, what myriads rise,
Each stamps its image on the other's eyes."

I place my hands upon these tender chords and cease their vibrations, turning to matters of current importance to myself personally, for I was soon to have the untried experience of sleeping for the first time in a tent.

The very thought of it, in comparison with the ambulance, which I hoped never to see again, not unmindful of past uses but from sheer weariness at the thought of one, brought cheerful anticipation as I looked forward to the exchange! Logical in theory; as a matter of practice—we shall see!

A detail of men from our company soon began operations. Two "A tents," set up and drawn together, were soon in shape for our occupancy, the front one for trunks, two rather dilapidated camp stools and a disfigured mess-chest, the other for two hospital bunks which filled nearly all the space, a small heating stove opposite, leaving a narrow passageway to a tarpaulin beyond, under which was a cook-stove placed ready for the preparation of the next morning's breakfast.

The prospect did really seem inviting, and when the night sentry called out the hour, the number of his post, and "All's well," surely I could make a hearty personal response and retire with a measure of complacency of mind and repose of body.

CHAPTER XII.

GARRISON LIFE BEGUN.

The sudden change of temperature incident to the high altitude and climate of our new home caused a deep snow to fall during the very night of our arrival, and the tents having been insecurely drawn together, combined with the penetrating wind to supply an extremely novel experience. The snow drifted in, covered my face, and there melting trickled down my cheeks until if I had shed tears they would have been indistinguishable. The cheering proverb, "weeping may endure for a night, but joy cometh in the morning," had neither solace nor comfort for me, just then!

When I arose from fitful slumber and had sufficiently cleared my eyes and face from snow to take my bearings deliberately it was only to find that pillows, bedding, and even the stove and the ground within the tent were also covered. Notwithstanding my misery, there was something actually ludicrous in the situation. I did afterwards intimate to friends that the fancy of thus prematurely donning snow-white robes did not occur to me at that moment, for neither levity nor philosophy could adequately meet the occasion. Shaking out stockings and emptying shoes filled with fine snow was earthly and practical in the extreme.

A soldier from our company had been detailed to make fires and render other domestic service as best he could, and the cook-stove required the first attention both for its heat and its more appetizing functions. That stove proved to be a success. Its warmth soon melted the snow, but in passing from the stove-tent to the mess-chest in the other tent, a slip-shod step became from actual necessity my trying resort. It would seem, and indeed it did seem, as if I had reached the extreme limit of endurance, but no, I had not.

I can speak of it now in calm terms, but at the moment I had such a sensation of actual desperation come over me that with butcher-knife in hand for preparation of something for breakfast I almost threatened then and there to end it all, and I could have settled the question "to be, or not to be " in short order. And then the second thought was of a less morbid vein and I resolved to "take up arms against this sea of trouble " and master the situation.

My first decided action resulted in the manufacture of some very hard biscuit from flour, salt, and water; and then bacon and coffee. All these in course of time were deposited upon the mess-chest for our first morning meal and the bacon and coffee were first served. Then for the biscuit. No hatchet chanced to be conveniently near to aid in separating them in halves, but the work had to be done. Impulsively I seized the butcher-knife, so recently associated with a vague idea of other use, but in the endeavor to do hatchet-work with it the blade slipped and almost severed my thumb, mingling both blood and tears. Had I any doubt of the truth of my statement or the memory thereof I have only to look at the scar which I still wear after the lapse of more than the third of a century.

One morning I started a brisk fire with shavings abundant when a sudden wind blew the sparks under the foundations of the commanding officer's quarters where the débris from carpenter work had accumulated, setting the whole on fire and actually threatening the building itself; but quick discovery and prompt action on the part of someone passing by soon extinguished the flame. I suppose that it was thought to be unsafe for such risky experiments as mine in the cooking line, for almost immediately new quarters were assigned me in a large hospital tent recently vacated by the Colonel's family, which had moved into their headquarters building then about half finished. The change was a decidedly agreeable one, that of a large tent with a safer cooking arrangement and better protection from future snow and wind blasts.

For some time after that we had no snow and the weather continued fine for weeks, so that in that invigorating climate there was a quick response to the delightful change, at least from a physical point of view. It did not, and could not, bring unalloyed happiness, for Indian alarms were almost constant and attacks upon the wood trains were so frequent that I had a horror of living in a tent, however large or convenient, so near the stockade as the officers' line of quarters had been located.

The stockade itself was rapidly nearing completion, notwithstanding all other work went on, and the skirmishing continued to be accepted as a part of the daily discipline and experience. It was made of heavy pine trunks eleven feet in length hewn to a touching surface of four inches, so as to join closely, all pointed, loop-holed, and imbedded in the ground for four feet. Block-houses were at two diagonal corners and one at the water-gate, and massive double gates of double plank, with small sally-wickets and substantial bars and locks opened on three fronts, while the fourth directly behind the officers' quarters had but a small sally-port, for the officers' use only. My constant fear was that the Indians would work their way over the stockade under cover of the darkness at night. Opening from this, the fort proper, was a rough cottonwood stockade, or corral, known as the quartermaster's yard, which contained quarters for teamsters, stock, wagons, hay ricks, and shops for wagon-makers, saddlers, and other general apparatus and conveniences usual in a large frontier fort. I often heard the crack of a rifle, so near that it seemed to be just at the back of my tent. The evident plan of the Indians was to harass the fort constantly by running off stock, to cut off any soldier or citizen who ventured any distance from the gates, and also to entice soldiers from the protection of the stockade and then lead them into some fatal ambush. As yet it was perfectly certain that the leading chiefs had not settled upon any plan to attack the fort itself in mass. Why they did not do so earlier and before the fort was completed is still a mystery.

The mountain scenery about the post was grand,

and the beautiful Tongue River Valley, with its countless bright streams, was full of charms. With the Panther Mountains beyond to the westward the Big Horn Mountains to the southward, and the Black Hills, soon after made so famous for golded treasure, to the eastward, surely Fort Phil. Kearney was beautiful for situation. Lowering my gaze to the hills immediately near us, my eyes more frequently rested with pleasure upon Pilot Hill, only a few hundred yards from the fort. This shapely conical summit was the real watch-tower from which the faithful picket guard would signal danger as his watchful eye caught glimpses and his waving flag announced an approaching foe.

As our world revolved in a very small space there were no happenings that were unrelated, and the stories of miners, trappers, and guides were more intensely interesting as told by word of mouth than when filtered through the printed page.

It was my good fortune to meet with old Jim Bridger, already past his three-score and ten, who had been the chief guide to Colonel Carrington in the opening of the country. He was a typical "plainsman" and his name is perpetuated by such types as Fort Bridger and Bridger's Ferry. He had been a chief among the friendly Crows and the guide to Brigham Young in earlier days, and his biography, if written, would make a ponderous volume of tragic and startling events. Although uneducated, he spoke both Spanish and English, as well as many Indian tongues, and his genial manners and simplicity of bearing commanded respect as well as the attachment and confidence of all who knew him well.

A quaint story is related of Bridger that when Laramie was but a small frontier outpost it was visited by a rich Irish nobleman who was upon a great hunting expedition among the Rockies and had secured Bridger for his guide. His outfit was made up of six wagons, twenty-one carts, twelve yoke of cattle, twelve horses, fourteen dogs and forty servants. He made Laramie the base of his supplies for several months during the hunting season. Bridger was a very revelation of a genuine sportsman to the lordly Irishman, who especially admired him for his honesty, simplicity, and shrewdness, as well as his knowledge of woodcraft and game. The contrast between the Irish gentleman and his train and the rude Bridger, who had depended upon his rifle for his livelihood from early childhood, was at times very amusing. The Irishman would lie in bed until a late hour, then take his hunt and return late at night, but however late he returned he would bring meat and insist upon having a late dinner to which he would invite Bridger. After the meal was over Sir George Gore, for that was his name, was in the habit of reading aloud to draw out Bridger's ideas of the author. On one ocasion when reading from Shakespeare and about Fallstaff, Bridger broke out with the exclamation: "That's too hyfalutin for me; that thar Fullstuff was a leettle too fond o' lager beer!" Sir George read the adventures of Baron Munchausen one evening. Bridger shook his head a moment and then remarked, "I'll be dog-goned if I ken swaller everything that **Baron** sez. I believe he's a liar.'' A moment afterwards he added, that, ''some of his own adventures among the Blackfoot Indians, in old times, would read just as wonderful if they were jest writ down in a book.''

He used to tell us stories occasionally at the fort. He ridiculed the frontiersmen for their ''gold craze'' and laughed himself as he told a hunter once that ''there was a diamond out near the Yellowstone Country that was on a mountain and if any one was lucky enough to get the right range it could be seen fifty miles, and one fool offered him a new rifle and a fine horse if he would put him on the right track to go for that diamond.''

Bridger would walk about, constantly scanning the opposite hills that commanded a good view of the fort, as if he suspected Indians of having scouts behind every sage clump, or fallen cottonwood; and toward evening, as well as in the early morning, it was not strange that we caught flashes of small hand mirrors, which were used by the Indians in giving signals to other Indians who were invisible from the fort. Indeed all sights and sounds were of constant interest, if not of dread, living so constantly in the region of the senses, keyed to their highest tone by the life external. I often wondered why a post so isolated was not swept away by a rush of mighty numbers of the surrounding savages, to avenge in one vast holocaust the invasion of their finest hunting grounds. Only our strong defenses prevented an assault, and the depletion of our numbers by attacks upon our exposed wood trains seemed to be their sole hope of finding some opportunity by which to find the way to final extermination of the garrison itself.

The nights were made hideous at times by the hungry wolves who gathered in hordes about the slaughter-yard of the quartermaster, without the stockade, and near the Little Piney Creek. The only reassuring comfort was the statement of Bridger and others that Indians were rarely near when many wolves were present, and that they could distinguish the howl of the wolf from the cry of the Indian, by the fact that the former produced no echo. Once indeed, Indians, knowing that the soldiers were accustomed to put poison on the offal at the slaughter-yard to secure the pelts of the wolves for robes, crawled up close to the stockade, crawling under wolf-skins that covered their bodies, and a sentry was actually shot from the *banquet* that lay along the stockade, by an arrow, before any knowledge of the vicinity of the enemy came to the garrison.

In contrast with howling wolves and screeching savages who on one occasion rode in full view along the summit opposite the fort, waving their blankets and yelling their fierce bravadoes, we had the fine music of our splendid band of forty pieces, which played at guard-mounting in the morning and at dress-parade at sunset, while their afternoon drills and evening entertainments were in strange contrast with the solemn conditions that were constantly suggestive of war and sacrifice of life. If unable to soothe the savage breast, our music did soothe our civilized dread and force cheer in spite of ever present danger.

An Indian superstition maintained that a man killed in the darkness must spend eternity in darkness, and if that enured to our benefit, all right; but it did not deter Indians from making demonstrations by moonlight. On one occasion, just after dark, an alarm called attention to a large fire built on the top of Sullivant Hills, where Indians were visible, dancing about the flames where they were supposed to be taking a substantial meal of basted venison. No alarm was given, but the Colonel turned three howitzers upon the spot, cut fuses for the right time of flight, and all were fired at the same instant. Two spherical case shot exploded just over the fire scattering the bullets which they carried, and the fire was instantly trampled out as the Indians swiftly disappeared. It was a novel surprise to the redman that at a distance of several hundred yards the white soldier could drop into their midst such masterful vollies as eighty-four one-ounce bullets at every discharge. To us who watched the flight and witnessed the flash of the explosion in their very midst there was a satisfaction in the conviction that the Indians would hardly venture to come nearer when the "guns that shoot twice," as they called our howitzers, could do so much fighting even at night at so great a distance.

CHAPTER XIII.

THE residents of Fort Phil. Kearney were not troubled with *ennui*. While the men were busy in their departments of labor, the ladies were no less occupied in their accustomed activities. "Baking, brewing, stewing, and sewing" was the alliterative expression of the daily routine. With little fresh meat other than juiceless wild game, buffalo, elk, deer, or mountain sheep, and no vegetables, canned stuffs were in immediate and constant requisition. Once, indeed, Mr. Bozeman sent a few sacks of potatoes from his ranch in Montana to headquarters, as precious as grain in the sacks of Israel's sons in Egypt; but these were doled out in small quantities to officers' families, while the remainder, the major part, was sent to the hospital for men afflicted or threatened with scurvy.

The preparation of edible from canned fruits, meats, and vegetables taxed all ingenuity to evolve some product, independent of mere stewing, for successful results. Calico, flannel, and linsey woolsey, procured from the sutler's store, with gray army blankets as material for little boys' overcoats, composed the staple goods required, and ladies' garments, evolved after the "hit or miss" style, came in due time without the aid of sewing machines, of which none were at the post. Our buffalo boots were of a pattern emanating from or necessitated

99

by our frontier locality, a counterpart of the leggings worn by the men, except that theirs did not have the shoe attachment. They were made by the company shoemakers of harness leather, to which was attached buffalo skin, with the hair inside, reaching almost to the knee and fastened on the outside with leather straps and brass buttons. The brass buttons were not for ornament, but a necessity in lieu of any other available kind. Nothing could exceed them in comfort, as a means adapted to an end.

There were hours when one could sit down composedly for a bit of sewing in a comfortable chair, with additional pleasure in the possession of a table sufficiently large for the double duty of dining and work table. With the few books I had carried with me for companionship distributed about, there was just a bit of homelikeness in tent life. My cooking experiments were never a great success, especially in the attempt at making pies, though I tried to emulate the ladies of larger experience in the effort. The cook-stove rested upon boards somewhat inclined, which was fatal to pie-making, which I did attempt a few times from canned fruit only to find in due time well developed crusts minus the fruit, which had oozed out gradually during the process, still in evidence of my good intentions, and to be eaten with as much philosophy as one could command with a straight face, disguising laughter, or tears.

Through the kind consideration of Mrs. Carrington, a large double bedstead was made by the carpenters, a luxury indeed, with mattress stuffed with dried grass, army blankets, and a large gay-colored shawl for counterpane, and surely no four-poster of mahogany, with valences of richest texture and downy pillows, and, for that matter, no Chippendale table, with these furniture accessories, could have been more prized during my life at the fort, as a demonstration of the simple life theory in every detail, whether enforced or otherwise.

Often, while reading or sewing quietly by myself, I would be startled by a rustling at my tent door, but fears were soon allayed when I discovered the beautiful head of Mrs. Horton's pet antelope protruding within. Its large, melting eyes would look at me appealingly, and, with sufficient encouragement, it would approach for the accustomed caress and favorite bite to eat.

Of the little children at the fort there were four boys, and many pleasant hours were spent in my tent with Jimmy Carrington, my little favorite, whose loving disposition made him a welcome guest. No picknickers of the pine woods ever enjoyed a repast so much as we did, after our simple preparations, involving a trip to the sutler's store, where cans of sugar were obtained, each with a mysterious-looking little bottle of lemon essence deposited therein, from which we produced lemonade, and this, together with ginger-snaps and nuts, made a "dainty dish fit for a King," never mind about the birds. After the repast was the song. He possessed a remarkably sweet voice, and together we sang familiar Sunday School hymns his mother had taught him, one of which I especially recall, "There is a light in the window for me," and his sweet childish tones sang the words deeply into my heart.

Sunday evening singing at headquarters was a feature of the day. Neither was Sunday morning service neglected, for, though no chapel had as yet been erected, each new building in turn was utilized for the service. With a fine string band to accompany the voices, and sometimes additional instruments, the presence of God was felt and recognized in this impromptu worship. Several of the band were German Catholics and good singers. On one occasion especial pains had been taken by the Colonel to make the music an attractive specialty to interest the men. The chaplain, Rev. David White, was a devout Methodist, of good heart and excellent in teaching the soldiers' children at the fort, for there were several, but very unsophisticated in general society matters. On one occasion, when great care had secured the rendition of "Te Deum Laudamus," in which the band took part, he very solemnly asked the Colonel, "Isn't that a Catholic tune?" and upon answer by the Colonel, "Why, that is one of the oldest and most glorious hymns of the Church all over Christendon," he expressed surprise, but thought himself that "it seemed to be quite religious, but it was new to him."

With a coterie of five ladies at the post, each had four places to visit, and the most was made of it in comparing notes upon the important matters of cooking, sewing, and our various steps of advancement in the different arts, quite independently of prevailing fashions of dress in the States, and yet this did not signify entire emancipation, for the problem was still a little perplexing in the evolution of new ideas, while mutual helpfulness simplified all our efforts. There was often an all-round social dance, games of cards, the "author's game," and other contrivances for recreation and amusement, in addition to the receptions at headquarters, which were spirited and congenial, and, with a band having the deserved reputation of being the finest in the army, their choice music was no small feature in the cheer on the frontier.

CHAPTER XIV.

SOCIALITIES AND ALARMS—A DREADFUL EXPERIENCE.

"Dwelling in tents," as suggested by the name, was a passing phase in the life of all at the Fort. When the day arrived for another move on my part, it was not made after the manner of the Arabs. In the transition, I simply left the tent standing, confidently took up my goods and chattels, as many as I could carry, and bore them silently to the little house built for my special use.

The house was made of pine logs, recently felled and not quite dry, and small pine poles closely set for the best possible protection were covered with clay for the roof. Beneath were three,—yes, actually three,—rooms. I could hardly realize this luxury. In my haste to move I could not wait for any further drying process, but tacked blankets around the bed-space and took the chances. Pieces of sheeting answered for window shades in two rooms and old newspapers, a very rare article, covered the kitchen windows. The company tailor sewed gunny sacks from which the corn had been hurriedly emptied, and I soon had a carpet. My residence seemed palatial. The kitchen stove was now upon a level, and yet in spite of this assurance I was too discouraged to renew my efforts at pie-making and turned my attention, not less ambitiously, and with more hope of success, to puddings.

Fortunately, bread could be procured from the

baker and "packed butter" from the sutler's store at the moderate price of 75 cents per pound. I had never made any butter, but at this period of my experience, I learned to "make it over." It was neither artificially colored nor flavored, but its chief characteristic was its strength. This element suggested that by pouring hot water over the mass to reduce its excessive saltness and kneading it well, I might restore the residuum to a fair grade of excellent butter. I set to work industriously, and my first pudding, of butter and bread, sugar, raisins, and water, was soon ready for the oven. The time-limit for baking depended upon circumstances. The pine wood fire would burn out so quickly, so suddenly, that unremitting attention was necessary for good results, and that I did not seem able to bestow with the accumulation of other duties, but when the sunset gun was fired and "Retreat" sounded, my pudding, having been in the oven for six hours, was considered done, and sufficiently browned at least to justify its removal. The sauce was not so complicated in preparation. A portion of flour, sugar, and water, not too much flour, was soon ready for disposal, milk being a later acquisition. As my fruit pudding proved adequate for two meals, the next day I turned my attention to cooking "desiccated" vegetables, of all sorts, compressed into a large cake, thoroughly dried, requiring but a *small quantity* for a meal, but this item of knowledge was to come later. At my first experiment, I broke off a very generous piece and deposited it in a large pot, happy to achieve both cooked vegetables and soup.

When the vegetables got down to business, boiling and swelling at every moment, the situation became alarming. I began to dip out, at intervals, depositing in other vessels, till I wondered what was going to happen, when I called my husband. He laughed uproariously at my dilemma and suggested that already I had cooked enough to feed all the cows in the garrison. The Indians had run off so much stock that milk was a precious commodity. An egg was occasionally sent in by the kind ladies, and it was my fervent wish that no ruthless hand would kill the hen that laid those precious eggs. It seems, that when the expedition left old Fort Kearney in May, the Commander had purchased several hundred beeves which accompanied the train, including seven cows for officers' families; a few turkeys and chickens, also, but on my arrival few were left and the cattle, not stolen, were so thin as to be almost valueless.

I felt glad that all of the ladies were not so dependent upon themselves as was my lot. Mrs. Carrington had a colored man-servant, who when dressed at his best, looked not unlike a head-waiter in a more pretentious hotel capacity. Mrs. Wands brought with her a colored maid, resembling a Pawnee, barring her characteristic hair, and the flirtations between this pair were often a source of merriment, but never taken seriously. Captain Ten Eyck had secured the services of a colored woman who had the distinctive qualification for her position, that she could make sausages, and good sausages, out of almost every kind of meat, except impossible pork. Mrs. Bisbee found no difficulty in evolving mince pies, "Phil. Kearney mince pies," from beef-heart, dried apples, raisins, and sweetened vinegar, for she seemed to possess natural talent in that direction. Mrs. Horton, in her sweet winning way, so companionable and ready to render sympathy and help, from the fashioning of a dress to the making of a pudding sauce in minutest detail, would offer from her little store, a precious egg, labelled as to date when laid, and endeared herself to me in many ways. Her lover-husband stood ready always to second her efforts in my direction and reward them with encouragement and praise. All this, apart from his skill as a physician, holds to this day a warm place in my heart.

But there is one element of desolation in garrison life on the frontier, brighten it how you will, never to be ignored. The soldier had not the stimulus of getting gold that induced the original pioneers of the west to brave all dangers in its acquirement. He had to make the best he could of life where the fundamental lesson to be learned is simply that of strict obedience to authority, whatever of discipline, self-denial, or hardness it involves. Whether he sees the working out of plans according to his own ideas, or otherwise, it is not for him to question. It was well known that there was gold to be found in all the creeks near us, and a few pannings in the nearest branch abundantly proved it; but not a soldier deserted the post, or shirked his duty in its pursuit. Never did a garrison of United States troops on the frontier more implicitly and honorably regard the regulations made and enforced for their protection, and the safety of the expedition. Its very organization contemplated almost an entire isolation in a country surrounded by thousands of hostile and desperate savages. The conduct of the officers themselves, with one or two exceptions, was admirable, though some were hasty at times, and impatient for more aggressive operations against this ubiquitous and numberless combination of all the Indians of the Northwest.

The character study of the true trapper, hunter, or typical plains-man, so different from that of the dependent private soldier, is a source of perennial enjoyment as he has pursued his own independent way, fascinated by a life amid dangers, hardships and trials, and yet, with it all, planting civilization on plain and mountain, all "without your leave," to the Indian, and doing his part in winning the West. The duties of the army officer and soldier were, in general, the same; but over a different trail, while the dust of both mingled in the struggle.

"Full many a gem of purest ray serene" the dark unfathomed gorge of mountain hides, and this prairie sea, of earth, holds the dust of heroes unsung, and oft unhonored, except as here and there some memorial stone, river, island, or fort commemorates a particular deed or name.

CHAPTER XV.

As the month of October drew near its close a
general order was read one evening at parade, then
at each company quarters, and bulletined at the
guard-house and the sutler's store, announcing that
on the last day of the month, which would be the
regular muster day for pay and inspection, there
would be special exercises for the formal dedication
to its proper use of the fine flag-staff which Chief
Musician Barnes, a former ship-carpenter, and
William Daley had long been preparing for the Post.
The order also especially gratified the men, no less
than the company officers, that the preceding day,
October 30th, would be a "Preparation Day," one
of rest from general duty, as the muster for inspection and pay would be in full dress and followed by
a formal review.

Owing to the exacting nature of well-denominated
"fatigue duty," day after day, officers as well as
men, except at guard-mounting in the morning,
usually wore undress uniforms, but the exactness of
neatness, even as to blacking boots, shining buttons
and belt plates for the guard details, were never
relaxed. My husband often spoke of this strictness
as especially calculated to stimulate the men to
remember that they were still soldiers of the Old
Eighteenth of the Civil War, although the most

severe conditions of physical labor were parts of inevitable duty at the time. The very sight of the band, as it appeared daily at guard-mounting, as fully equipped as if on duty at Governor's Island, West Point, or any other eastern Post, was a joy and cheer to everybody, and, as the three most tidy soldiers at guard inspection were chosen as Orderlies for District and Post Commander as well as for the Officer of the Day, the competition was sometimes very eager.

The order, therefore, announced a most thorough inspection, so as to determine the exact condition of every man, every animal, and every property. Wear and tear had been constant, and in spite of all the armorers could do more than one hundred rifles had become unserviceable, over twenty of them in my husband's own company. The completion of the fort up to the full conception of the original plan was a pleasure to us all, as it did seem as if its defensive qualities would be almost equal to a reinforcement of troops. The Colonel had established slender poles tipped with small strips of white cloth at various ranges, including the maximum howitzer range, so that soldiers on the parade ground, in block-house, or on the stockade sentry platform, would know exactly when an Indian would come within his accurate firing distance and not waste his precious ammunition without effect. All this inspired confidence in the men and equally strengthened the confidence of the commander in them.

There had been very little rest up to that time. Usually on the Sabbath there was only temporary duty to be done, and at the guard-mounting, Sundays, the band itself usually played standard hymn tunes, such as "Old Hundred," "Nearer my God to Thee," and similiar pieces, sometimes adding "Annie Laurie," "When the Swallows Homeward Fly," and other restful, quieting airs. Much of the earnest and painstaking service of the men was in part due to this considerate regard for the memories and associations of former homelife, and all this was strengthened by a stern order called by some "Bully 38" (for such was its number), which was occasioned by the brutal striking of a soldier by his sergeant and some profane endorsement of the sergeant by his own lieutenant. A single paragraph will give its spirit.

"That perversion of authority on the part of non-commissioned officers which displays itself in profane swearing, verbal abuse, kicks and blows, and which violates every social, moral, and military principle, will be dealt with in the most decided manner." . . . "No less useless is vulgar, profane and abusive language. It never can command respect. It never will prompt a cheerful obedience, where the soldier retains a spark of manhood, though he may implicitly obey the very letter of the order given." . . .

"Whatever (not his own act) degrades a man, destroys the soldier, and it is perfectly compatible with strict discipline, and the highest order of military subordination, to command that the personal rights of the soldier be held as sacred as those of officers."

The ladies of the garrison were horrified when the incident thus reprimanded occurred in their full view one morning; and the public reprimand, read at the afternoon parade, and placed on the bulletin at the guard-house, distasteful as it was to the subjects of the rebuke, required no further penalty to enforce its observance.

"Preparation Day" came at last, and the morrow was anticipated as if it were a veritable Thanksgiving in the States.

With main-mast and top-mast scientifically in place, rising one hundred and twenty-four feet above the parade surface, halliards reeved, a large, octagonal bandstand around its foot, and a well-adjusted and seated platform just in front of headquarters, for us ladies to form one side of a hollow square, to be supplemented by the garrison for the other sides, "the assembly" was sounded at the hour fixed in orders.

Lieutenant Adair, who had succeeded Captain Fred Phisterer (a most beloved officer ordered east on his approaching promotion) as assistant adjutant-general of the district and as adjutant of the Eighteenth, had the adjutant's call sounded. Companies promptly formed before their respective quarters, then in line of battle, and then the divisions moved to their allotted positions.

"Attention" was sounded by the chief bugler, followed by the Colonel's "order arms!" "parade rest!" and Chaplain White invoked the divine blessing upon the exercises to follow.

Then followed the Commander's Address, which is given in full.*

* From Coutant's History of Wyoming from the Earliest Known Discoveries. In three volumes. Vol. i, pp. 563–5. When

OUR FRONTIER HOME

" Officers and Men!

" Three and one-half months ago stakes were driven for the now perfected outlines of Fort Phillip Kearney. Aggressive Indians threatened to exterminate the command. Our advent cost us blood! Private Livenberger of F Company was the first victim, July 17, 1866. Lieutenant Daniels, Private Callery of G Company, Gilchrist and Johnson of E Company, Fitzpatrick of H Company, and Oberly and Hauser, have also, in the order named, given their lives to redeem our pledge to never yield one foot of advance, but to guarantee a safe passage for all who seek a home in the lands beyond.

" Fifteen weeks have passed, varied by many skirmishes and by both day and night alarms, but that pledge holds good. In every work done, your arms have been in hand. In the pine tracts or in the hay fields, on picket or general guard duty, no one has failed to find a constant exposure to some hostile shaft, and to feel that a cunning adversary was watching every chance to harass and kill.

" And yet, that pledge holds good. Stockade and blockhouse, embrasure and loop-hole, shell and bullet, have warned off danger, so that women and children now notice the savage only to look for fresh occasion for you to punish him and, with righteous anger, to avenge the dead.

" The Indian dead numbers yours, fourfold, while your acquired experience and better cause afford you constant success in every encounter. This is not all. Substantial warehouses, containing a year's supply, spacious and enduring quarters and a well-appointed magazine are other proofs of your diligence and spirit. The steam whistle and the rattle of the mower have followed your steps in this westward march of empire. You have built a central post that will bear comparison with any for

---

Address was delivered, and Col. Carrington placed the halliards in the hands of young William Daley, he did not know as fully as he did later, that the mechanical work on the flag-staff was almost wholly that of Daley; but his verbal recognition appears in the Address that follows, *italicized.*

security, completeness and adaptation to the end in view, wherever the other may be located or however long in erection.*

"Surrounded by temptations to hunt the choicest game, and allured by tales of gold just beyond you,† you have spared your powder for your foes and have given the labor of your hands to your proper work. Passing from guard-mounting to fatigue-work, and often, after one night in bed, returning to your post as sentry, attempting with success all trades and callings, and handling the broad axe and hammer, the saw and the chisel, with the same success with which you have sent the bullet, your work has proven how well deserved was the confidence I repose in all of you, and that same old pledge holds good.

"Coincident with your march to this point was the occupation of Fort Reno, first by B Company of this battalion, afterwards reinforced by F Company, and the advance of Companies D and G to Fort C. F. Smith, nearly one hundred miles farther west. All these, like yourselves, having a share in the labor, the exposure and the conflicts that throughout the whole length of the line attended its occupation, have sustained the good record of the 18th Infantry, and thus, also, have vindicated your pledges.

"And now, this day, laying aside the worn and battered garments, which have done their part through weeks of toil and struggle,‡ this veteran battalion of the 18th Infantry, from which perhaps I shall be parted in the changes of army life and organization, puts on the full dress attire for muster and review.

"The crowning office, without which you would regard your work as scarcely begun, is now to be performed, and to its fulfilment I assign soldiers, neither discharging the duty myself nor

---

* Brigadier General W. B. Hazen, upon his tour of inspection, pronounced this stockade the best he had ever known, excepting one in British America built by the Hudson Bay Company at great labor and expense.

† Gold color panning out quite plainly was in every creek near us.

‡ New uniforms were issued to the entire command.

delegating it to some brother officer; but some veteran soldier of good repute shall share with a sergeant from each of their companies and the worthy men whose work rises high above us, the honor of raising our new and beautiful Garrison Flag to the top of the handsomest flag-staff in America.

"It is the first full "Garrison Flag" that has floated between the Platte and Montana; and this beautiful pole, perfect in detail as if wrought and finished in the navy yards of New York, Philadelphia, or Boston, will be to Sergeant Barnes, whose appropriate verses will be read to you and William Daley, a long remembered trophy of their patriotism and skill; a new impulse to your own future exertions; a new cause for pride as its stars and stripes are daily unfolded; a new source of courage to each traveller westward, and a new terror to foes who dare to assail you.

"With music and the roar of cannon we will greet its unfoldings—

"This day shall be a holiday and a fresh starting point for future endeavor.

"And yet, all is not said that I wish to say! While we exalt the National standard and rejoice in its glory and power, let us not forget the true source of that glory and power.

"For our unexampled health and continued success; for that 'land of the free and home of the brave;' for our institutions and their fruits, we owe all to the Great Ruler who made and has preserved us.

"Let us, then, ask all, with uncovered heads and grateful hearts, to pause in our act of consecration while the Chaplain shall invoke God's own blessing upon that act, so that while this banner rises heavenward, and so shall rise with each recurring sun, all hearts shall rise to the throne of the Infinite, and for this day, its duties and its pleasures, we shall become better men and better soldiers of the great Republic."

For a few moments perfect silence prevailed. The group of selected sergeants and enlisted men gathered about the halliards in the hands of Daley;

the men in position stood at "parade-rest" with right hands raised to their plumed hats; and officers, as well as ourselves and the staff on the platform, with Mrs. Carrington in the centre, and the little boys at our front, remained in a reverential attitude while the Chaplain offered prayer.

Then, in quick succession, rang out the orders, "Attention!" "Present, arms!" "Play!" "Hoist!" "Fire!"

With the simultaneous *snap* of presented arms in salute, the "long roll" of the combined drum-corps was followed by the full band playing "The Star Spangled Banner," the guns opened fire, and the magnificent flag with its "thirty-six-foot fly" and its "twenty-foot *hoist*" slowly rose to mast-head and was broken out in one glorious flame of red, white, and blue!

The thrill of contending emotions was almost overpowering for the moment. The day itself was simply glorious! The air was soft and balmy, requiring no protecting outer wrappings, and the sun was so bright that several of the ladies used para-sols. The epaulets and decorations of the officers and the freshly burnished brass shoulder scales of the troops added intense brilliancy to the groupings around the compact centre. The very shadow of the immense flag, as it floated at full length in the breeze, seemed to answer back our waving handker-chiefs; and while cheers were not permitted to break the dignified exultation of the occasion, we *did* invol-untarily clap our hands, and our beating hearts did respond to the vibrations of the guns, whose echoes among the hills seemed to magnify their number as if a battle were raging all about us. Then, every officer on the alert, at the order, "pass in review," the formal inspection having been affected in the morning, column was formed, the review received, and with the order "parade dismissed" each company marched to its quarters, the band playing "Hail Columbia" until the troops disappeared.

And yet the day was not without its acute reminder that we were not to long dwell in peace. Long before the evening gun was fired Indians appeared in unusual numbers on the hills and attempted several demonstrations, without doing any mischief or disturbing the general order of the Post; but their flashing little mirror-signals were visible at many points for more than an hour before the sun went down.

As a precautionary measure, however, extra ammunition was sent to each company quarters, and tired as the men were a slight increase of the guard was made in anticipation of any possible combined attack from without. As for us ladies, all were on the *"qui vive"* for the customary *levee* at headquarters, where, under Mrs. Carrington's genial administration, dancing, singing, and general merrymaking enlivened the evening until the chain of sentries, in quick succession, repeated "Twelve o'clock at night and all's well," and "Flag Day" at Fort Phil. Kearney, Dakota, the 31st day of October, 1866, closed its functions!

CHAPTER XVI.

The promised and long expected reinforcement of companies of the Regular Cavalry was announced as approaching, and the total strength of the body that actually arrived consisted of sixty-five men of Company C, under the command of Lieutenant Bingham. More than half of this force were raw recruits joining for the first time, and because their carbines had not reached Laramie at their departure they were armed with muzzle-loading Springfield rifles. The promised reinforcement of infantry, instead of being from other companies of the Eighteenth Infantry, consisted of ninety-five recruits for the eight companies of the Second Battalion of the Eighteenth, to be distributed among the companies at three widely separated posts in the Mountain District. Any addition, however, was reassuring and most welcome, and temporarily relieved the tension. This painful disappointment was not for the want of information at Laramie or Omaha of our isolated condition and need of both troops and ammunition, for the commanding officer had sent detailed reports showing the hostile attitude of the Indians around each of the three posts in the district, and during all this time there were twelve com-

118

panies at Laramie, a point of no immediate danger whatever.

The women, with tearful eyes and sinking hearts wondered why the War Department and the Commanding General at Omaha, or whoever was responsible, could leave us in such imminent danger during all these terrible days. The arrival of this handful of men did not do away with the constant excitement of Indian alarms, which they shared with us; but freshly arrived as they were they misconceived the danger and seemed to think that a little more aggressiveness in fighting Indians was needed, in the immediate vicinity of the fort, as if the Indians were an organized force to be fought, at the pleasure of the garrison, to their own disadvantage.

Brevet Lieutenant Colonel Fetterman, recently arrived from recruiting service, with no antecedent experience on the frontier, expressed the opinion that a "single company of Regulars could whip a thousand Indians, and that a full regiment, officially announced from headquarters to be on the way to reinforce the troops, could whip the entire array of hostile tribes." He was warmly seconded by Captain Brown and Lieutenant Grummond. Captain Fetterman submitted to the Colonel his own plan, which he had carefully devised, as certain of decisive results. His plan was to take a detachment, that very night, to the cottonwood thicket along Big Piney Creek in front of the fort, secrete his men, hobble some mules between the thicket and the fort, as a *live bait*, and decoy the Indians into his hands.

It was a bright night (moonlight) so that the

119

Indians could distinctly see that the mules were unprotected and fully exposed to their attack; but the Indians did not appear. They were not surprised and destroyed; but within three hours of the return of Fetterman they ran off a herd not a mile distant. Whether they suspected Fetterman's intentions or not was never learned. The wonder was that Fetterman's own select party were not surprised and massacred through taking such a risk. The entire garrison was keenfully watchful of this experiment. The presumption is that the Indians well knew that to attempt an attack within reach of the howitzers of the fort was a risk too "extra hazardous" for their notice, but as above noted they went outside of howitzer range and accomplished their work unassailed.

The most notable exception to this prudence on their part occurred before our arrival and it certainly illustrates the fact that the possession of the mountain howitzers by Colonel Carrington, in the handling of which he was an expert, practically assured security from attack during the building of the stockade, as well as attack upon the stockade itself.

The exception as given in full after my arrival is as follows:

Soon after Red Cloud had occupied the old Bozeman Trail, a large party of miners under the leadership of William Bailey, an expert scout, took refuge near the stockade, reporting that two of their number had been killed by Indians and they asked protection for themselves and their stock.

They had good teams, good horses, good arms, and agreed to render service for a moderate compensation in return for being given quarters immediately under the protection of the fort. They numbered about fifty. They conducted a small party to bring in their dead, who were buried near the fort, and then pitched their tents directly in front of the fort, just across Piney Creek at the foot of the slope rising to the north.

One morning just after the breakfast hour, while the miners were scattered along the creek, quite a large body of Indians suddenly appeared at the summit of the hill in full war-paint, brandishing their spears, giving loud yells, and lifting their blankets high in the air as they moved down slowly in an attempted charge upon the miners' camp. Between one and two hundred Indians were scattered along the crest of that hill, but hardly three minutes had elapsed after they first came in view before the smoke and crack of the miners' rifles, out from the cottonwood brush that lined the bank of the creek, had emptied half a dozen warriors' seats and brought down three times as many ponies, while the cheers of the miners and their perfect confidence in defending their camp were enlivened by the music of the Eighteenth Band, which Colonel Carrington had play on the parade ground, while the whole garrison was under arms ready for a fight, and three howitzers were ready to open their fire in case of need. A small detachment had been sent to support the miners, but no shells were fired from the fort lest they might inflict as much injury upon friends as foes beyond the creek.

On another occasion Lieutenant Bisbee and even Captain Ten Eyck, himself, hardly realizing how closely Indians watched movements, accompanied Fetterman and other fresh arrivals at the Post with the wood train to the Pinery to advise them of existing conditions and take observations as to the progress of work. Venturing in advance of their escort they were fired upon from ambush and although unhurt were compelled to do some lively skirmishing down the Island, getting completely out of sight of the wood party guard.

I recall, as if of yesterday, the blanched face of Mrs. Bisbee, knowing as she did that her husband was with the wood party, when a little bugler boy dashed up to the door where we were standing with the exciting announcement that "all were killed." The Colonel with a relieving party dashed out at once at a fierce gallop but soon returned with the party, whom they met not far from the fort, thus relieving our minds of the fear of an anticipated tragedy.

I shall never forget how this incident, at the time of its occurrence, illustrated the fact of such experiences in the army, as well as those so common with almost all tragedies or even deaths in other human experience. Nearly all fatal casualties involve many far-reaching changes in the relations, duties, and rank of army officers. A single death even involves not only the promotion of the next lower in rank to the deceased officer but a change of regiment, a change of assignment to duty, and often the sudden removal of more than one officer with his family to some distant post and at large expense, while an entirely new field of activity and a new circle of acquaintances are the result. When the Colonel returned from this ride which he took under such ominous circumstances, he spoke in pathetic terms of the fact that officers who accompanied him discussed the matter of promotion that would ensue in case the alarm given proved to be correct, and that when he checked them they spoke very tenderly of their endangered brothers-in-arms and said, "You are right Colonel, this is not the time for such suggestions."

Lieutenant Bingham, of Company C, Second Cavalry, was a fine young fellow, and my husband and myself grew very fond of him. He spent many a social hour with us, talking over our garrison experience, and as an assurance of our friendly feeling we extended our hospitality so far as to invite him, occasionally, to a meal. Considering my status in the matter of preparing *menus,* this was an abundant evidence of our sincerity.

The November days took their wonted course, but it seemed as if the Indians were more alert and aggressive, if possible, than before, possibly because of increasing numbers, or they may have noticed that few additional troops came to the post. It cannot be known whether they considered the "Flag-Raising" as a taunt; but their clearly increased numbers were more than a match for our own, many, many times over.

Red Cloud, the intrepid chief, was in personal command of more than three thousand warriors, as was subsequently learned, and this force was constantly augmented by tribes that had been disaffected by the negotiations at Laramie, if not already prepared to fight against any concession of a right of way through that section.

On one occasion a pursuing party of mounted men captured a pony loaded with presents received at Laramie, but it is to the credit of the great chief that his purpose was undisguised from the first.

Mrs. Carrington gave me this incident in connection with their halt at Laramie during the sessions of the Peace Commission: "I wanted to do a little shopping for myself and the boys at the Laramie sutler's, as it was a place of great note for frontier supplies on the Plains, and after the troops were in camp, five miles below the fort, my ambulance accompanied the advance party, as my husband must report to the Commission which had passed us on the journey, and learn from them whether peace was to be really assured. He dismounted from his horse and ascended the platform in front of Post Headquarters where about some tables, placed on an extension of the porch, the Commission and several chiefs were seated, or standing. In front, seated upon extemporized benches, for protection from the sun, were hundreds of the warriors and hundreds more of squaws. I could not hear what was said but there was evidently some trouble which caused a sudden adjournment of the conference for the afternoon. Henry soon left the platform, walking rapidly towards his horse, which an orderly was lightly holding by the rein near the ambulance, and at his left were two Indians, one of them Red Cloud, who had his right hand upon a large knife at his side, and looking at Grey Eagle. I thought the Indian was going to stab Henry in the back, and perhaps jump on Grey Eagle and ride off. I called out in my fright, ''Oh! Henry.'' He caught my warning, and motion with my hand, and slacking his step so the Indians would come within range drew his revolver belt to the front, keeping his hand upon it, then slowed his step, looking side-wise at the Indians and allowing them to pass. Whatever their first plan, they stolidly passed on as if they did not notice him, and when once clear of the parade ground, or plaza, went to work and made the squaws take down and pack their tepees. Colonel Maynadier, the commandant and chief member of the Commission, told us that evening that Indians always have those tantrums, and that Red Cloud was no chief when he first came here, but as the old warriors said that he was at the head of the young men whom they called 'Bad Faces,' always fighting other tribes and stealing their horses, the Commission would appoint him a chief, as they did Spotted Tail and other Indians of influence, and make him our friend.''

Her recollection of the passing through Laramie was much like my own, with the same assurances that whatever might be the sullen dissent of the Indians to the roadway, they would not fight, even if they made raids. This blind over-confidence involved all the bloodshed that followed. I have always wondered that when Colonel Carrington had distinctly asked of the Government permission to halt near Laramie until the question could be settled some way, he was ordered peremptorily to move without a moment's delay. Hence, Sunday, as it was, they had to leave Laramie without completing the little trading for which Mrs. Carrington had visited the post.

And without injustice to any, or an attempt to explain the ignorance of the authorities, I must mention one alarm late at night, which explains much, otherwise inexplicable. It was just after a skirmish that had cost one valuable life, and many head of stock, that couriers from down the road were challenged by the watchful sentries at the front gate, who reported that they came from a train that had gone into corral surrounded by Indians, just below Lake De Smedt, and called for assistance. The "assembly" was sounded, but, in the most quiet way possible, nearly a full company, taking a howitzer and ammunition with them, went to rescue that train. The train itself was simply bringing our mail (and no troops). Strangely enough it brought written documents from the Laramie Commision that "a satisfactory treaty with all the Indians of the Northwest had been made, and to notify all the Indians to come to Laramie for their presents." This reached Phil. Kearney in the midst of some of the most trying hours of danger and concern. We learned afterwards that this very Red Cloud, of whom I am now writing, declared that "he would war to the death until every white man left the country.''

At every recollection of the vast numbers that threatened us, it still remains a mystery why, with their superior numbers and better arms, they did not overwhelm and kill every one of us. I know that Indians generally fight under cover and by stealth, and rarely in the open field unless when in great numbers they have decoyed the whites into separate parties, to destroy them in detail. But that does not solve the mystery of their holding back until after the fort was completed, when the troops living in tents might have been an easy prey.

I always felt so much sympathy with the private soldier and the faithful picket guard. And then the hard-worked wood-parties, guarded though they were by an armed escort, witnessed one or more of their number killed, almost every day. And yet, never murmuring, they toiled on, faithful to duty and their trust which their commander had given to their charge. They showed a zeal and overmastering purpose to get the timber for the saw-mills and completion of the buildings and to lay in a supply of logs for winter fuel beyond the reach of my pen to describe. During all these sudden attacks our men always stopped to rescue the wounded and dead, except in one instance, where one of their number disappeared and never was heard from afterwards. He had probably been captured by the Indians and reserved for torture and food for wolves.

I felt most grateful in behalf of the common soldiers that the Colonel commanding in his eloquent speech had so signalized their worth and service on the eventful day of the flag-raising.

Among the many incidents of Indian craft, just a few are worthy of special notice.

On one bright day, when hay-cutting was in progress along Goose Creek, where the grass and wild oats were so dense that a horse could hardly be forced to a trot, and while the unyoked cattle were feeding at the noon hour, the Indians made a "surround" of a buffalo herd, forced them into the valley, and stampeded and drove off the cattle along with the buffalo. More than once they crawled up to the stockade covered with wolf-skins and imitating the wolf cry, and on one occasion actually shot a sentry from his platform with an arrow that noiselessly pierced his heart. The "call of his post by number" not having sounded, summoned the guard, but the soldier was silent. Once, crawling to the block-house in the Pinery, they sent an arrow through a loop-hole at night, wounding one of its inmates. Once, with keen knowledge of their business, they ran off the "bell-mare" which was used to lead mules while grazing, and the mules followed their accustomed leader.

There was one faithful, honest, and simple-minded white man at the post, the Colonel's confidential guide at all times, who seemed instinctively to know the invisible as well as the visible operations of the Indian, good old Jim Bridger. His devotion to the ladies and children and his willingness to cheer them the best he could were as prized as were his quaint tales of his experience among the Crow

Indians where, having a Crow wife, he was also an honored chief while in their midst. I learned afterwards, from the Colonel, that the Department Commander, Philip St. George Cooke, living at Omaha, even at the time of our greatest peril, ordered the discharge of Bridger, because of the expense, and that on the back of the order was endorsed by the Colonel *"Impossible of execution"* and Bridger was retained on full duty.

CHAPTER XVII.

THE FIGHT OF DECEMBER 6, AND ITS TRAGEDY.

The organs of sight and hearing grew to be extremely acute in that dry and rarefied atmosphere, involving an almost overpowering sense of stillness, especially at night when ordinary conversation could be heard and understood at a long distance. Even the crack of a rifle would seem to be near one's bed, during tent life, and as before intimated every sound exacted attention. The sight of the daily wood-party leaving for their accustomed duty, the interval of anxious waiting, and the reassuring bugle-notes signalizing their safe return, relieved tension in that respect and found a responsive echo in the soul, as did that of the captive knight in Paynim's tower, "Sound again, clarion, clarion, loud and shrill." No less grateful was the sentry's call at night, "All's well."

On the 6th of December the wood-train was again attacked as early as nine o'clock in the morning, not long after its departure from our view. The signal was kept in motion by the mounted picket on Pilot Hill, for they continued to wheel their horses in rapid circles, admonishing the garrison that an attack in force was pending.

Captain Fetterman, always eager for a fight, was immediately started with a detachment of mounted infantry and a part of Lieutenant Bingham's cavalry, to drive the Indians northward over Lodge

Trail Ridge and relieve the train, while Colonel
Carrington and Lieutenant Grummond with thirty
mounted men moved to intercept the retreat of the
Indians if repulsed by Fetterman and Bingham.
When Colonel Carrington's party gained the summit
between the fort and the Ridge, Fetterman's steady
firing was in clear view, about two hundred Indians
being gradually driven back to the valley northward.
In pushing to the front to gain the rear of this body
and descending to the intervening creek, there suddenly appeared in the low ground, dismounted and
without an officer, fifteen men of the cavalry force
which had acted with Fetterman. The dismounted
cavalry, when challenged and ordered to mount and
fall in behind the Colonel's detachment, replied that
Lieutenant Bingham, together with Lieutenant
Grummond and a few men, had turned a point and
gone forward. It was then noticed for the first time
that Lieutenant Grummond in eagerness of pursuit
had joined Lieutenant Bingham. Upon turning the
concealing point the retreating Indians were seen to
be in considerable force and the bugle was sounded
to guide Fetterman in joining the Colonel. To do
this, it appeared afterwards that he had to make
quite a circuit to avoid meeting the Indians too early
for combined action. The cavalry also followed
slowly, probably awaiting Fetterman's arrival, to
whose detachment they had first been assigned. The
official report as published by the Government
shows that the Colonel followed the original plan,
by the valley, until an opening disclosed a large
force gathering, as he rightly supposed, for the

purpose of entrapping his own small party, as others had been caught previously.

The following extract from his Official Report as published by the Government, more fully explains the critical moment of the day's movements. "But six men turned the point with me, one a young bugler of the Second Cavalry, who told me that Lieutenant Bingham had gone down the road around the hill to my right. This seemed impossible, as he belonged to Fetterman's command. I sounded the recall on this report but in vain. One of my men, Carnahan, fell, and his horse on him. The principal chief operating during the day attempted to secure his scalp, but dismounting, with one man to hold the horses and reserving fire, I succeeded in saving the man and holding the position until joined by Fetterman, twenty minutes later. The cavalry that had abandoned him had not followed me, though the distance was short; but the Indians, circling round and yelling, nearly one hundred in number, with one saddle emptied by a single shot fired by myself, did not venture to close in."

Lieutenant Wands was to have started with Colonel Carrington's party, but being delayed to exchange his horse, by mistake joined Fetterman. He had been grazed by a ball and it was reported that his coolness and Henry rifle saved Fetterman's detachment after Bingham left it.

Captain Brown was also with Fetterman, voluntarily, though under orders to report at Department Headquarters, but was anxious, as he expressed it, "to have Red Cloud's scalp before he left."

When the recall was sounded it was reported that Bingham had certainly gone beyond the second hill, though there were at least eighty Indians in sight before that hill and intervening the place of his disappearance. One cavalry man said that "Bingham's horse ran away with him and he could not restrain him." The Colonel thus confronted by a superior force took higher ground and soon found the body of Lieutenant Bingham, as well as that of Sergeant Bowers, who was still living though his skull had been cleft by a hatchet. Several men were still missing, but where was Lieutenant Grummond? Suddenly a shout was heard, "For God's sake come down quick," and through a gulch where the road was visible, seven Indians were seen with their spear heads close to the backs of four of the men of whom Lieutenant Grummond was one. They had been cut off in their dash of pursuit and were now making a desperate effort to cut through and save their lives, as their mad ride indicated. By the death of Bingham all clue was lost, and his reason for leaving Fetterman will always be an unsolved mystery. He must have ridden farther in advance than he realized, but he met the death of a soldier brave and true.

After the finding of the two bodies an ambulance was sent for as well as reinforcements, and these, under command of Lieutenant Arnold, went to join the Colonel. The *written order,* that came, was for Captain Powell to bring the fresh troops, but that officer requested of Captain Ten Eyck that a lieutenant be sent, and Captain Powell remained in his

quarters. It was not until nine o'clock in the evening
that the bugle-note sounded the return of the troops,
but the extent of casualties and history of the day's
experiences was not communicated until the ambulance bearing the dead revealed all, yet not all, for
I was to learn from my husband, Lieutenant Grummond's, own lips, the dreadful story of the experience that nearly cost him his life. How I endured
the shock I don't know, but in mercy I seemed to be
paralyzed for the time and we both sat for a long
time in silence, then mingled our tears in gratitude
for the wonderful deliverance.

A sense of apprehension that I seemed to have
been conscious of ever since my arrival at the Post,
deepened from that hour. No sleep came to my
weary eyes, except fitfully, for many nights, and
even then in my dreams I could see him riding
madly from me with the Indians in pursuit.

I cannot forbear making allusion to the good
fleet horse that bore him so faithfully on that fren-
zied ride. In telling the story he said that he abandoned the use of spurs and jammed his sword into
the weary beast to urge him to greater effort, followed by the chief, in full war-dress, with spear at
his back so near that but for his good horse he would
then and there have met a terrible fate.

Lieutenant Bingham and Sergeant Bowers were
buried with military and Masonic honors, my husband, himself a Mason, with others, conducting that
portion of the service. Captain Brown placed his
own badge, that of the Army of the Cumberland,
upon the breast of the dead sergeant, whom he had

known during the Civil War and to whom he was greatly attached.

And thus, at last, but not the last, after all the random skirmishes and frequent pursuits of stock-stealing parties, there had been a pitched fight to increase and intensify the Commandant's assurances, backed up by guide Bridger, that the enemy was increasing in force and watchful of every exposure or recklessness of parties leaving the fort, for whatever purpose, to destroy us utterly. Out-of-door life in that climate was conducive to health, and sickness other than scurvy, was rare, so a cemetery became necessary only for graves caused by violence.

After this fight, while Indians appeared in their usual manner on the surrounding hills, no special demonstration was made until the 19th, when they again attacked the wood-party.

There were two obvious reasons for their persistent attacks on this party, first, to kill off in detail all isolated parties and so reduce the force of the garrison and wear it out, and the other was to prevent the hauling of timber for lumber to complete the fort and the accumulation of a winter's supply of logs for the fuel at the post. Several times they attempted to burn the saw-mills, with the same purpose in mind, but the garrison was too alert for their success.

On the 19th, a quick response was made to the alarm and the detachment was sent out under command of Captain Powell, for the first time, to rescue the threatened train, but with orders "not to pursue

the Indians but to heed the lesson of the sixth.''
Powell strictly obeyed his orders and all returned
safely; but he reported that at least two or three
hundred Indians were in sight. All of us were
apprised frankly of the exact state of affairs and
assured that there was no immediate danger at the
post if all were prudent and avoided gossip and
nervous agitation, so that the women, no longer kept
in doubt of the facts that occurred, were stimulated
to new hope and confidence for the future.

All buildings had in fact been completed except
the hospital, and that would require but one more
train of logs to complete the work. Directly behind
our quarters, outside of the stockade, but commanded by a block-house at the angle close by, where
a howitzer could sweep the whole field of vision, an
immense collection of slabs from the saw-mills and
logs unfit for lumber, amounting to many hundred
cords, had been accumulated for winter's fuel, so
that we were all glad that wood-parties were no
longer to keep us in constant alarm. On the following day, the 20th, Colonel Carrington with a carefully selected party of eighty men, took personal
command of the train. Upon reaching Pine Island,
the nearest point for cutting timber, but the Big
Piney requiring to be crossed, he first cut timber
stringers and then small pines for a corduroy floor
and built a bridge to facilitate crossing, while the
choppers cut the desired timber, preparing the way
for the following day's work, to complete all outside
labor for the winter. The respite from attack since
the 6th, coupled with Powell's report of the 19th,

was so unusual that it seemed ominous of the future, for while our force was constantly though slowly depleted, we had the greater reason to believe that the Indian force was being augmented by the concentration of various war parties with identical intent to destroy the garrison utterly.

Ambitious young officers could not realize the real facts. All told, our strength was represented by only 350 men. This included soldiers, civilians, employees, teamsters, and prisoners in the guardhouse, not a very imposing force to match the warriors of Red Cloud, ten times their strength. And this force, as shown in the morning reports, which my husband studied with great care, included mail parties and escorts, of every kind, present or on the road between the Post and Fort Laramie. Already several mail-parties had been cut off, and finally, Van Volzah, who had come out with us, had been killed with his escort and the mail matter in his charge was found scattered along the trail.

And then came a cruel order that aroused intense feeling. A dispatch from Omaha was received and communicated to all of us, that "the Commander must send a mail once a week, at the rate of not less than fifty miles per day, or stand a court martial for failure to do so."

All this time long-expected ammunition failed to reach the Post and the supply, though carefully concealed from general knowledge, was not a cartridge box full to every man. It had to be conserved with the utmost care, but whether sleeping or awake, there was no such respite as truly restful repose.

CHAPTER XVIII.

PARTING WITH ONE FAMILY, NOTICED.

WE had experienced varieties in temperature amid snows and cold, but the cold was not so sensibly felt at our altitude of over 5000 feet above sea level. Really, at times we could not realize the extreme of cold without consulting the thermometer, and a barometer that hung in the vestibule of headquarters was always accessible for reference when any change seemed pending that might affect preparations for increased comfort. The men's ears were often frost-bitten in crossing the parade ground, but men were ready in all such cases to apply snow promptly to prevent serious freezing.

After December 6th, and for more than two weeks, the weather was remarkably fine, even temperate, though snow covered the mountain heights, and we settled down with as much equanimity as we could possibly command and went about our usual tasks, domestic and otherwise. Rally we must from threatened depression, no matter what might be its occasion, and by philosophical converse and mental effort seek to bring something of cheer. To this end the ladies contributed no inconspicuous part.

Early in December our circle was broken by the departure of Captain Bisbee and family, he having been promoted to a captaincy and ordered to Department Headquarters at Omaha. Linsey-woolsey garments and buffalo boots proved an invaluable comfort for their journey, as they had been priceless, with the thermometer below zero. Frontier life, above all other conditions of living, illustrates the truth of the somewhat trite maxim that "necessity is the mother of invention," and while we might deplore the necessity, we took comfort in the invention of these buffalo boots.

The change of quarters and readjustment of domestic affairs involved in Mrs. Bisbee's departure meant hardly less to her than to myself; notably, I came into possession of her little black cow. I have read somewhere that footprints on the sand first suggested the art of printing and the poet speaks eloquently of "footprints on the sands of time," teaching thereby a beautiful moral lesson, by figure of speech, but the literal foot-prints in the sand about my back door made by my little cow were of more material value to me than any discovery of art or lesson from poetical effusion, for they were an assurance that we were still within civilized environment and not yet wholly appropriated by savage neighbors.

"Milking cows" was not my prerogative, though a possible future acomplishment. Army life on the frontier was not identical with the life of the plains woman. While in many ways parallel, in the former case it did not include milking, though there were many other practical and homely duties to learn. The services of a soldier were called in requisition, and though he might not have been one of "Sherman's Bummers," or even one of those who milked my mother's cows into canteens many times during the Civil War, yet he proved sufficiently adept, and that precluded debate or doubt in the matter. A convenient milk-stand was improvised for the reception of pans of milk, and no ambitious farmer's wife ever anticipated the process of cream-rising with more interest than did I, rising early, day by day, to garner results of quiet formations for the morning "cup that cheers."

Another donation of interest was some crockery, a needed addition to my small stock in hand, whether chipped or not was immaterial, also a box with shelves to hold it, instead of the kitchen table, with dish-towel accompaniment—I was surely rising in the world. No child after a recent visit of Santa Claus enjoyed toys more than I did my little dishes when spread for the daily meal. And now I did not feel so timid in having a friend drop in for an occasional meal, and the housewife's perturbance of inadequate crockery became a thing of the past.

After all how little one requires for genuine happiness when the very most, the maximum good, is made of present possession! The charm too often vanishes with greater acquisition; but the real charm remains of *"much in little."*

I have taken occasion to speak of the climate and its bracing air, whatever the temperature, with almost no sickness, though Mrs. Wands was ever on the alert to divest little Bobby's pockets of the candy procured at the sutler's or presented by admiring friends.

Out-of-door life and exercise, though, limited to

the stockade enclosure or its immediate vicinity, were certainly conducive to health, and one is reminded of the story of the surprise and remonstrance of an early tourist in California who was charged by a tradesman with twenty-five cents per dozen for cheap buttons for which "ten cents was a big price at home," who was met by the prompt reply, "The charge, sir, is for the climate, and the buttons thrown in." Perhaps we ought to have been equally reconciled to the charge of seventy-five cents per pound for packed and rather ancient butter, and feel that the healthy invigorating climate was more than a compensation by the logic of relative values.

CHAPTER XIX.

THE usual "reveille" broke the stillness of the sunrise hour, to be followed in turn by "sick call" and "guard-mounting," the latter accompanied by the music of the full band, always a grateful and cheering accompaniment. Had the vision been limited to our immediate environment it would only suggest the ordinary routine exercises and functions of almost any frontier garrison in time of peace.

The wood-train moved out a little later than usual to the Pinery to begin the formal duty of the day, but with a stronger guard than before, numbering ninety men. It had gone but a short distance beyond view from the fort when the picket on Pilot Hill signalled many Indians, and that the train already had been forced to go into corral. This was not an unusual alarm, but a never-failing signal that would bring every man out of quarters with eyes and ears alert until a detail could be suitably organized and sent to its relief. Indians actually appeared for the first time, on several hills at once, although in small numbers; but the glass of Colonel Carrington revealed others in the thickets along the Big Piney Creek just in front of the fort. Their object seemed to be to test the watchfulness of the garrison and gain information as to the strength of the force that would leave the stockade in aid of the endangered wood-party. Several case-shot fired from a mountain howitzer exploded over their hiding-places, dismounted some and scattered others who broke for the hills and ravines to the north in hot haste. The "gun that shoots twice" and distributes more than eighty one-ounce balls as though dropped from the sky was entirely too mysterious and realistic for the Indian to linger within its range.

In the meantime, Brevet Lieutenant Colonel Fetterman, the senior Captain at the Post, claimed that his seniority as captain entitled him to command the relieving party, and his request was complied with. He also was given the choice of his own company and such additional details as he might select for himself. Captain Frederick Brown, just promoted and about to leave for the East, had been the district and regimental quartermaster in charge of all stock and properties and was always foremost in their protection, so that he asked for "one more chance," as he called it, "to bring in the scalp of Red Cloud himself." Permission was given, and Lieutenant Grummond, who had commanded the mounted infantry and cavalry after the death of Lieutenant Bingham, asked leave to take the cavalry detachment. His request also was granted. The entire force thus assembled at headquarters, therefore, consisted of eighty-one men, including three officers and two citizen frontiersmen, who were already acting as scouts in the quartermaster's department.

I was standing in front of my door next the commanding officer's headquarters and both saw and heard all that transpired. I was filled with dread and horror at the thought that after my husband's hairbreadth escape scarcely three weeks before he could be so eager to fight the Indians again.

The instructions of Colonel Carrington to Fetterman were distinctly and peremptorily given within my hearing and were repeated on the parade-ground when the line was formed, "Support the wood-train, relieve it, and report to me." To my husband was given the order, "Report to Captain Fetterman, implicitly obey orders, and never leave him." Solicitude on my behalf prompted Lieutenant Wands to urge my husband "for his family's sake to be prudent and avoid rash movements, or any pursuit;" and with these orders ringing in their ears they left the gate. Before they were out of hearing Colonel Carrington sprang upon the *banquet* inside the stockade (the sentry walk), halted the column, and in clear tones, heard by everybody, repeated his orders more minutely, "Under no circumstances must you cross Lodge Trail Ridge;" and the column moved quickly from sight.

I stood for a time, moments indeed, almost dazed, my heart filled with strange forebodings, then turned, entered my little house, and closed my door. The ladies, in turn, soon called to cheer me and, as I thought, with labored effort, to satisfy me that all would be well. They insisted that there was no more cause than usual for anxiety when troops were sent out, and the orders had been so explicit that any serious fight seemed absolutely impossible. And yet the recollection of the fateful action on the 6th and the danger experienced at that time came over me with such a tide of apprehension that no reassuring words could dissipate its gloom.

Shortly after the detachment left the gates, the Colonel, finding that Fetterman in his haste had gone without a surgeon ordered one to overtake the command forthwith. He started indeed, but soon returned with the information that the wood-train had broken corral and moved on safely to the Pinery, but that Fetterman had gone beyond the crest of Lodge Trail Ridge and that so many Indians were in sight he could not possibly reach him.

It became evident that the train had been threatened by a decoy party, and that when Fetterman followed its retirement thousands who had lain in ambush were assembling for his destruction.

Before leaving the watch-tower on his house, the Colonel sounded the general alarm and every man in the garrison either reported to his company's quarters or such other position assigned to him in an extreme emergency. It was a fixed rule that girths should be loosened and bits taken from the mouths of the horses so that there would never be delay when they were required for active service. Captain Ten Eyck was ordered to move at once with utmost speed with infantry and a supply wagon, and such mounted men as could be spared to guard the wagon and act as scouts. The Colonel himself inspected the men, and they were ready in very few minutes and moved at double-quick step all in a solid body to the crossing. At this crossing, as at the previous fight on the 6th of December, the ice broke through over the swift current, but without serious injury to men or horses and they pushed on.

Meanwhile, suddenly, out of silence so intense as to be torture to all who watched for any sound however slight, from the field of exposure a few shots were heard, followed up by increasing rapidity, and showing that a desperate fight was going on in the valley beyond the ridge just in the locality of the fight of the 6th, and in the very place where the command was forbidden to go. Then followed a few quick volleys, then scattering shots, and then, dead silence.

Less than half an hour had passed, and the silence was dreadful.

Of course we could see nothing of Captain Ten Eyck's men after they crossed the creek, and from his position in the wooded low ground and ravine opening just beyond the crossing he could neither hear nor see anything to guide his march until gaining some higher position which could be reached both by his loaded wagon and his mounted men. Much depended upon the actual distance from the fort where the last shots were fired and whether the sudden ceasing of the firing did not indicate a complete repulse of the Indian attack.

Hope sprang up in our aching hearts with the thought that Captain Ten Eyck had probably reached them in good time, and that the Indians had been repulsed. I shall never forget the face of Colonel Carrington as he descended from the lookout when the firing ceased. The howitzers were put in position and loaded with grape, or case-shot, and all things were in readiness for whatever might betide. He seemed to try to impress us with the assurance that no apprehension could be entertained as to the safety of the fort itself, but encouraged all to wait patiently and be ready for the return of the troops.

How different was the reality, soon to be realized!

Ten Eyck's relieving command, which had disappeared in the brush at the crossing of the creek, reached the summit of the hill opposite the fort, when all at once we saw the Colonel's Orderly, Sample, who had been sent with Ten Eyck, mounted upon one of the commander's own horses, break away from the command and dash down the hill towards the fort as fast as he could urge his horse.

Sample brought the written message from Captain Ten Eyck that "Reno Valley was full of Indians, that several hundred were on the road below, and westward, yelling and challenging him to come down to battle, but that nothing could be seen of Fetterman." He asked for a howitzer, but no one of his company could handle its ammunition and men could not be spared to move it.

The Indians who thus dared him to another fight were, as was afterwards learned, on the very field of the dreadful carnage finishing their deadly work. The message was not allowed to be published in full, but its tenor was tacitly understood to be that a terrible disaster had taken place. The evening gun was fired at sunset as usual, but what of us women! Agonizing fear possessed me! The ladies clustered in Mrs. Wands' cabin as night drew on, all speech-less from absolute stagnation and terror. Then the crunching of wagon wheels startled us to our feet. The gates opened. Wagons were slowly driven within, bearing their dead but precious har-vest from the field of blood and carrying forty-nine lifeless bodies to the hospital, with the heart-rending news, almost tenderly whispered by the soldiers themselves, that *"no more were to come in,"* and that "probably not a man of Fetterman's command survived."

In answer to the despatch brought by Sample the Colonel replied in part as follows:

"Forty well-armed men, with 3000 rounds, ambu-lances, etc., left before your courier came in. You must unite with Fetterman, fire slowly, and keep men in hand. I ordered the wood-train in, which will give fifty men to spare."

Ten Eyck at once advanced toward the threaten-ing Indians, who quickly vacated the field of struggle, and he was thus enabled to rescue as many as he did, and bring them in safely without the loss of a man. If the Indians had renewed the battle, his party also would have been among the victims.

Mrs. Carrington herself tenderly took me to her arms and home where in silence we awaited the unfolding of this deadly sorrow.

CHAPTER XX.

ITS SAD DETAILS.

HENCEFORTH my home was with Mrs. Carrington. There she conducted me with sisterly affection for shelter and comfort to await further light to guide me out of the enveloping gloom.

Early in the evening, after the mutilated bodies of the dead had been placed in hospital and spare buildings, and while a sense of apprehension and gloom were all pervading, there was a quickening of purpose in the heart of one brave man to dare and to do for relief or sacrifice his life in the attempt.

A knock at my door brought me to my feet. An orderly, brave and faithful Sample, announced that a man was waiting in the adjoining room wishing especially to see Mrs. Grummond. There I was met by an entire stranger, John Phillips by name, a miner and frontiersman, in the employ of the quartermaster, clad in the dress of a scout, who had something to communicate. So impressed was he by the gravity of the situation of the garrison that he extended his hand to me, with tears in his eyes, and in brief but pathetic language said, "I am going to Laramie for help, with despatches, as special messenger, if it costs me my life. I am going for your sake! Here is my wolf robe. I brought it for you to keep and remember me by it if you never see me again." There was no price put upon John Phillips' services. He asked no reward. The only condition he imposed was that he be allowed to choose his own horse. That choice, promptly conceded by its owner, was a fine thoroughbred belonging to the Colonel. He started, splendidly mounted, under cover of the night-time, to travel a distance of two hundred and thirty-five miles to Fort Laramie, through cold and snow, danger and probably death, with rations of crackers only, and a limited supply of provender for his horse. The sally-port gate was unbarred and relocked by the Colonel himself, and John Phillips passed out, and beyond. . . .

Nature herself seemed shocked by the awful tragedy of the day, for that very night the weather became unparalleled in its severity, almost too extreme for man or beast, but the faithful sentinels went their rounds of exacting and dangerous duty, at every risk, and it was from them alone that our ears caught, half hourly, the call of the hour, the number of the post, and the cheering words, "All's well!"

There was little repose, however, for any one that dreadful night. All ears were expectant of a momentary alarm. Subdued discussion of whether some of the missing ones might not have fallen into the hands of the savages as prisoners, a worse fate than death itself, continued late into the night, as some of the bodies had not been discovered by the party returning from the battle-field, and yet it was somehow borne in upon our minds that all were dead.

From grief, exhaustion, and inexpressible horror I retired at last, but not to sleep, until the morning sunrise gun, followed by bugles and then drums, sounding the "reveille," announced the dawn of another day, the Post intact, and the men fully aroused for duty, whatever that duty might be.

And then, promptly, came a Council of Officers, to meet the commanding officer as to a search for the bodies of the remaining dead.

There was a unanimous disinclination to undertake the work. It was argued with undisguised solemnity that a small party would not be safe while the Indians were still gloating over so complete a victory, and that if a large force left the stockade the lives of all left behind might be in peril. It was felt that if the Indians, with their largely superior force, should take advantage of a sally to rescue the dead, there might be a bold and irresistible onset upon the fort itself and its few defenders. And thus the matter was gravely discussed until Colonel Carrington quietly announced his decision, "I will not let the Indians entertain the conviction that the dead cannot and will not be rescued. If we cannot rescue our dead, as the Indians always do at whatever risk, how can you send details out for any purpose, and the single fact would give them an idea of weakness here, and would only stimulate them to risk an assault."

"Assembly" was sounded immediately, and officers reported back for orders. We, in the next room, could hear every word that was spoken, and soon the Colonel's "Grey Eagle" was at the door and details from all companies, picked men, formed in front of the house to enter upon their sad and sacred mission.

The women had not been consulted. A rap at our door was startling, as we knew of the conference, and, responding to the knock, the Colonel himself entered to announce to his wife and myself his decision.

Mrs. Carrington was sitting near the window, deep in thought, as the hastening details of soldiers came from all quarters. I was lying down, equally absorbed by the momentous question at stake, while we were debating what was best to be done. When the door opened, we sprang trembling to our feet. The Colonel advanced to his wife and quietly announced his decision. Pale, but calm and womanly, with her hands upon his shoulders, she replied, "Yes, it is your duty. God bless you! He will care for us. Go and rescue the dead, Henry."

Turning to me, he said, "Mrs. Grummond, I shall go in person, and will bring back to you the remains of your husband." I could only reply, "They are beyond all suffering now. You must not imperil other precious lives and make other women as miserable as myself." But his decision was fixed, and bidding his wife a tender good-by, and a word of hopeful confidence, he mounted his horse and the bugle sounded its "Forward march" as if on a parade. He left with the "God speed" of every soul in that aroused and endangered garrison.

With the Colonel were Captain Ten Eyck, Lieutenant Matson, Dr. Gould, and eighty men. We soon learned that when the men were selected for this extra hazardous detail, every single soldier, fit for duty, begged permission to join it.

Thus, once again, we were to witness the departure of our brave guardians, possibly to share the fate of others at the hands of the elated savage hordes about us.

With the last good-by, the gates were shut and bolted. Anxious eyes watched their departure and with equal intentness the picket-guards which the Colonel was to station on successive hills to keep up communication with the garrison itself, to call for reinforcements if needed or to fall back to the fort if it should be attacked in his absence. To the Officer of the Day orders were given, in pencil, which were afterwards preserved with care. They were these:

"Fire the usual sunset gun, running a white lamp to mast head on the flag-staff. If the Indians appear, fire three guns from the twelve-pounder (a large field howitzer) at minute intervals and later substitute a red lantern for the white."

Before leaving the fort on this mission of rescue, unknown to us at the time, the Colonel had opened the magazine and cut the Boorman fuses of spherical case-shot, such as were usually used against Indians prowling in the woods or thickets near by, and so adjusted the ammunition in store by the opening of boxes that by the application of a single match all could be destroyed. His secret instructions, still preserved, were these:

"If, in my absence, Indians in overwhelming numbers attack, put the women and children in the magazine with supplies of water, bread, crackers and other supplies that seem best, and, in the event of a last desperate struggle, destroy all together, rather than have any captured alive.''

We two women sat mute before the front windows, vaguely suspecting the possible intent of busy workers around the magazine, as they took barrels and boxes thither, and it began to be whispered about among the women as to the reasons for these activities, and a strange hope sprang up, as we watched with calmness and assurance the progress of the work, for it indicated the preparation for an unparalleled defense.

And there we watched, for hours, through the long, long day! Retreat, followed by the sunset gun, came as usual, and a white light shone from the mast-head. The Colonel told us, on his return, that ''no sight was ever so beautiful to the troops, as they reached the summit overlooking the fort, as that white lantern at mast-head, gleaming so like the Star of Bethlehem, guiding to safety and peace.'' And no sound that ever fell on mortal ears carried a more grateful message to us than did that of his bugles, sounding the ''Assembly'' as if to say, ''Fear not, all is safe.'' *

Then our tears mingled, for the whole garrison was under arms, as we watched, unavoidably

---

* Captain Brown rode '' Calico,'' a little pony he gave Harry and Jimmy Carrington in 1865 at Fort Leavenworth for their use in marching to Old Fort Kearney, and afterwards to their final destination at Fort Phil. Kearney. When the bodies were rescued, the pony lay at the foot of the hill, and the last act of the Colonel was to order that if the pony were not dead to put him out of his misery with a bullet.

watched, the wagons moving slowly to the hospital bearing the remaining dead.

How true it is that "One touch of nature makes the whole world akin." Soldiers brought out their best uniforms to decently clothe their dead comrades. Colonel Carrington came to my room, almost before the mournful procession had fully passed, and taking from his breast an envelope, handed it to me, and left before it was opened. I opened it with eager but trembling hands. It contained a lock of my husband's hair. He had redeemed his pledge!

And then the horrors of the following days, the making of coffins and digging in the hard, frozen earth for a burial place, when the cold was so intense that the men worked in fifteen-minute reliefs, and a guard was constantly on the alert lest Indians should interrupt their service.

One-half of the headquarters building, which was my temporary home, was unfinished, and this part was utilized by carpenters for making pine cases for the dead. I knew that my husband's coffin was being made, and the sound of hammers and the grating of saws was torture to my sensitive nerves.

The burial of the dead was accomplished, calmly, systematically, and safely, each case being numbered and full data, recorded for any future re-burial, if desired by the Government or friends of the dead.

Just here I transcribe a paragraph written by my dearest friend, already a matter of record in her volume, "The Experience of an Officer's Wife on the Plains," which recalls the undertone of a spirit of faith felt by many of us in a protecting Providence, "a light in the darkness of those dark days." She thus writes, "To a woman whose home and heart received the widow as a sister, and whose office it was to advise her of the facts, the recital of the scenes of that day, even at this late period (1868), is full of pain; but at that time the Christian fortitude and holy calmness with which Mrs. Grummond looked upward to our Heavenly Father for wisdom and strength inspired all with something of her same patience, to know the worst and meet the issue."

I never returned to my own quarters. One look in that direction was sufficient, and the presence of the mountain howitzers in position before the door, which, from its elevation, commanded both within and over the stockade in all directions, while the rooms were occupied by soldiers being trained by the Colonel in the gun and shell practice, preparatory for a possible siege, was the dominant thought.

Lights burned in all the quarters. Every man had his designated loop-hole, or other position, and one non-commissioned officer was on constant duty in each building, so that in case of alarm there would not be an instant's delay in the use of the entire command. The Colonel himself did not remove his clothing for sleep for more than a week and was constantly going "the grand rounds" to see that every man was on the alert.

My husband had a picture of myself in a choice setting that he always wore, and I have often wondered what Indian Chief had it now in possession to wear as a trophy of those days of desperate battle.

At that trying hour, when, as in all army experience, the conditions change as quickly as when the
band itself returns from a burial, exchanging the
quick-step music for the solemn dirge, the ladies
were thoughtful of myself, and combined with Mrs.
Carrington in the hasty preparation of such garments as would be in harmony with my lonely condition, and thus ward off thoughtless intrusion from
whatever source.

CHAPTER XXI.

On the sad and solemn days of December, 1866, the pervading gloom, shared alike by all, permitted none of the social meetings, levees, and miscellaneous entertainments that had been redeeming features of our isolated garrison life.

During the nights I would dream of Indians, of being captured and carried away by Red Cloud himself while frantically screaming for help, and then awaken in terror only to spring from my bed involuntarily to listen if the near-by sentry would still voice the welcome cry, "All's well." Sleeping draughts and the kind ministrations of Dr. Horton seemed rather to aggravate than reduce the nervous tension, and during all those wearisome days of waiting we chiefly wondered whether Phillips had safely performed his mission, whether reinforcements would surely come, and when or whether we must abide a dreadful common fate.

The constantly increasing and drifting snowstorms made it possible for the men to walk over the stockade in some places and the constant clearing of a ten-foot trench in the snow seemed to be almost a useless task for the overworked garrison, as the next snow would immediately fill the gap. Still, it was absolutely necessary to prevent so easy an access by an insidous foe and the work was kept up under the Colonel's personal supervision by the faithful men who were no longer detailed for cutting timber. Not a soul ventured beyond the limits of the stockade except to bring in wood for which the winter's supply was abundantly ample. Any antecedent lack of provision in so vital a matter would have indeed added terrors to the siege. Everybody's senses seemed under fair control, at last, with a single exception and that was in the person of Mrs. Carrington's colored servant Dennis, who seemed to be actually possessed by a demon, and in his frantic efforts to exorcise the specter and relieve the tension by efforts of his own he would strike his head with all possible force against the boards of the partition which separated the kitchen from my own room, until they trembled with the shock. Finally he continued this mania by butting his head against the stove-pipe and even the stove itself, like a veritable mad-man. It was not until the appearance of the Colonel with the muzzle of a cocked revolver touching his head that the equilibrium was restored and Dennis became contented to live a while longer and discharge the normal functions of his usual employment.

And yet during his frantic dread of the surrounding Indians there was something so similar to their wild demonstrations even in sight from the fort, brandishing spears, yelling like very demons, and desperate for our blood, that there was not a little sympathy for Dennis, as we sought sympathy in our distress from those in authority who held our own fate in the balance of a speedy or neglected interference in our behalf.

There was mingled with all this anxiety an undercurrent of feeling that the widely heralded announcement all over the country that the Laramie Treaty had been followed by a universal peace with the Indians of the Northwest, so speedily followed by the despatches borne by Phillips, would bring a burst of hateful criticism upon all the survivors of the fight, because of the surprise for which the public was unprepared.

Bridger's good sense was rarely at fault and he never had any confidence in the success of the treaty.

On one occasion a midnight alarm compelled the Colonel to send a howitzer and a hundred men down the road to rescue a coralled train, bringing to the Colonel an official notice of perfected peace and freely to make presents to these Indians; as this falsehood had been announced through the land, no wonder that troops and ammunition were deliberately withheld from our relief.

Some would persist that the extraordinary cold and stormy spell of weather that immediately followed the battle would check Indian aggressions, and that the hour of danger, if we kept behind the stockade, had passed. Others argued that the Indian loss must have been so severe that the savages would never risk so wild a venture as to attack the stockade with artillery ready to discharge grape-shot and canister from block-house and parade-ground. It was evident, however, to all, that any aggressive action to avenge the loss would be suicidal, while we could not fail to know, or suspect, guarded as the secret was, that not only were the Indians better armed and more numerous, but that there was scarcely small ammunition enough at the Post to maintain an action against a vigorous and bold assault.

Even while writing this narrative a letter has been received from a competent author, who has undertaken to prepare a history of all the Indian wars at the West, in which he supplies additional information as to the incidents connected with the Indian plan of that campaign.

He writes as follows:

"I take the liberty of sending you 'Two Moons,' account of the Fetterman disaster. Two Moons was visiting his Indian friends at Oklahoma last winter, and I secured this account through his brother-in-law, a half-breed who speaks Cheyenne.

"Two Moons says that 'he and a small party of friendly Cheyenne Indians were sent to the fort to spy about and see if it could be taken by storm. Here he saw old Bridger, the former scout and guide, and had quite a nice visit. When he returned to the hostile camp he reported the fort too strong to be taken without great loss, so the chiefs decided to draw the garrison out, by detachments, and surprise them, a plan which the recent recklessness of some of the troops in chasing Indians convinced them would succeed.

"'So they attacked the wood-train that day, and, when Fetterman's command came out they sent a few men mounted on their best ponies to decoy them into the hills. Fetterman followed and then the Indians swarmed out from all sides.'

"Two Moons adds, 'At this time more troops were coming up behind Fetterman;* Fetterman turned and tried to get away. Then he dismounted his men and the horses either broke away or were turned loose. After this," continues Two Moons, " Fet-

---

* The Indian pickets had evidently watched Ten Eyck's relieving party from the time they left the fort.

terman couldn't do anything else but fight, and it was soon all
over.' "

This letter has a most striking verification from
the fact that the visit of the friendly Cheyennes was
made of record, at the time of their visit, and the
whole was narrated to us after our arrival as proof
that all the Indians were not at that time hostile to
the occupation of that country.

But, as a matter of fact, Bridger, who was present
at the Council with the Indians which was marked
by very formal exhibition of the defenses and the
guns, took special pains to warn the visitors that
"the fort was impregnable," and the Cheyennes, in
fact, offered to furnish one hundred warriors to go
with another hundred of the troops and exterminate
their own, old enemies, Red Cloud's band of Sioux.

It is also a vindication, most complete, of the
conservative policy in the management of the entire
campaign, which, if fully sustained by all subordinates would have prevented the disaster of the
21st of December, 1866.

It is but just to add, even in anticipation, that the
Special Commission from Washington which was
despatched as early as possible to investigate these
matters in full, summed up its elaborate Report as
to the Fort Phil. Kearney disaster, in these laconic
words:

"The difficulty, in a nut-shell, was that the Commanding Officer, Colonel Carrington, was furnished
with no more troops, nor supplies, for this state of
war, than had been provided and furnished for a
state of profound peace."

CHAPTER XXII.

THERE was nothing of a festive character to usher in the dawning of the New Year, 1867. The hours dragged slowly and painfully along. Ten days had passed since Phillips started upon his perilous mission and we still wondered as on Christmas Day whether he had safely fulfilled his pledge and whether our earnest prayers for reinforcements of troops were to be answered through his co-operation and his guidance to our relief.

New Year's Day, however, was signalized by formal exercises through an order read before the assembled garrison, and the dedication of a well-defined Military Reservation, giving to the burial place of the victims of the massacre a memorial character. Brief but appropriate words were spoken of the departed ones, but they seemed only to increase the solemnity of the day. If we could have felt assured that reinforcements were already on the way to our relief, our sighs would have been translated into a "Te Deum"; but no supernal voice cleft the sky to announce such a longed-for message, and the Angel of Patience alone, in whispered tones, bade us "wait."

But one day there was a sudden, almost a tumultuous, hurrying out of quarters, with excitement and bustle as intense as if we were called to

163

arms against an advancing foe. First, the Pilot Hill picket, and then the sentry before headquarters, and the lookout on the headquarters tower, announced the unmistakable appearance of troops, five miles distant. The bugle-call and the "long roll" were never more gladly echoed in hearts. Our spontaneous cry was, "Open wide the gates, and admit our deliverers." We hardly had patience to don protective outer-garments because of the glow of our quickened blood, and our common outbreak of joy was simply, "At last! At last! We are saved! We are saved! Phillips was saved, saved, for us!" Can a more dramatic life episode be imagined! The emotion of joy was too deep and all-absorbing for more than ejaculations of grateful delight, but tearful eyes and hand-shaking, with mutual welcome we were soon to accord our friends and deliverers.

The band was on hand with its preparations for a share in that welcome and an escort was hastened from the gates to facilitate their arrival. As for myself, I felt that I could have hugged every half-frozen man as he entered, and I still feel that their story as it unfolded would have justified the impulse, if not the action.

And this is the story of John Phillips' ride:

Picking his way cautiously until day began to dawn, then hiding himself and horse in bushes or ravine in some solitary place until the succeeding night came on, he had plodded on night after night, with the greatest of all thoughts uppermost in his brain, "salvation for the perishing!" If not so crystallized in his "inner soul chambers," it was the very spirit of the sublime truth, that "death means life; sorrow brings joy; and the Cross leads to the Crown!"

This hardy, brave, self-sacrificing pioneer might not have been conscious of this God-likeness, but there was within his breast an element of strength and will equal to this stupendous effort and its full accomplishment. The country was indeed familiar, in its general features, when daylight gave him the bearings of the mountain ranges, but there was the great risk that in tramping deep ravines and crossing many streams, all obscured by drifted snows, and only at night, he might lose his way, or became frozen, helpless, and beyond human power to fulfil his task. He proved himself to be his own sufficient guide, and surely if he had no angel's guidance, such a messenger, or such a message, was well worthy of celestial guardianship.

His own narration of his journey was intensely simple.

He stopped at Fort Reno for rest and information as to whether Indians were in the vicinity of that post, and to secure fresh supplies, and with a brief despatch from General Wessels, who had recently taken command of that sub-post, pushed on with more speed and less danger from Indian attacks. At the Horse Shoe Creek telegraph station, on the line between Laramie and Casper, he delivered General Wessels' brief despatch, which reached Fort Laramie at 2 o'clock on Christmas Day. The operator at the Horse Shoe Creek station was unwilling to risk so long a despatch as that of Colonel

Carrington,* but Phillips pressed on with this despatch, reaching Fort Laramie at 11 o'clock with icicles hanging from his clothing; both beard and hair matted with snow and ice. He delivered the despatch, and relieved of that responsibility he fell, exhausted and unconscious.

I am aware that four or five other men claim that they accompanied him. He might have met other travellers at Bridger's Ferry where it was comparatively safe and they might have ridden with him a part of the way, and dropped off before he reached Laramie, but he left Fort Phil. Kearney alone and also reached Fort Reno alone. Whatever may be the reasons of any making the claim of sharing the trip with him, John Phillips was the messenger who

---

* Colonel Carrington's despatch:

(Duplicates to Generals Grant and Cooke.)

" FORT PHIL. KEARNEY, D. T., December 21, 1866.
" By Courier to Fort Laramie.

" Do send me reinforcements forthwith. Expedition now with my force, impossible. I risk everything but the Post and its stores. I venture as much as any one can, but I have had a fight to-day unexampled in Indian warfare. My loss is ninety-four men." [Should have been eighty-one.] "I have recovered forty-nine bodies, and thirty-five more are to be brought in in the morning, that have been found.

" Among the killed are Brevet Lieutenant Colonel Fetterman, Captain F. H. Brown, and Lieutenant Grummond. The Indians engaged were about three thousand, being apparently the force reported as on Tongue River in my despatches of November 5th, and subsequent thereto. This line, so important, can and must be held. It will take four times the force in the spring to reopen it if it be broken up this winter. I hear nothing of my arms

singly braved the toils and dangers of the service rendered and no man can share the glory of his achievement. For daring heroism, neither the Ride of Paul Revere nor that of Sheridan can be compared with it, although not commemorated either by poetry or song, and he deserves undying fame for his *midnight ride.*

In this connection I would note, for the satisfaction of all who are interested in the story as well as due to the memory of Phillips himself, the matter of compensation for his services to include payment for goods and stock stolen from him by Indians while in the Government employ was undertaken for the benefit of his widow. The Congressional

---

that left Leavenworth September 15th. Additional cavalry ordered to join have not reported their arrival. Would have saved us much loss to-day.

"The Indians lost beyond precedent. I need prompt reinforcements and improved arms. Every officer of the battalion should join it to-day. I have every teamster on duty, and at best only one hundred and nineteen left at Post. I hardly need urge this matter, it speaks for itself. Give me at least two companies of cavalry forthwith, well armed, or four companies of infantry exclusive of what I need at Reno and C. F. Smith. I did not over-estimate my early application a single company. Promptness will save the line, but our killed show that any remissness will result in mutilation and butchery beyond precedent. No such mutilation as that to-day is on record. Depend on it that the Post will be held as long as a man or round is left. Promptness is the great thing. Give me officers and men. Only the new Spencer arms should be sent. The Indians are desperate and they save none.

"HENRY B. CARRINGTON,
"Colonel Eighteenth Infantry Commanding."

Globe, while the Bill was pending, gives this extract from the favorable report of the House Committee, "that in all the annals of heroism, in the face of unusual dangers and difficulties on the frontier, or in the world, there are few that exceed in gallantry, heroism, self-devotion, and patriotism the ride made by John Phillips from Fort Phil. Kearney in December, 1866, to Fort Laramie, carrying despatches which gave the first intelligence to the outside world of the terrible massacre near the former Post and which saved the lives of the people garrisoned there, men, women, and children, by starting reinforcements to their relief."

The closing paragraph of the affidavit of Colonel Carrington who commanded the fort, and entrusted his despatches to Phillips, thus closes:

"It is impossible to state more strongly the value of his services, which were never adequately requited, and affiant knows of no soldier of the army whose services more absolutely demand reognition for the sake of his family than do those of the brave, modest, John Phillips, since deceased, leaving his widow in a destitute condition."

The writer of this narrative was called upon to furnish an affidavit for the consideration of Congress and the following is an extract from the Congressional Globe, when the Bill came up on its final passage:

"On the 21st day of December, 1866, her husband, Lieutenant George W. Grummond of the Eighteenth U. S. Infantry was killed in action with Sioux Indians near Fort Phil. Kearney in what is now known as the State of Wyoming; that, she was the guest of Colonel Carrington's family when all the troops were

rallied for convenience of defense; that, during that terrible
night, when an attack in overwhelming numbers was constantly
expected, John Phillips called to express his sympathy with her;
that, overcome by his interest in her condition and the imminent
danger of all concerned and weeping with sorrow over her loss,
he said, ' I will go as the messenger if it costs me my life,' and
then presented to her his own wolf robe to remember him by if
he was never heard from again!

"His whole bearing was manly, brave, unselfish, and self-
sacrificing, beyond all praise. He had been respected by all the
officers for the quiet courage he always exhibited and was the only
man of the garrison who realized the danger of the garrison to
the extent of daring to offer his own life in the desperate attempt
to cut through the savage hordes that surrounded us, with any
faith in such a mission. He left with the good wishes of all, and
it is the smallest possible reward that Congress can offer to
provide a suitable support for the widow in her lone and desolate
condition."

The days of anxious waiting for arrival of aid
from Fort Laramie was a period of peculiar trial
because the commanding officer could not spare a
detail adequate to protect a sufficient escort for a
soldier messenger without precipitating an attack
in overwhelming force from the enemy, and there
was insufficient ammunition in store even for a protracted defence by every one able to assist in its
ordeal. Hence it was that not only our little group
of women but every soldier in the fort was as interested as ourselves in the daily gossip and speculation as to where the brave messenger was located
on each succeeding day of his absence.

JIM BRIDGER, LEGENDARY MOUNTAIN MAN AND GUIDE
(Wyoming State Archives, Museums and Historical Department)

COLONEL HENRY B. CARRINGTON
(American Heritage Center, University of Wyoming)

MARGARET CARRINGTON
(American Heritage Center, University of Wyoming)

FORT PHIL KEARNY
Sketch by Antonio Nicoli, Second Cavalry bugler
(National Archives)

RED CLOUD, THE OGLALA SIOUX LEADER
(Bureau of American Ethnology, Smithsonian Institution)

CAPTAIN WILLIAM J. FETTERMAN
(National Archives)

LIEUTENANT GEORGE W. GRUMMOND
(Wyoming State Archives, Museums and Historical Department)

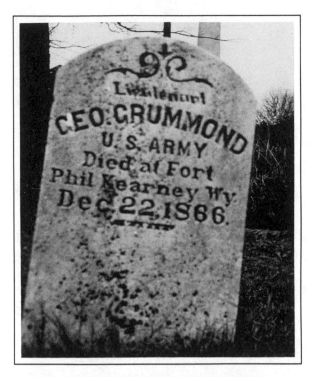

GRAVE OF LIEUTENANT GEORGE GRUMMOND
(American Heritage Center, University of Wyoming)

JOHN "PORTUGEE" PHILLIPS
(Wyoming State Archives, Museums and Historical Department)

THE "PORTUGEE" PHILLIPS MARKER NEAR FORT PHIL KEARNY
(Jerry Keenan)

GENERAL HENRY CARRINGTON AND S.S. PETERS
At 1908 reunion
(Wyoming State Archives, Museums and Historical Department)

THE 1908 REUNION
Left to right: Bugler Pabloski, Lieutenant Wheeler, William Murphy, William Daley,
General Carrington, S.S. Gibson, Mrs. Carrington, J. Stawn, S.S. Peters, J. Owen
(Wyoming State Archives, Museums and Historical Department)

FORT RENO, WYOMING
Sketch by Schonborn
(American Heritage Center, University of Wyoming)

William Daley

RECEPTION AT OMAHA
Left to right: Mrs. Carrington, Samuel Gibson, General Carrington, Maurice Barnes,
General Morton, J.D. McKinnie, and S.S. Peters

PART III
HOMEWARD BOUND
FROM FORT PHIL. KEARNEY, DAKOTA, TO TENNESSEE

CHAPTER XXIII.

LIEUTENANT Colonel Wessels, of the Eighteenth U. S. Infantry, Brevet Brigadier-General, brought to our relief two companies of cavalry and four companies of the First Battalion of the Eighteenth, for which the Colonel had so long importuned, being the exact force also which he had called for in his telegram for relief. The whole story of their march was self-revealed without word of explanation as they entered the main gate. They had waded or dug their way through snows, knee deep, and often waist deep, while the mercury ranged from 25 to 40° below zero, and with both hands and feet frost-bitten they were as happy as ourselves to reach friends and friendly shelter. Bright fires were blazing in all quarters and the ample supply of wood anticipated in the autumn was a cheering assurance that any further weather exposure was amply provided for. General Wessels spoke of the warmth of his welcome as in a double sense most satisfactory.

Immediate activity in the assignment of the fresh troops to comfortable quarters was replaced by another incident of importance to us, only second to the arrival of reinforcements, an incident of real excitement, and that was the opening of a huge wagon-load of mail matter long accumulated at Fort

173

Laramie. Nor was this excitement abated when it was at once realized that important changes were to take place in the life of the fort itself.

My own personal mail, so long looked for, brought letters from my distant Southern home. One letter from my sister astonished me by this strange passage: "What can be the matter? I have had such terrible forebodings, consequent upon dreams that have troubled me. I have witnessed horrible battles with Indians. I have seen them drinking blood from the skulls of the slain. I sincerely hope that such dreams may go by contraries, as we are often reminded, and that you cannot be exposed to such dangers as are suggested by such horrible dreams."

Her letter made me quiver, for it really seemed that she must have possessed some clairvoyant power thus to interpret so closely the state of affairs, not indeed in exact detail, but only approximating the truth, since the reality of massacre, mutilation, and scalping was beyond the imagination to conceive, even in dreams, by any one distant from the theatre of action itself. This letter was written before the massacre occurred, and now I was trying to adjust myself to conditions so much worse than her fears.

Ours was a busy place during the adjustment of quarters, with orderlies passing back and forth and the men of the reunited Battalions of the Eighteenth renewing old friendships and telling over camp-fire stories of old-time marches and hardships during the Civil War for which the Old Eighteenth was famous. It was not long, however, before all the troops were settled to the usual routine of garrison duty, and the new-comers were eager for more social reunions that they might introduce something more of spirit to cheer our drear and solemn surroundings. With our splendid band ever ready to furnish music for all occasions and destined soon to leave the Post with changing regimental headquarters, impromptu dances and musicales again became the chief features of social entertainment, and yet, so kindly, as I shall never forget, not without my wishes first being consulted in the matter. It was not in the spirit of "after us the deluge" at all, and certainly the propriety of such things at such a time could not be judged from the view-point of ordinary civilized life in the States. There was, I am sure, a measure of protest down in my heart, but it never rose to the surface in conscious feeling that such merry-making could in any sense touch me, and gratitude for their presence and our rescue from threatened destruction prompted a kind of pleasure that they at least would find some relief from the strain of their fearful march in our behalf. Without demurrer therefore on my part, they planned and carried out their entertainments in a moderate fashion and quite independently removed from my immediate quarters.

The newspaper mail brought by the command contained very surprising statements as to ourselves. It was marvellous to see how enterprising and original certain news editors could be, when removed from all access to real facts, when they

set their brains at real work. General news, already
stale in the States, was remarkably fresh to us, and
certainly very novel, as concerning ourselves. No
correct accounts could have reached them except
through the commanding officer's couriers to Laramie, 235 miles from his headquarters. As the subject has been partially anticipated in a previous
chapter I will cite but two ludicrous conceptions
that had been promptly supplied Congress immediately after receipt of the Colonel's telegram of
December 21, 1866. Mr. Lewis V. Bogy, Commissioner of Indian Affairs, on the 4th of January,
informed Congress of his own views, as follows:

" Now, I understand this was the fact. These Indians being
absolutely in want of guns and ammunition to make their winter
hunt, were on a friendly visit to the fort, desiring to communicate
with the commanding officer, to get the order refusing them
guns and ammunition rescinded, so that they might be able to
procure their winter supply of buffalo. It has been reported
that some 3000 to 5000 warriors were assembled to invest the
fort. This is not and cannot by any possibility be true. The
number of Indians is not there. The whole is an exaggeration,
and although I regret the unfortunate death of so many brave
soldiers, yet there can be no doubt that it is owing to the foolish
and rash management of the officer in command at that Post."

The second piece of news, by the same mail, had
this key to the situation which bewildered Congress-
men had to explain, viz., that "the commanding officer was constantly *giving powder* to the Indians,"
which was true in a *different sense,* and that "the
ladies of the garrison were in the habit of throwing
packages of sugar and powder over the stockade to

the squaws." Pictorial papers illustrated the whole affair after a wild fashion, so that we wondered if there had not been some other similar fight somewhere else of which we had no knowledge.

I have alluded to a Military Commission of Inquiry, but there was another which met at Lee's Ranche on the South Platte, where wagon loads of presents were distributed to all Indians who came in, and were "good Indians," though the "bad Indians" by their absence lost their best choice opportunity for plunder, or gain. The Secretary of that Commission, Henry M. Stanley, afterwards became the world-wide explorer, and Mr. Coutant, the accomplished Historian of Wyoming, says that "Mr. Stanley acquired his love for that wild adventure which afterward led him to fortune and fame, in that country." *

Orders came by the same mail for the immediate removal of the headquarters of the Eighteenth Infantry to Fort Casper, as the Second Battalion was to become a complete regiment by itself in the reorganization of the Army, and this, in the midst of winter, of the kind already described. The order had to be obeyed, of course, at once, regardless of weather conditions, which those in authority either could not appreciate or did not in fact consider.

It was indeed a grave question for the women to consider how to make such a journey with the care of three children, Harry and Jimmie Carrington and Bobby Wands, to make comfortable as well

---

* Vol. I, Coutant's History of Wyoming.

as ourselves in addition to the families of several of the Band, for the Band and Regimental Staff were headquarters accessories embraced within this imperious order. "How can it be done?" was the first inquiry. But the element of "could not be done" has no place in the Army Code. *How* it should be done, when it *must* be done, involved grave thought and planning. In the first place, the augmented garrison was already too large for the men needing cover, and in the second place the supplies of all kinds, including provisions, had not been considered in the haste of forwarding reinforcements, and already a plan was on foot to send wagons back to Fort Reno for additional commissary supplies.

My own mind was racked by the thought, for it was a desperate question for me to decide. The alternate problems were, "Why should I stay?" and "How can I go?" "How, under existing circumstances, can I undertake the journey homeward in the dead of winter?" which involved much more than need go on record. Homeless, at least for the present, and seemingly helpless, as I thought of the journey in all aspects, what wonder that it staggered my judgment. But,

> " When faith grows weak and courage fails,
> When grief or doubt, the soul assails,
> Who can, like Thee, the spirit cheer!
> Great Comforter, be ever near! "

The die was cast! I must go! Neither was I deserted in that solemn hour by worldly friends, who loved me for the dangers I had already passed through. I loved those who did so pity and with sympathetic heart rendered such grateful service. Oh! that springing, germinating power that belongs to the sanguine temperament of youth, and my prayer was that we might all preserve it as the years should go by.

CHAPTER XXIV.

In the preparation for our journey very much
of personal individuality developed as the problem
of ways and means unfolded its mysteries and not a
few humorous incidents occurred. Having been
accustomed to the tricks and manners of negro servants all my life, they still interested me. Mrs.
Carrington's colored man, Dennis, had fully recovered his normal mental poise with the arrival of
fresh troops and the matter of his own personal
outfit gave him much concern. He must have had
some original notions of the proprieties, judging
from his conduct. This was no less marked in the
case of Laura, Mrs. Wands' colored maid, who first
of all improvised for herself a travelling hat, quite
unique in its style, made of white rabbit skins but
adorned with pink roses, already very much crushed.
When Mrs. Wands first discovered her intention and
her equipment, thus picturesquely to express her
exuberance of joy *through her hat,* so to speak, she
made no objection to the fur hat proper but drew a
decided line as to the roses, greatly to Laura's
chagrin and disappointment.

All were blessed with buffalo boots, which we had
long worn and which fortunately were not worn out.
Standing in these and bundled with shawls, cloaks,

and every available adjustment of furs, topping off
with hoods of beaver fur, our friends in the States,
if they could have seen us thus garbed, would have
hesitated long before fixing our identity. Not only
buffalo but mink and otter as well as beaver skins,
well tanned, were to be utilized for bedding and
other comfort while on the journey.

The ladies were very considerate, after I left
my little log house to become Mrs. Carrington's
guest, in purchasing my moderate stock of furniture
and dishes, paying double their value, that I might
have ready means at hand for so long and painful a
journey, and their generous action was timely and
doubly prized.

General George B. Dandy who had accompanied
the troops as quartermaster was just the man for
the hour and especially in tender consideration for
the women and children in anticipating their needs.
At each recurring memory of those days, as we
recall his skill and discernment in fitting up our
wagons in a manner that proved our very salvation
on such a journey, we render him grateful thanks.
It was a novel caravan, indeed. The wagon covers
of cloth were first doubled, and both sides and ends
of the wagon bodies were boarded up, with a window
in each end. A door at the back of each wagon
swung on hinges to admit of easy ingress and egress,
and near the door was a small sheet iron stove made
from stove-pipe, with a carefully adjusted smoke
escape through the wagon-cover above. Pine blocks
and knots had been sawed in proper lengths and
packed in the corner, only requiring the stroke of a

hatchet to reduce them to a proper size, while a full wagon-load of extra blocks followed.

My mattress, stuffed with straw, was first laid upon the wagon-bed and upon it an extra one from the hospital, and a buffalo rug presented by Mrs. Carrington extended beyond the bed space to the stove, while the wolf-robe given me by Phillips, and one chair, completed the furnishing of my *"travelling house."*

It certainly was with a very desolate feeling, even after packing was done and the loaded wagons were drawn up before headquarters, each waiting her turn for embarking, that we evacuated our quarters and bade good-by to our friends, new and old, and then took a last look at those familiar surroundings which held so much of tragic interest in their keeping, never to be revisited except through memory's guarded recognition.

With all importance attached to actual and visible preparations for our creature comforts, there was, subconsciously, a sense of the under-girding of the Everlasting Arms. In one sense, that slowly moving train was a funeral procession, for my husband's remains were placed in one wagon, that they might accompany me to my home in Tennessee for a resting place until the final Roll Call.

We started, shortly after noon on the 23rd of January, 1867, in a snow-storm, accompanied by an escort of forty infantry and twenty cavalry, and many empty wagons which were to return from Reno with supplies for the garrison at Phil. Kearney, all under the command of Lieutenant

Alpheus H. Bowman.* We had seen nothing but snow on mountain, ravine, and valley for weeks, and the whirling, driving flakes on that day were no novelty except as they added a sense of discomfort if not of apprehension at the beginning of so long and slow a march as lay before us with no possibility of stopping under any conditions until Fort Casper would be reached. A wagon loaded with tools of various kinds for repairs, axes, shovels, and picks was sent in advance, and by dint of shovelling on the part of the pioneer corps, the road was made visible or created, until at ten o'clock at night we halted for rest, having advanced but six miles from the fort, which we left more than eight hours before.

The train was carefully corralled on a high hill for the sake of a better defensive position if attacked by Indians, where, also, wild gusts of snow driven by a fierce wind almost prostrated the men. Here also the stock received a little grain. All were waiting until the rising moon would admit a distinct progress over the low lands beyond.

At one o'clock the bugle sounded and by three o'clock we were again in motion under lead of Bailey, our intrepid guide. Bridger, old and infirm, had been left behind.

I certainly *thanked the stars,* as if they were "my stars," for their appearance, and they seemed to twinkle a willing companionship; and the moon, as well, for the storm had ceased and the night was bright at last.

---

* Retired as Brigadier General, 1903.

On the 25th we reached Crazy Woman's Fork and went into camp in a bend of the river where from the adjoining hill a careful lookout was maintained against any possible surprise. Every halting place on this return eastward had its earlier association. I seemed to reproduce them all and connect them with the present in a single moment, but the immediate environment compelled thought upon making the chilling flesh comfortable, and life endurable. The co-operation of all, actively, was our instant necessity. Before full morning we learned that the thermometer in headquarter wagon had given out, the mercury having congealed in the bulb in spite of all that Dennis could do to keep the stove at a red heat. We no longer had artificial means to determine *how cold it was*. Blessings upon General Dandy's head were hearty for our equipment as we corralled in the snow and the pine knots were dropped into the little stoves to facilitate the boiling of water for coffee. Then came the laborious work of half-frozen men to cut through the ice on the creek, after shovelling off the accumulated drifts of snow, even to get water itself, for the kegs we carried had only a limited supply and they also had succumbed in a large measure to the cold. The driver of Mrs. Carrington's wagon had knocked at the little window in the front of her wagon to have her call the Colonel and have him relieved as "his feet had gone to sleep." When the man was lifted from the saddle he was unable to stand for he was frozen almost to his knees. He was cared for as well as possible, but did not survive the amputation of both limbs two days later at Fort Reno.

Mrs. Wands had a curious fancy and would fire up her stove to its utmost capacity when we passed dangerous places under the strange conceit that if the Indians saw the black smoke it indicated that *cannon* were near.

Actual cooking was a suspended function. The best modern kitchen-range could not secure as far-reaching results as our little sheet-iron stoves, with hatchets our only utensils as we prepared a frugal meal. And then, while one steeped the coffee, another utilized the hatchet for breaking bread and severing knobs of the frozen remnants of our last dinner at the fort. Bacon was thawed also, the accompaniment being the crying of the little boys because of the stinging cold. Being unable to help except by passing pine knots, they were fed intermittently as they crouched as near the stove as the process of cooking would permit. They stood it like young heroes, anxious but powerless to do substantial service.

The camp-scene of the men as viewed from my window had its own distinctive features. There was of course abundance of wood from long-fallen dead timber, but this was procurable only through the supreme efforts of the men, who dug it out and dragged it through drifts within the corral. Even then, when these snow-clad logs were lifted in heaps as high as the men could reach and the flames shot high into the over-hanging pines, the melting snow at their base would change into solid ice. Never by the most unrelaxed effort, could more than one side of a man have warmth at one time. I opened my own wagon door more than once to give my own driver a chance to warm his benumbed hands at the stove, and give him a sip of hot coffee, just to start the circulation, as the sudden heat might, as the surgeons said, only do harm.

The protection of the hill behind us shielded us, otherwise we must have frozen to death. I am sure that the crazy woman whose mental aberration had suggested a fitting name for this stream must have halted here involuntarily under adverse conditions similar to our own, as no sane woman could have tarried long in this place in midwinter.

Some of the men, old soldiers too, men who had come from Lookout Mountain to join the Eighteenth when it was on the eve of departure from Louisville, Kentucky, in the fall of 1865 for the frontier, grew desperate and swore that they "would not budge another inch" so intense was the cold and their need of refreshing sleep.

And thus the night wore on, only relieved by the call of the half-frozen sentries who were changed half-hourly, until "reveille" sounded and every man was expected to report promptly. Repeated bugle-calls failed to arouse men who were wrapped in blankets for rest. Verbal orders loudly sounded, that "all who did not report for duty, would be left," were met by begging pleas for "one more nap." When told that it was not sleepiness, but slow freezing that they felt, they could not be aroused until the Colonel ordered their legs to be lashed with whips, to start the circulation and bring them to their feet.

And then it was slow work for frozen hands to put on icy harness, for the teamsters as well as half the escort had frozen ears, fingers, and feet, while the hands of Dr. Hinds, one of our surgeons, had black fingers already from the excessive cold.

The army mule had figured in my experience and developed latent capacities at every new opportunity. Ours on this occasion acted naturally, however, by getting mad, breaking loose from their tether, dashing where they pleased, kicking, biting, and stamping to keep themselves warm,—mule nature was not so unlike human nature after all, as one could readily observe, and circumstances often develop the best and the poorest qualities we possess, so that under existing conditions the testimony favored our faithful beasts.

When at last we broke camp we experienced entirely new sensations in the attempt to gain the summit of the bluff and pursue the journey. It was nearly sixty feet above the river-bed and only one wagon could ascend at a time, so that it was not until teams were doubled for each in turn, with men tugging at the wheels and others pulling with ropes, that the train after three hours of severe labor was able to resume the "forward-march."

When my turn came I rolled over on my bed, clung for dear life to the sides of the wagon, with eyes shut and jaws clamped, to assist or ignore the situation, both being equally ineffective, for it all depended upon those mules. By dint of whipping, prodding, pushing, pulling, and emphatic shouts from the teamsters suited to mule handling, we reached level ground at last.

Instantly Lieutenant Wands galloped to my wagon, hurriedly opened the door, and thrusting his pleasant face within, hailed me with his usual cheering "How are you now?" Meeting a favorable response, as nearly as I could give my reckonings on so short a notice, he slammed the door, off for similar kindly greetings elsewhere.

But we had hardly begun the march through drifted snow-banks when we had our first "Indian alarm." The word was passed along the lines by a mounted orderly that the rear of the train was threatened. The half-frozen men sprang to the wagons for their arms, which were there stored to protect them from snow and wet and the Colonel dashed back to close up the rear, while the wagons went into corral, but it was soon discovered that the supposed Indians in file were immense herds of buffalo, which of itself disabused us of the idea that Indians were near. Mrs. Wands did not even have the satisfaction of firing up her stove, but directed all her energies to holding it in position so as not to lose it altogether, for the door swung wildly on its hinges and there was no time to close it.

Of all rides I ever had taken in army life or out of it, this one in an army wagon without springs, with mules on a gallop over such a road, or no road, exceeded all in utter misery. One learns something from such an experience and I had learned to seize the sideboards of the wagon firmly, half reclining on the mattress with pillows compactly adjusted, and holding my breath abide the result. Thence onward we travelled through immense herds of buffalo, the bulls wallowing in and tearing up the snow to uncover the buffalo grass for the cows and calves which the bulls protected, and all the time the drivers were forbidden by the Colonel either to crack their whips or "holler" lest the disturbed buffalo should become frightened and stampede the train. Such a stampede had been almost as dangerous as an Indian attack, and less than a year before the First Battalion lost several mules, men, and wagons by a similar experience.

At last the bugle sounded "halt." Drivers cried "whoa," and the column slowly approached the entrance to Fort Reno.

CHAPTER XXV.

As we were to be three days at Fort Reno we were quite ready to adapt ourselves to changed conditions and would have been equally so for a single day's halt, exchanging comfortable quarters for army wagons, and yet if any one had ventured a word of disparagement of the style in which we travelled it would have been defended in strongest terms as the only possible way by which the journey could have been safely made.

I have a quite distinct impression of half rolling out of my wagon and being caught by friendly arms before reaching the ground and being assisted in the effort to stand upon my benumbed feet as well as of being supported until restored circulation enabled me to take a single step toward the comfortable quarters provided for me by the officers of the fort.

While our wants were being looked after with all promptness it was not long before the surgeons were equally engaged in their merciful ministrations to the men, in some cases requiring the amputations of fingers, toes, and even legs, with two fatal results, Mrs. Carrington's driver being one of the fatal cases. Kindly and efficient service was rendered to all. Blessings on those kind physicians,

190

ever ready to render aid and skill in behalf of the suffering, whether through wounds, accident, or other cause.

Our poor hungry mules did a most unnatural thing. I had heard of goats being indifferent to their fare and very promiscuous in their indulgence of appetite when thoroughly famished, but this was the first instance in which I ever heard or knew of mules chewing wagon covers, gnawing mess-chests, spokes of wheels, and wagon-tongues as they attempted that first night at Reno before their time came to be fed. The best possible was done for them on the journey but the supply of fodder and food of all kinds was limited. The troops that relieved us, as already intimated, did not bring adequate supplies for more than their march, in their hasty departure, so that when our train left Fort Phil. Kearney it was augmented by forty empty wagons to return with commissary supplies from Fort Reno.

But this novel experience for our mules was but for a night, and "joy came in the morning," not in the mule's brain cells but in the mule's empty stomach, which in the nature of the mule meant the same thing. On the journey outward in the autumn nothing transpired at Reno to suggest pleasant memories except the kindness of Captain Proctor and Lieutenant Kirtland, but on the return and during the very first night there remains one sweet memory that will ever, as now, linger, notwithstanding the flight of years. As Mrs. Carrington, Mrs. Wands, and myself sat chatting by a comfortable fire over the many incidents and scenes of the preceding weeks and were about retiring for greatly needed sleep, I took from my bag a Bible which had been unopened on the march. Opening it at random my eyes fell upon the thirty-fourth Psalm, which I read aloud, and when I came to the words, "The Angel of the Lord encampeth around them that fear Him and delivereth them," we were all moved to tears, for it seemed as if the comforting reassuring words had been written for our special benefit. They could not have been more fitting as to time or place.

I at once registered on the open page the date, "Fort Reno, January, 1867," and from that date to this, in each succeeding Bible used, never fail to copy the same words from the old one still in my possession. In years long subsequent to that date I had the pleasure of meeting Captain Proctor, who had left the army, in Massachusetts, his native State. After reminiscences of former times I alluded to this incident, and in his response, "You could have read none better," there was the unconscious testimony as to his familiarity with the passage.

But our stop was to end abruptly. The trains were brought to the gates with the shout, "All aboard for Casper," as the signal for all to move lively. A chair was deposited against my wagon, two well-directed steps were taken and the order was obeyed.

There was some readjustments in reduction of the escort which for the most part must return to Fort Phil. Kearney with supplies, but we took up our line of march under charge of Lieutenant Joshua W. Jacobs,* bidding hearty adieus to our hospitable hosts, but with no regret on my part at leaving, as each mile would bear me nearer home,— nearer home, but still so far, far away.

For three days each camp-scene was like another except the fourth which was signalized by our arrival at Deer Creek, a telegraph station which had been burned by Indians. In the ruins, however, there was a large fireplace still serviceable and close by it a heap of blocks of tar which had been used for insulation in building the new line between Fort Laramie and Fort Casper. It was indeed a pleasant task to build a fire with something that would readily burn, and unmindful of both smoke and odor we congratulated ourselves upon its light and warmth. We also celebrated the occasion by the prosaic ceremony of boiling water in a real fireplace, for our coffee, sufficient for all, escort included. Our reduced number was not, after all, so important now, as the band, numbering thirty, had been well armed by the Colonel with Spencer carbines before they left Fort Leavenworth in the fall of 1865 on their early march to Old Fort Kearney. They were proud of their carbines and as glad as ourselves to get beyond the reach of Indian enemies.

I had eaten corn meal cooked in every possible shape, as I supposed, at my old home in Tennessee, but none ever had the taste and flavor of that pre-

---

* Lieutenant Jacobs lived to become a Brigadier General of the United States Army and died in New Jersey, late in 1905.

pared by Mrs. Carrington at this camp-fire on Deer Creek. I actually fed upon her corn dodgers and fried bacon with such relish that memory has the very savor of that journey and her enduring friendship.

CHAPTER XXVI.

" THUS far " on the march we had not seen an
Indian. The buffalo that swarmed the country north
and west of Reno and which were mistaken for
Indians at one time because of their single trail, so
like that of Indians in their migrations, were missing, and our guide took for granted through their
absence that Indians were not in pursuit, or near
our line of march. We had left the special haunt of
the buffalo, he argued, and were in sight of Casper,
but not as near in distance as appeared to the eye.
But the moving of dark objects in separate Indian
files were at this anxious moment very suggestive
because so similar to buffalo trails.

The headquarters of the Eighteenth Infantry
were again approaching an appointed home, six
miles distant.

Lieutenant Wands and guide Bailey rode forward to announce our speedy arrival. Very suddenly, without a word of warning, I realized that our
teams were on a quick trot, and upon looking
through the front window of my wagon the cause
was soon apparent, for I caught sight of Indians.
They had dashed between us and the fort and run
off the stock of horses belonging to the fort just
after the officers had dismounted and entered the

enclosure. They had evidently followed us, but had never ventured an attack.

Thus between the announcement of our coming and our "getting there" occurred this terrifying episode.

The Colonel, who was riding somewhat in advance of the train, ordered it closed up with speed and we moved steadily on. The teams soon formed a moving corral with six teams at front, and as many in the rear with flanking teams in single file so that in an emergency all would form a compact hollow square. My fear was intensified by the fact that my wagon was on the outside upon a hilly surface, where the road was too narrow for all to be on level ground, and my instant conclusion was that if the Indians attacked us suddenly my position would be one of great peril. Thoughts come quickly at such times, as to a "drowning man snatching at a straw." All the wagons had become shackling and not as secure for defense as when we started. While these thoughts were rapidly increasing our anxiety we were relieved by seeing the Indians dash for the hills across the Platte to the northward, not venturing to attack our train and risk losing the stock already in their possession. It is not improbable, as we learned after our arrival, that the Indians who had watched the stock of the fort presumed that our arrival would disarm the garrison of any suspicion that their own stock, so near by, would be in any danger. At any rate we had the excitement of a genuine scare, and groans of relief, not translated into words, came from the women who had to pacify the children as we moved toward the gates. It seems that the Colonel, who had seen Indians on the other side of the river, had not sounded the bugle, and had quietly closed up the train by way of precaution, but avoided a general alarm, which to us was as real as if the Indians were making for our train itself.

Fort Casper was a historic place, and named from a worthy hero, Casper Collins, who lost his life near there before he was twenty-one years of age, and about a year before our arrival. When General Pope heard of his gallant fight and death, and of the brave men under his command, he issued an order to commemorate the event in these words:

"The Military Post situated at Platte Bridge on Platte River will hereafter be known as "Fort Casper," in honor of Lieutenant Casper Collins of the Eleventh Ohio Cavalry, who lost his life in gallantly attacking a superior force of Indians at this place."

Fort Collins of Colorado already existed, named for his father, Lieutenant Colonel Collins of the Eleventh Ohio Cavalry, a noted Indian fighter in Wyoming, previous to his young son's connection with the army. Casper Collins was a worthy son of a worthy sire, and Wyoming does honor to the name of Casper by perpetuating his memory.

We were warmly welcomed on our arrival by Major Norris, Lieutenant Carpenter, Captain Freeman and his wife, Captain Potter and his wife, and their little son Carrol, who made the quartette of four little boys full again, consisting of Harry and

Jimmy Carrington, and Bobbie Wands.* We were assigned to as pleasant quarters as possible, some of the officers doubling up to give the ladies more room. Mrs. Freeman was particularly considerate of myself, preparing every possible delicacy in the way of food within reach.

The most was made of our short stay at Casper, for very soon after our arrival it was learned that after all it was to be but transient. A few trunks were unpacked that the ladies might make a more presentable appearance at the mess-table, and linsey-woolsey travelling dresses, flannel sacques, and cumbersome articles of dress were doffed for others more appropriate for Casper society. Our band, or those members whose hands and frozen fingers had sufficiently recovered for the purpose, discoursed fine music, as a more congenial exercise than the handling of the carbine, though disciplined to use both mouth and fingers as the case required. With equal skill in the use of either brass or stringed instruments, they were ready to respond to any call. They surprised us one evening by giving a concert-program made up of overtures and arias from several leading operas. The barrack was a strange "stage-setting" for the overture from "William Tell," though some of these brave performers had

---

* Lieutenant Carpenter (Gilbert S.) lived to become not only Colonel of the 18th Infantry, but at his quite recent death had reached the rank of Brigadier-General. Captain Freeman, elsewhere noticed as Brigadier-General, was with us at Sheridan, in 1908. Jimmy Carrington (James Beebee) is, and for years has been, on the editorial staff of *Scribner's Magazine*, New York City.

done heroic deeds surpassing those of the immortal William himself. Then followed some inspiriting waltz that was irresistible to some who had been in that frontier post with only drum and fife and bugle for music, and then was heard the sound of tripping feet, as if to verify the old adage, "if you have a day to be happy in, be happy for the day."

There were few episodes of special interest, or worthy of mention at Casper, each person viewing the situation philosophically according to temper, temperament, or situation, as incidental to army life. We soon learned that orders had been received to change headquarters to the handsomely rebuilt Fort McPherson. If this had not miscarried, the trip, that terrible winter trip to Fort Casper, at least would have been needless. There was, however, one case of incipient rebellion, not serious, because soon quelled, in the line of domestic service. Mrs. Wands' Laura, previously honored with notice, protested in most emphatic terms that "she wouldn't budge another step." In plain words, she "swore" she would not go further with the command, and was otherwise so obstreperous and independent as to exasperate her mistress beyond longer endurance. One morning Mrs. Wands gave a hurried rap at my door and requested me to go to her room with her as she was going to flail Laura into subordination by the help of a "trunk strap." No means had been devised at army posts, or fixed by army regulations for the punishment of women. Soldiers having wives, as garrison laundresses, regulated their domestic discipline aside from fixed methods, though sternly punished for indecent bossing. In this instance gagging would seem to be suitable, but aside from any fixed standard or precedent it might have required more physical force than Mrs. Wands had at command, so that Mrs. Wands resolved to try what virtue there might be in the impromptu application of a strap.

I was not expected to assist in the operation, only to lend my presence as a sort of moral force to the situation. I do not remember to have responded with any great alacrity, much as I loved Mrs. Wands, but nevertheless went to her room as requested.

I recall the drama: Act one; scene one; Mrs. Wands, with a double strap and hand uplifted ready for the fray; Laura with menacing attitude, yet with furtive glances toward the exit. Then frequent changes of position from one side of the stage to the other with quite appropriate action something in the nature of sparring. One could readily perceive that this little domestic drama would be quite short, while at the same time having the dramatic unity of beginning, middle, and end. In military parlance, there was considerable skirmishing for so small a field of action, when, by one supremely misdirected aim, the door was struck instead of Laura, while the enemy hastily retreated through the door, bringing active hostilities to an abrupt close. The moral victory was assured, for when the time of our departure arrived Laura was as ready to leave as the rest of the party, only that her rabbit-skin hat was somewhat demoralized though not so seriously as to be unfit for the journey.

Wagons had to be repaired and other necessary duties were to be performed preparatory to doubling our tracks to Sage Creek and thence to Laramie. Our party was augmented by the company of Mrs. Potter and little Carrol, as her husband had been appointed to headquarters staff as the Adjutant of the Eighteenth Infantry. He had been once the Colonel of one of the "Galvanized Regiments" (made up of paroled Confederates to serve on the Plains), and had served as assistant adjutant-general to General Heintzelman, when our Colonel, then a brigadier general of volunteers, served under Heintzelman, so that the appointment was a fortunate one every way. His wife was a lovely addition to the coterie of ladies that usually attach to an Army headquarters.

"As half is shade, and half is sun, this world along its course advances," so we retained pleasant memories of Fort Casper as we fell into line for our cold march to Sage Creek, the first allotted camping place.

Every one was cheerful, or tried to be, as every step brought us nearer to Laramie and all fear of Indians gradually lessened. And yet we were not to be thus speedily emancipated from all danger, as we found upon approaching Sage Creek, a famous place for Indian attacks.

Suddenly an alarm was sounded of Indians attempting the ford and all was quickly put in shape for an attack, and the corral ordered to be formed instantly and compactly. While galloping swiftly to hasten the movement, Colonel Carrington had the misfortune to be wounded by the accidental discharge of his revolver, which, in its repair at Casper, left one hammer-pin broken, so that the quick motion of the revolver while riding at a gallop to close the train discharged it in his left leg. He had just passed my wagon, and as I watched from the window I heard the shot and saw him fall upon the neck of his horse, Grey Eagle, and the horse as suddenly stopped. I felt that something serious had happened to his master. Intense excitement prevailed for a while until he was dismounted and conveyed to an ambulance, for the result could not be immediately known. Surgeons were in attendance at once. Leather straps were swung across the ambulance from side to side for greater comfort, but the surgeons, whose hands were still almost without feeling from previous freezing, could not safely probe for the ball. Whatever might be the result, the Colonel ordered the train not to return to Casper, the nearest post, but force the march to Laramie.

That night in camp was a solemn one indeed and in the morning the gloom took on another and deeper shade when a sergeant unable to control his tears announced that ''he knew the Colonel never would ride again, for Grey Eagle, who had fed all night from the bark of a fallen cottonwood, lay dead from horse-colic.''

Grey Eagle was a blooded dapple-gray horse, nearly seventeen hands high, from the best Kentucky stock, and had been presented to the Colonel by the City of Indianapolis when he left Indiana to rejoin the Army of the Cumberland, and was actually loved by every soldier of the command.

The train pushed forward, stopping at Bridger's Ferry, where I had the inexpressible joy of meeting my brother William, who had promptly responded to my call of distress, from far-away Tennessee and had been waiting for me during our needless march to Fort Casper.

Although I had received so much of brotherly attention from officers at the fort and all along the journey, here was a real brother, of flesh and blood, bringing so much of the home-spirit with him that the distance seemed to have been instantly shortened though there was still much more than a thousand miles of travel before me. My mother in Tennessee had received a long telegram from Laramie with details of the disaster and when the telegram came brother was attending a Masonic Celebration. He doffed his regalia instantly, boarded the first train for the North, and had nearly reached me when he learned of the changes at Casper and awaited my arrival.

CHAPTER XXVII.

AGAIN AT LARAMIE AND McPHERSON—GOOD-BYE
COURTESIES AT OMAHA.

ONCE more at Laramie, but how changed in many ways since I bade farewell to kind friends on that beautiful September morning to join our regiment, so far away! I did indeed meet a few former friends, most of the officers I had gladly greeted when they arrived with reinforcements that came to our relief at Phil. Kearney.

My husband's body was tenderly borne to a little house where it remained under a "guard of honor" during our temporary stay at the post.

Colonel Carrington was borne to the sutler's own house, that of Mr. Bullock, and there I learned from his wife more particularly of the previous two days' march, while she attended upon him and my brother William kept me in his charge. Had I not been so utterly prostrated I should have been by her side. It had been a willing service to minister to the wounded after that Battle of Franklin, but I seemed paralyzed by my own personal experience, and was no longer a nurse, for the occasion, but a woman with a broken heart, carried along as circumstances, under God, shaped my course.

She told me that his surgeons, whose hands had been so frost-bitten on the march to Reno, felt that they were not safe in probing the wound, as the ball had entered the inner side of the thigh in what they called the scarpal place, actually grazing the coating of the main artery, that they feared that any administration might induce secondary hemorrhage, with a fatal result, and besides that, they insisted that the ball had passed out of the leg, although there was but one orifice. They said that the ball heeled, and went out just when it struck. The Colonel claimed that the ball was still in his limb; in spite of their protests he was carried in a sling in his wife's wagon, but the left limb was paralyzed and opiates were administered to quiet his system until help could be had at Fort Laramie.

When the Post surgeon was called in he declined to act, in deference to the surgeons with the command, until the Colonel half jocosely asked him "whether he would assist sufficiently to answer a question, viz., "whether lead in the human system could be regarded as a normal element of advantage to the patient?"

This was followed by asking the loan of the surgeon's finger, which he placed upon the flattened ball that rested under the nerve on the opposite side of the limb. Then he demanded its immediate removal, watching the process with interest, and when the ball was removed the limb was relieved and restored to its normal functions.

When I called to bid them both good-by, he was cheerful, urged my immediate departure and, as from the first hour after he fell from his horse, renewed his assurance that he would soon be on duty with the new Regimental Headquarters at Fort McPherson.

Although Mrs. Carrington remained, of course, with her husband, Mrs. Wands and Mrs. Potter, whose husbands were on the Regimental Staff were to accompany them as far as the new Headquarters, and so we began our journey together.

Scott's Bluffs, Fortification Rocks, Chimney Rock, and Court House Rock, already noticed in the outward journey, as well as Fort Mitchell, were passed without noteworthy incident, but they were no less dreary now that they were covered, mountain and valley alike, with deep and drifted snow. Scott's Bluff, however, did indeed present new and alarming features. The drifted snows almost obscured its precipitous embankments, which rose many feet on either side, and the deep ravines now packed with snow made the driving through the gorge a perilous risk. A slight deflection from the proper course, especially where the track was on an inclined plane, would have been destruction. The mules, urged to their utmost, would dash forward and then fall prostrate, but as soon as they felt the weight of the heavy wagon following them they would scramble to their feet, throw the snow in blinding clouds above their heads and then pitch forward again by frantic leaps. Finally, by coaxing and leading, for they could not be driven, they made the final exit, and were halted for the next wagon, as but one could pass at a time.

We were indeed glad to leave Scott's Bluffs, with the conscious assurance that a similar experience could never be repeated by either of us.

Ranchmen along the road were very eager to

render any service that would promote physical comfort and there were times when a restful breathing delay at such hospitable, unpretending homes, actually made us reluctant to leave their shelter.

But the ubiquitous Platte, already feebly described in the narrative of our outward journey, was to add one more incident to the category of our experience of western frontier life. As we drove down the bank we found that the river was more than half frozen over. Here, as elsewhere, only one wagon was to pass in turn. I took my post of observation at the window, and clinging to the sides with tenacious grip, watched the process. When we came to the edge of the ice, the mules refused to jump into the water. They tore madly to one side and then the other, leaving the wagon poised on the ice; but at last, by the use of whip and language suited to the mules' comprehension, the final plunge was made, but my stove, fortunately not lighted, my chair, and everything movable was overturned, while the mules kept on with one wild dash to the southern shore, where the equilibrium of all, that of the mules included, was fairly well restored.

Lieutenant Wands greeted us, as he rode up to my door, with his usual "Hello, how are you?" reassuring, as always, of his solicitation for my comfort.

Fort Sedgwick was soon reached and right glad we were to disembark for more agreeable quarters. Captain Mix of the Second Cavalry and his lovely little wife seemed to typify both the Priscilla of poetic song and the rough and kindly Standish,

MY ARMY LIFE

"great of heart, magnanimous, courtly, and courageous" with never a John Alden to intervene.

I had seen no apples since leaving the States and
my brother was despatched to the sutler's to purchase this greatly-coveted fruit. He returned with
the unwelcome report that the supply was reduced
to a few that were both decayed and frozen.

This did not deter me from my purpose, and then
I began to appreciate the hunger of our mules at
Fort Reno, when they attempted to eat mess-chests
and wagon-covers. I had eaten queer things on the
frontier, not forgetting "desiccated vegetables,"
but this was the first time that the range of diet
included frozen, rotten apples. If they contained
bacilli their power for injury was possibly negatived
in that climate by the freeezing process. I really do
not know, for I had never heard of bacilli at that
time, and at any rate if harm resulted it fell to the
bacilli and not to myself.

The poet sings "new occasions teach new duties."
New occasions certainly bring novel experiences,
and each adds to the general store. One, at least,
awaited me at Sedgwick. While chatting one evening with Mrs. Mix in her sitting-room, footsteps
were heard in the hall, followed by a hurried and
simultaneous rap on the door, which when opened
admitted Mrs. Sokalski and a young lieutenant, her
escort, both of whom had just arrived from Laramie.
This lady is worthy of more than passing notice.
As she flourished into the room with her two favorite
dogs, Romeo and Juliet, she unbuckled her belt from
which two revolvers were suspended and handed

them to the lieutenant with these laconic instructions: "Have these pistols repaired at once, and see to it that the same are returned, for if exchanged or otherwise appropriated I can identify them anywhere in the United States." She was the widow of Captain George Sokalski, on her way to the States. Her husband had been before a Court Martial at Fort Kearney, and she managed his case before the court. Her experience with our own officers, before they left Kearney the previous spring, was related to me in part. There she not only had Romeo and Juliet, but other dogs to the number of thirteen, " the exact number of stripes in the American Flag," as she facetiously counted them up. She was a noted and dexterous horse woman. During General Sherman's visit at the Post she dashed into the parade-ground one day clad in a wolf-skin riding habit, with wolf-tails at the bottom of the skirt almost sweeping the ground, and a fur hat from which floated another bunch of wolf-tails. As she galloped swiftly past headquarters where the General was standing, he raised his hands in astonishment and with this ejaculation addressed his host: "What the devil of a creature is that? Is she a wild woman, a Pawnee, or a Sioux, or what?"

Mrs. Mix did not on this occasion have an extra room for the accommodation of the lady, but she contentedly occupied a mattress on the floor, which "suited her well enough." She only stipulated that "Romeo and Juliet should sleep at the foot of the bed."

Mrs. Sokalski kept up a lively conversation half the night, relating incidents of her exposures in army life, and as the partitions were very thin, the officers in the morning inquired "what we found so entertaining to talk about all night and keep them from sleep?"

This episode of our home journey, like so many of the unnatural freaks of life experience where the grotesque and diverting seemed designed to arrest melancholy by striking contrasts, was followed by an affectionate and considerate farewell, and dear Mrs. Mix stored our basket with such delicacies as would minister to our comfort as we took our departure.

CHAPTER XXVIII.

HOME AGAIN.

THE destination of the new headquarters of the Eighteenth having been changed to Fort McPherson, Nebraska, only one hundred miles west from the starting-point of its march during the previous year, we pushed on, making but two halts by the way, arriving late in February, and, as we afterwards learned, the Colonel was able to be moved to the Post on the 2nd day of March. Opposite this very station, as we were rejoiced to learn, the Union Pacific Railroad had established its immediate terminus; and, reminded of our early experience on its first passenger car from Omaha, we appreciated the fact that the continuance of our homeward journey would be after modern, civilized methods.

Mrs. Mizener, the wife of Colonel J. K. Mizener, was our generous hostess and gave a cordial welcome to their pleasant home, and her accomplished sister, Miss Stevens, shared in that welcome. There was no lack of sympathizing words and friendly acts during our brief stay, never to be forgotten so long as life lasts.

Other changes, matters of course in army life, had to follow, Mrs. Potter remaining at headquarters, while Mrs. Wands was to go as far as Omaha in company with us, on her way to her former home, near Albany, New York. Her husband, our kind friend, remained with the headquarters staff, as a matter of duty.

Fort McPherson had been beautifully rebuilt from the red cedar wood abundant in that vicinity, so that not only doors, sash and furniture, but even shingles had been made from this lumber; and the interiors when varnished bore the air of costly furniture. The old record of the "Cedars of Lebanon" as of surpassing beauty, in very ancient times, had new suggestions as to their practical use.

Several officers had been sent eastward on recruiting service, although greatly needed with their companies, but they were surely entitled to that relief; and among them was Captain Arnold, just promoted, who had been assigned as my special escort, always prompt to render grateful service to myself and brother until we could reach usual lines of travel.

It seemed as if a century had elapsed since we were first at Omaha, as we again sat down to a bountiful table amid peaceful surroundings. With the American characteristic, wherever located, and under whatever conditions, times or hardships, many trials seemed for the moment to have been obliterated as other topics of conversation obtruded their subject-matter, and one seemed to live in another sense of old times, and contrasting environment. It was once said of a Confederate soldier returning home after peace had been declared that when stopping at a hotel restaurant where meals were lavishly furnished, upon being asked by the colored waiter who offered him the menu, "What will you have Sir?" he invariably gave the single response. "Give me pie." Mrs. Wands had her own special *penchant;* but, for "sausage" instead of pie, and was rather abashed by the polite but quizzical inquiry of Captain Arnold, "Mrs. Wands, have you faith?" A kind of sausage had been made for us from canned meats and desiccated potatoes, on the frontier, and his question was not pressed.

At Omaha, however, we had the pleasure of again meeting Mrs. Bisbee, who left Fort Phil. Kearney late in the fall, when her husband was promoted to a Captaincy and became attached to the Department Staff at Omaha. With pleasant rides and introductions to her friends she contributed largely to the relief of my mind from the pressure of the journey upon my nervous system. But it was with peculiar sadness under the most kindly attentions that I left Omaha and old army association with no prospect that we would ever meet again. The good wishes of those left behind did serve to mitigate the sorrow of the parting, and the star of hope never sets, once for all, in the human breast.

I was indeed from that parting appreciably "Homeward bound." But, so far as travelling conveyance was concerned, I assumed that when I left both ambulance and army wagon, the future method of travel was unequivocally settled. And so it would have been but for the Missouri River, the Rubicon to be crossed in the winter while no bridge spanned its swift and variable conditions. We felt as anxious as did Cæsar in his achievement and the personal motive was no less serious to us than

213

was his own. We had been sufficiently familiar with boat travel on the Missouri River and ambulance and wagon appliances on the Platte River, but when driven to the ordinary steamboat landing, we found that the river was frozen from bank to bank with ice of variable thickness and that the passage could only be made by wheels.

I confess to a downright sinking of heart. Here was an ordeal entirely unanticipated. I had become convinced that I had done forever with crossing strange rivers and tortuous drives through snow-stuffed gorges, but the assuring thought that I had recently crossed the Platte itself, when only half frozen over, was suggestive that the Missouri might not be so bad after all. So, gathering strength for the crossing and bidding a last good-by, the last indeed, to dear Mrs. Wands and other friends, my brother and myself took seats in the stage. The driver kept his four stalwart horses well in hand and, with a flourish of his cracking whip, instead of a trumpet, away we went on a spirited gallop, almost suspending breath, but landing safely on the opposite river side.

I have never taken a trip in an ice-boat nor yet tried the experience of travelling in an air-ship, but aerial suspension would lose something of its certain novelty, in my humble judgment, after the excitement over the ice-bound Missouri.

On our arrival at the hotel at Council Bluffs for a temporary sojourn for rest and recreation preparatory to our remaining journey, it came over me with increased persistence that I was now indeed separated from all the past, except in memory, and that I must turn more earnest thought toward the future that involved so much, and yet must check such thoughts, lest they speed too far into the unknown and lose that strengthening grace that is so surely promised for the immediate present.

Among the guests at the hotel were members of the Commission on their way to investigate Indian affairs and especially that of the Fort Phil. Kearney Massacre. They sought an interview, which I declined. It seemed a rude shock to my sensibilities that in the presence of strangers I should be called upon to revive the past scenes and give historic details as to events for their enlightenment. Their motive was a proper one and they were good men, but such an interview was ill-timed and they withdrew the request. My brother William was able from our mutual confidences in the matter to inform them of my own feelings, as the chief surviving sufferer, and to let them know that no censure could attach to the commanding officer. Indeed, there was perfect unity of opinion that ''failure to obey orders strictly and unequivocally given, caused it all.'' But my heart was too sore over the great sacrifice the dead had made to publicly censure their action, and so far as I was concerned the Commission was left to do their work in their own appointed time and way.

It is but just to add to that already stated as to the exoneration of the Commanding Officer of all blame, that after a year of absence to recover from his wound he was immediately ordered back to the

Plains, with headquarters at Fort Sedgwick, where he resumed command of his regiment and operations within the range of that command.

Once more on the east and south-bound train, with courage revived and all the comfort that a modern Pullman car could furnish. Without attempting to draw aside the veil from the future, only just a little, we safely reached home in March, 1867, after a journey of seven weeks.

A month later a son was born.

"The Lord preserveth thy going out and thy coming in!"

My welcome home again, with my faithful brother and our precious charge, was most tender as well as pathetic, and both neighbors and our people generally extended their sympathetic greetings.

When adjusted to these new conditions the very surroundings became once more so intimately associated with the closing scenes of the Civil War in and about Franklin that my mind was somewhat diverted from thought of those on the frontier whom I left behind on that cold and stormy winter's day in 1867.

During the following year, while visiting a sister in Cincinnati I read for the first time Mrs. Carrington's history of her own "Experiences of an Officer's Wife on the Plains" under the title "AB-SA-RA-KA," "The Land of the Crows," and also learned that her husband had been assigned to duty at Wabash College, Crawfordsville, Indiana, as

Professor of Military Science, that Chair having been established at that College where the family had fixed their home.

Later, when I saw the announcement of the death of a Mrs. Carrington, I wrote to learn if it were, indeed, the wife of our old commander. Correspondence ensued that resulted in our marriage in 1871, and my removal to his new home.

In 1882 we removed to Boston, and in 1885, to Hyde Park, where my husband, who had been retired from active service while at Wabash College, has continued his historical and literary studies, with occasional assignments in making treaties and taking the Census of various Indian Tribes.

PART IV
AFTER MANY DAYS
THE TRIUMPH OF PEACE

CHAPTER XXIX.

THE after-word, as will readily appear, fills only in part an interval of forty-two years in the history of Northern Wyoming, particularly Sheridan, and its vicinity. This modern, up-to-date little city, the product of virile western enterprise, had its beginning only twenty-five years ago, when "the site of the city was a stretch of bunch grass and sage-brush, peopled by prairie dogs in greater number than the population of the city now standing on the ruins of their villages." Over four hundred towns have grown up since I first visited the present State. The life of the early pioneer is as novel to the present generation indigenous to the soil as present conditions are astonishing to those same pioneers who have not been part of the life and growth, yet sharing the blazed trail epoch, and only later-day witnesses to results, after the lapse of years.

The object of supplementing the foregoing narrative with an abridged account of the development of the country involving mutation in things temporal so impressive is not for the purpose of giving those alert citizens information concerning their own history aside from personal relations to that history,—"a carrying coals to New Castle," or Sheridan for that matter,—where in reality without figurative expression there exists the flourishing town of New

Castle and the home of their highly esteemed Congressman, Mr. Mondell, and Sheridan with its adjacent coal mines; but for the reason of its impressiveness as evidence of the fulfilment of prophecy in regard to this particular section, and noting the strides made in the development of the country, so magical and hardly capable of realization by those outside its pale, and not a part of it. And to generalize and take in a larger scope of the country west of the Mississippi, and even what has come to pass in the lifetime of the writer, as she reviews the past, the mission of the pathfinders through the west suggests the figure of a chain of human links that bound together the underlying country between the Atlantic and Pacific Seas.

To the Indian fighters, the explorers, trappers, hunters, and particularly the settler folk, who carved States out of forest and prairie, the statement of one who has spent his life's best labors in the West is pertinent.

He says, "The great West is the heart of America, and out of it are the issues of national life. The East is surely but gradually becoming foreign. The alien is so much in evidence that in some cities one must know two or more languages to do business successfully;" and he further adds, "to one who remembers the trackless prairies and mighty forests tenanted by wild Indians, the West of to-day to such a one becomes the miracle of the nineteenth century."

More than a hundred years ago Joel Barlow in his Columbiad describes Columbus as "being led by Hesper out of prison to a hill of vision, and from that vantage ground is unfolded to him the future greatness of America.''

The poem is obsolete, yet the poet himself must have seen visions, and dreamed dreams, and, quoting at second-hand, Hawthorne playfully suggested that ''the Columbiad be set to the music of artillery and thunder and lightning, as a kind of national oratorio.''

For a complete review of our country's history the student, as Victor Hugo says of general history, ''will study the successive movements of humanity.'' The rival civilizations of Spanish, French, and English must be considered; and surely, as the good Bishop Berkley sang so many years ago of the westward course of empire, ''Time's noblest offering is the last, the native type, the American citizen.''

When I first went to that section of the country as the wife of an army officer, there was no such designation of the territory as Wyoming. It was later formed out of parts of Dakota, Montana, Utah, and Idaho, a State almost as large as Colorado, and almost twice the size of any State east of the Missouri River, with an area of ninety-seven thousand square miles; for the most part a beautiful State, with some bleak and barren looking regions, too often misjudged when these are the basis of conclusions, and the political and social conditions emphasized by the novelist, when the people were practically without law, or only such as was usurped by Vigilance Committees, and when evil deeds were restrained only by fear of violence at the hands of these self-appointed executors of law, without Judge or Jury.

Army officers, in their discussions of the new State to be, thought the name would be Absaraka, meaning in the Indian language "Home of the Crows," and the preponderance of opinion favored that designation. I recall one officer particularly who would become quite excited when the name of Wyoming was mentioned in connection with the christening of the new State. Equally strong arguments were maintained on the other side, led by the editor of a Nebraska paper called the "Pioneer Index," claiming that he first proposed the name of Wyoming from Campbell's poem "Gertrude of Wyoming"; while others claimed that the name was carried to the West by emigrants from the Wyoming Valley in Pennsylvania, in its native location, the word itself being derived from the Delaware Indians, meaning "Great Plains," or "the large plains."

In the State's nomenclature, as in the chemical formula, "that the structure of the terms employed expresses the composition of the substance to which they are applied," the Delaware meaning would be eminently consistent, yet the suggestion of the emigrants bearing their old home name to the home of the new appeals to the poetic sentiment. From distant quarters the name of Lincoln was suggested, but voted down as in the case of Colorado, and later pending as the name for the proposed State of New Mexico, when she enters the sisterhood. But Wyoming it is, beautiful for situation and the glory of her people.

I had often dreamed of returning to the spot so full of tragic interest, and the thought evolved from the dream was intensified by reports of later day developments; yet it seemed not possible unless perchance in some reincarnation, when it really came to pass, for the alert citizens of that particular section bestirred themselves to have a combined celebration on the third and fourth of July, 1908; each, of local and national interest.

The old proverb "that all things come to those who wait" was certainly verified in this instance.

Coincident with the cordial invitation to be present on the occasion, and indeed to be a feature of the celebration, the generous guarantee of financial provision made my dream come true, and my thought crystallized with actual preparation for the journey and final settling down into comfortable drawing room compartment with the satisfaction that we were actually setting out on a journey to Wyoming.

The chief interest of the celebration on the 3rd of July centered around the presence of the few survivors of the Fort Phil. Kearney Massacre that occurred in 1866, emphasized by the gathering of nearly two thousand people with them, around the monument dedicated to the memory of the heroes who lost their lives on that field of slaughter.

These survivors did not take part in the battle, for not one was left to tell the tale of woe, but were among those who risked their lives to rescue the dead while the Indians were in possession of the field.

Unless, perhaps, that as sudden realization of present conditions might prove too bewildering it was arranged through the authorities of Omaha that a stop-over for a night and day should be made at that city. At all events we stopped.

At the Burlington Station, awaiting our coming were S. S. Peters of the Omaha Bee, and Sergeant Samuel Gibson (both retired), old soldiers of forty years ago, Maurice Barnes, son of Drum-major Barnes, who helped fashion the flag-staff way back in October, 1866, and J. D. McKinnie, as well as Pat Desmond, each of whom served in the Eighteenth U. S. Infantry during the entire Civil War and came to Omaha to meet their old Commander. Several photographers were present to take a snapshot of the party, and were not satisfied with anything less than several "posings" before the camera.

General Charles Morton commanding the department of the Missouri in behalf of the Army, and his accomplished wife were also present to welcome us. Mr. Gould Dietz and Mr. Henry Foster, in behalf of the Commercial Club and Omaha Club, and the Knights of Ak-sar-ben (Nebraska spelled backwards), Governors, made us feel that we were indeed among friends. We were taken to General Morton's residence in Mr. Dietz's automobile to be their guests during our short sojourn, and General Carrington was entertained at luncheon at the Omaha Club by Mr. Dietz, and Mr. H. J. Penfold of the Board of Governors of the Ak-sar-ben. The additional guests included General Morton, and General Charles F. Manderson, the staff-officers of the "Department of

the Missouri," a number of the Regular Army officers stationed at Forts Crook and Omaha, the Board
of Governors of the Ak-sar-ben, also Commissioners
Guild of the Commercial Club, as well as Mr. S. S.
Peters and Sergeant Samuel Gibson, old comrades,
and Mr. Jones, another old Civil War veteran of the
Eighteenth Infantry.

General Manderson acted as toastmaster, intro-
ducing the speakers, each of whom responded in
characteristic vein, relating the early opening of
Nebraska to settlement and other past army experiences that have already become a part of the history
of the old Eighteenth Infantry.

Major D. E. McCarthy, Chief Quartermaster of
the Department, closed the program with a song entitled, "The Christening of Danry," which brought
down the house, and literally brought the guests to
the door where automobiles were in readiness to
take the party to the "Den of the Knights," the old
Coliseum, as the special guests of the Knights of
Ak-sar-ben, Mr. Frederickson contributing his big
four-seated touring-car for the occasion.

The evening was christened "Military Night,"
and a large crowd was present to do honor to the
distinguished visitors.

General Carrington, General Manderson, and
General Morton, the only speakers of the evening,
were each greeted with an ovation as they appeared
on the platform. General Carrington paid a high
tribute to the progress and enterprise of Nebraska,
and the magnificent spirit of fraternity and comradeship that prevailed in the Ak-sar-ben. He gave a

short history of his organization of the Pawnee Scouts, under Major Frank North, and the excellent service rendered by that organization against the hostile Sioux. He told briefly of the early days of old Fort Kearney in their own State, and "Doby-town," when he was in command of the District of Nebraska, then a territory, that were of historic interest.

General Manderson's address was a brilliant and deserved tribute to the work accomplished by Aksar-ben, and he told further of his plug hat experiences at old Julesburg in 1869, when the wearing of such headgear was not in conformity with the style of the West; that he loaned that hat to a comedian in a Julesburg theatre in which to sing "Lannigan's Ball," and that it was the drawing card of the entertainment.

General Morton expressed his pleasure at being present on this occasion and told briefly of the development of the West during the period he had served in Nebraska, and concluding his remarks with a tribute to the services of General Carrington in the days of the early building of the West.

As ladies were not expected to be present at such functions, I felt quite contented to be relegated to the home of our charming hostess, Mrs. Morton, and with a few invited guests spent the time where speech-making was not a feature, but reminiscences of the long past were quite in order, beginning with my first visit to the State, not then admitted to the Union, my former sojourn at Omaha, a town of eleven hundred inhabitants, now a magnificent city

of one hundred and sixty-five thousand, the Chicago
of the West; and here indeed began the first chapter
in revelations that were to be continued in its unfolding in the next upon resuming the journey. It
was no easy matter to adjust one's self to the real
fact and sense the feeling that at the Omaha Station
we were indeed boarding our car for Sheridan,
Wyoming, the next place to disembark.

CHAPTER XXX.

ESCORTED TO SHERIDAN—THE ROUTE A CONTRAST WITH FORMER DESERT WASTES.

ROLLING into the Sheridan Station July 1, 1908, was a long train of Pullman cars, not an unusual happening, unless on schedule time, and once described in Indian parlance as "coming over the iron road, with a horse that ate wood and breathed fire and smoke," though in this instance coal instead of wood was eaten; and bringing a few passengers at least, who received a cordial welcome from the citizens of the charming little city; and to them, at once began the next chapter of revelations continued from Omaha.

Advance into this section in July, 1866, was guarded by marching troops, themselves the only white faces in the country, with bristling bayonets, and mounted guns, the means of transportation only wagons and ambulances, with every inch of ground disputed by a savage and relentless foe.

Compensations for former experiences were not lacking through the unbounded hospitality of present occupants of this modern Canaan which like its ancient prototype "flowed with milk and honey," and sharply accentuated the difference between the *"Now"* and *"Then."* Really, the strain of present agreeable experiences possessed an element almost painful, so insistent were those of the past, a problem of psychology not easy of solution. A dual personality or reincarnation was a suggestion merely, that scarcely relieved the mind, but was entertained for the moment, irrespective of logic.

The same country, certainly, yet not altogether the same, for with restricted or extended vision nothing was familiar save the everlasting mountains with their snow-crowned crests, and dashing mountain streams that changed not with the changing life below.

With susceptibility to outward impressions, apprehensible through the eye, with the emotional nature stirred to its very depths, adequate expression of inward consciousness was futile. Commonplace exclamations of surprise and delight at the panorama unfolding to view must suffice for the present.

To think one's self back into the long past in a moment of time is an experience somewhat akin to that of suddenly facing death with unimpaired consciousness, drowning for instance, when all of life is reviewed. Even a more gradual poise required a mental dexterity not attainable on first arrival, even at the stimulating altitude of four thousand feet above the level of the sea. Subsequent time and occasion afforded opportunity for calmer review and a deeper sensing and appreciation of the changes that had been wrought with the passing of the years.

Sergeant Gibson, and Mr. S. S. Peters of the Omaha Bee accompanied us from Omaha, veterans both, of the Eighteenth Infantry, who bore their parts nobly in the conflicts of 1866–7 in wresting this country from its savage tenants, and shared the recital of reminiscences on the way, while no less unremitting in their attention to the comfort of their old commander on this peaceful journey to the locality of former struggle.

The car that bore us from Omaha had for its distinctive name, "Mt. Olympus," an unintentional coincidence of the journey, but suggested a fanciful conceit, as we were in verity ascending to a mountain region, and on arrival at our destination were served with nectar and ambrosia, otherwise iced tea and delicious coffee, by the Hebes' of the hospitable Inn; meeting here, also, a few of the gods, or heroes, who figured in the earthly life of the long ago. We were met at the station by a committee of citizens: the Mayor, Hon. J. S. Taylor, Mr. R. M. Walsh, President of the Chamber of Commerce, Mr. Geo. W. Perry, Secretary of the same, Colonel C. Z. A. Zander, Mr. C. B. Holmes, C. E. Stevenson, J. H. Helvey, Dr. William Frackelton, Harvey McKinly, and others, beside whom were the many kindly faces of those unofficially present, to bid us welcome, and were thus escorted to the Sheridan Inn as guests of "mine host," Mr. D. D. Warner.

At the conclusion of our repast Dr. Frackelton with Mr. Perry gave us the unique pleasure of an automobile ride through the city and suburbs, one attended with surprise and delight every foot of the way, returning "as the shades of night were falling fast" by the guidance of electric lights casting their soft radiance through the dense foliage of the trees along the way, making a scene at once weird and beautiful, and if we did not fall dead, under our banner "Excelsior" on reaching the Inn, we were quite overcome with a less ambitious excursion than that of the youth of the poem.

We were here joined by other survivors of the war experience of 1866: William Murphy of Spokane, John Strawn and his wife of Rosalie, Washington, and Dennis Driscol. We had the pleasure also of meeting Judge Parmelee of the District Court and his accomplished wife, whose father, Captain John A. Manly, served in the old Eighteenth during the Civil War, and other leading citizens at an informal reception, after which a serenade and fireworks closed the evening's welcome.

There was time enough before the morrow's actions began to recall the personal experiences of the first journey, out and back, whose itinerary is already recorded in this narrative, but to revisit this spot in the summer months was "a consummation devoutly to be wished," to review the country under all its most modern aspects.

The emigrant to this spot twenty-five or thirty years ago, and the younger generation born in its environment, or, an Eastern visitor of current date, may think descriptions over-drawn and the situation idealized.

I have other pictures in mind of scenes impossible of realization except to those who figured in the earlier life.

Picture number *one* would present the outward journey in the autumn of 1866, when nature was dun in color, sere and brown, except here and there clumps of trees near water courses whose leaves did not wither so early, and the long stretches of undulating prairie, which when stirred by the wind had the appearance of billows of dust, and our small caravan, like ships in the desert.

On the return journey in January, 1867, picture number *two* would describe snow storms, which had formed mountains for themselves, filling up ravines, passes, and the road for weeks at a time, and our pathway made by guides with pick and shovel; snow-blindness being a common experience of the men who made it possible to travel in those perilous mid-winter days.

Now, the *third* picture unfolds undulating plains with verdure clad, waving wheat, barley and other grains, whose cultivation and exuberant development have been made possible by a magnificent system of irrigation not surpassed in any other region.

The wild rose, and many other species of wild flowers were in evidence along the country roads, once the trail of the savage, reminding one of Isaiah and the wilderness; and the thought I had once heard expressed came to mind, ''And God said let us make the wild rose, and man said, let us make them double-leaved,'' as was suggested by the beautiful specimens cultivated in the city yards.

Garden vegetables and small fruits were everywhere prolific in their growth, for Sheridan County once took the prize for the greatest number of potatoes to the acre, and more recently, at Omaha, for the finest barley, the value of its beet crops reaching millions of dollars. Whether true of that particular locality, or in some adjacent field, there is a tradition in regard to rapid vegetable production, though reports are sometimes exaggerated, that "a farmer happened to be examining a cucumber, just when the season of rapid growth set in, and as he stepped back to give room, the growing vine followed him so rapidly, that he took to his heels, only to be soon overtaken. It grew around him, tangled up his legs and then threw him down. Reaching in great haste for his knife to cut himself loose he found that a cucumber had gone to seed in his breeches pocket."

Halting along the drives in the shade of waving trees, the surrounding verdure taking on its richest summer hues, in sight of giant mountains with snow-capped Cloud Peak rising majestically in the background, the poet's words express the thought in mind: "What channel needs our faith, except our eyes; God leaves no spot of earth unglorified!"

Comfortable and commodious houses were dotted here and there along the country roads with wire fence enclosure that had long since superseded the fences of an earlier date that were built "horse high," "bull strong," and "pig tight." Dwellers in these ranch homes are connected by telephone with each other, and the city, and with Uncle Sam's mail boxes distributed along the main routes of travel, the genii of Aladdin and his wonderful lamp seemed to have been responsible for the results; when, in reality, the process of development had been going forward by the toil and sweat of man, the self-denial, energy and endurance of women; the heroism of both, indeed epical! The pioneers who live in the present environment meet in reunion and recall their early struggles, when wild red men and wild beasts were sole occupants of this entire region, and conflict with blood-thirsty foes was a constant experience, and at a later day, when wild white men were the terror of the country, and can say "all of which I saw, part of which I was," in the process of evolution and adjustment to present conditions; and the children of the succeeding generation may, with equal surprise, when listening to the historical recital, ask as did the Hebrew children as to their historical Passover Feast, "What meaneth these things?"

One deeply interested in the development of our great Western Empire enthusiastically writes, "There is no epic like the making of a State! Beneath the hard, homely and even repugnant details of pioneer life are hidden all heroisms, all sacrifices, all achievements. The ox-team, the flat boat (the prairie schooner), and the log cabin, will some day become invested with the halo of the Golden Fleece, and they will be far nobler, historically, because symbols of a grander epoch, and the times of those days and those peoples, with their tragedies and their comedies were times of epic splendor, more vital with the stuff and color of life, I think, than any since the stubborn earth was made to yield its treasures."

The region of the Big Horn Mountains, larger than Massachusetts and Connecticut combined, possesses inexhaustible coal fields, valuable supplies of petroleum, with gold, silver and copper partially developed, and the State of Wyoming stands on equal footing with Montana in sheep raising.

Over four hundred towns have grown up since I first visited the State. Sheridan, while not the capital, has secured the appropriate sobriquet, "Queen City" of Northern Wyoming. I do not wonder that its citizens have great pride in their progressive little city; with pretty homes, well-kept streets, fine public buildings, the State Hospital, Carnegie Library, the finest Court House in the State, several manufacturing concerns, six banks, two hotels, a weather bureau, twelve clubs, nine school buildings, with thirty teachers and fourteen hundred pupils enrolled, nine churches of different sects in which the women are alert through their different societies, two semi-weekly newspapers, enterprising and active in local and State matters. The Women's Club of ninety-five members is a power for good in Sheridan, and for the State at large, a factor in its welfare. The Women's edition of the "Enterprise," one of the city papers issued last May, was a credit to them and indeed would have been a credit to any town or city. Surely the women that publish these things are a great host of themselves in all that makes the State honored and great.

I have no special interest in booming Sheridan and while its growth is surprising, it is along conservative lines, steady and sure, and while contemplating the possibilities of this undeveloped country, when attention is so largely drawn to aeroplane excursions above the earth, and subterranean enterprises in developing subway travel, there is found right here almost an infinity of opportunity for development on *terra firma,* and especially as there are no more worlds to conquer, or discoveries of earth to engage the explorer unless it be the north pole regions of dubious importance to the general whole. We need not, like Alexander the Great, sigh, or lay down and die, for that reason, since there is enough on hand to warrant the patient efforts of those who are patriotic, and have faith in the future, based on present achievement, the substance of things realized, the hope of the future.

I recall an old campaign song of the long ago, of which the refrain contains these words:

" Then come along, come along, make no delay,
Come from every nation, come from every way,
Our lands they are broad enough, don't be alarmed,
For Uncle Sam is rich enough, to give us all a farm!"

The ladies of Sheridan were charming hostesses in their well appointed homes. To one born and reared in the East, suddenly transported to the environment of our Western cities, she would observe that the people generally are refined, her equals,—if unprejudiced,—perhaps *crude* in some things, as I have heard said, but they are warm-hearted, the men gallant toward the women in characteristic Southern way, and while there is delightful freedom manifested in social intercourse the characteristic of "wild and woolly" is out of date and the expression must be recoined to meet present conditions of society.

A recent writer to one of our papers, himself a

well born and well educated cow-boy, in commenting on Owen Wister's book, the "Virginian," says, "Wister wastes his time in deploring the exit of the cow-puncher, forever gone! Mr. Cow Puncher in his high heeled boots, and jingling spurs, is here pretty numerous. All of it is, that Wister does not want you stampeding out here expecting to find every one of them a heroic character or even intruding."

As to the term "woolly," that did not apply, I found by the clean-shaven appearance of the men whom I met, and the dress of the women according to prevailing modes elsewhere, and with pompadoured hair; indeed the marcel wave was at high tide, the desideratum of women who make concessions to prevailing modes not determined by geographical lines. I saw no lions in this civilized region and no bears, except the "Teddy" variety, in various stages of dismemberment lying on piazza floors.

A bright Western woman recently said in an Eastern Convention of Women, that "there were but two classes in the West, the quick and the dead." Sufficient has been said on this point indicating that the ladies of Sheridan do not belong to the latter class.

Seated at worship in one of the pleasant churches, I felt impressed with the fact that in this region of material prosperity and development other forces were also at work, powerful but unobtrusive; that "Israel was lengthening her cords, and strengthening her stakes;" and, as must necessarily come to pass that in further lengthening of cords, stakes might be uprooted, I hope that the landmarks of Bible truths would emphasize the stability and influence of the Church, wherever planted or extended, and as water is the emblem of the Spirit, in the Scriptures, that this vast system of irrigation might also represent, in symbolic form, the necessity for corresponding Spiritual growth and power.

CHAPTER XXXI.

WELCOMED TO SHERIDAN.

THE words "then and now" were constantly recurring to mind, and like the swinging of a pendulum indicating the passing years instead of moments they were not less impressive or notable as marking the contrast in the conditions of military life and environment.

Through the courtesy of the Chamber of Commerce, automobiles were furnished for a trip to Fort Mackenzie, four miles from Sheridan and twenty-seven from the old Phil. Kearney Fort site. Mrs. Frankelton, graceful in equestrian costume, with her party on horseback, seemed to form a host of advance guard. We were more immediately accompanied by members of the Chamber of Commerce and a coterie of ladies, among them the genial Mrs. Stevenson, Mr. G. W. Perry being our special guide.

We had heard church bells, factory whistles, bands and other sounds until they had grown familiar, but the first sound of *guns* greeted our ears by the firing of a salute of eleven guns due the General, with the party, from a cannon located near headquarters building.

The garrison turned out on parade and were reviewed by the General. His surviving veterans (Eighteenth Infantry men) Gibson, Peters, Murphy,

Strawn, and Driscol, were given a place of honor as members of his extemporized staff.

The abundant supply of good water, wood, and coal, within the garrison enclosure renders guards, with guns and ammunition, unnecessary in securing these necessities in contrast with the experiences of forty-two years ago.

Fort Mackenzie has had over a million dollars spent upon its establishment during the eight years of its existence. Substantial brick buildings for quarters, hospital, gymnasium, and post exchange make it a permanent garrison, necessitated at first by the proximity of the Sioux, Cheyenne, and Crow reservations, and a possible war-path expedition. The new Fort was made possible and materialized through the efforts of Senator Warren, Chairman of military affairs in the U. S. Senate.

Captain Walton, the Commander of the Fort, was our gallant host at headquarters where light luncheon was served. A delightful social hour followed, the young officers of the Nineteenth Infantry greeting the surviving veterans of the old Eighteenth with camp-fire characteristics and reminiscenses that signalized the visit.

A leisurely return was made to the Sheridan Inn,—if the word *leisurely* could describe an automobile excursion. At any rate rest was sought preparatory for the afternoon journey by private conveyance to the site of old Fort Phil. Kearney. Our party was augmented by the presence of Judge T. J. Foster, our guide, philosopher and friend, a citizen of Sheridan, and a pioneer in the earlier days.

At our solicitation, during the drive, he regaled us with incidents of his experience when he first came to the country. One in particular is well worth recording as one of the tales told "by the wayside."

As has been stated Fort Phil. Kearney was built in 1866, evacuated two years later, and immediately burned by the Indians.

Judge Foster homesteaded the old site of the fort twelve years later, and he with wife, the first pioneer woman settler in northern Wyoming, and their young son, made their home there for over twenty years.

Their troubles were not with the Indians, but with so-called road agents and horse thieves, who infested the territory during that formative period of its history, the "James Brothers," and other congenial companions of their type figuring conspicuously, and their names have been embalmed in the dime novel literature to the detriment of American youth who have made many initial efforts to emulate their virtues.

One day the "road agents" made a descent on his log mansion, and ordered him "to hold up his hands," and the Judge with a twinkle in his eye said, "I obeyed orders promptly." No one but his wife and little boy were present, and (the Judge with his hands tied securely behind him) the three were ordered to face the wall, while the house was ransacked for money supposed to be concealed, resulting, however, in finding only a few dollars in the little son's bank. Not satisfied with their efforts, they marched the Judge to the barn, bound and blindfolded. Possessing themselves of a rope they proceeded to hang him by the neck allowing him to remain long enough to pass over the "big divide," which, he remarked, he "did to all intents and purposes." He was finally let down, and upon regaining consciousness, they again demanded of him where his money was hidden, emphasizing their demands by a series of kicks and blows. Upon being told that they had secured all that was available, and finding their threats of no avail, they again pulled on the rope, though not sufficiently long to produce unconsciousness. They closed their part of the drama by cocking a revolver, with the threat to "croak him, anyway," an additional stimulus to persuade him to "give away the cache." This move proved as unsuccessful as at first.

They finally returned with the Judge to the house and instituted another search, but failing to find anything they ordered supper, closing the little drama with the final act of possessing themselves of all remaining provisions, the Judge's three horses, with accoutrements, and all the fire arms in the house, and finally took their midnight departure with a fond adieu.

The afternoon journey was of pathetic and peculiar interest, especially as the heart beat was accentuated on reaching "Massacre Hill" five miles in advance of the old fort site itself.

"The tear, the groan, the pall, the bier, and all we dream or fear of agony," for personal relation to this scene, must be read between the lines.

The battle with an overpowering savage foe, the

hopeless struggle, the agony and horrible death, the ancient stones, still there, were mute witnesses, and histories (if not sermons) could be read in them.

Not one soul was left to tell the tale of the dreadful happenings of that day of battle! Parties sent to the rescue found bodies behind these stones with numberless empty cartridges that revealed the awful struggle around them and beyond this stretch of earth now hallowed by the erection of a monument of natural boulders, with bronze shield tablet, on which names and deeds are recorded.

We gathered clusters of wild flowers, our little party of old soldiers, wherewith to decorate the monument, and some were gathered to bear away in memory of those "who sleep their last sleep, who have fought their last battle."

Even if their spirits hovered near, the bodies have long since been removed to the National Cemetery, on the Custer battlefield, one hundred miles distant; a battlefield made ten years later than the Phil. Kearney Massacre, where more than two hundred others repose, awaiting the last trumpet sound.

The old fort site is now owned and occupied by Mr. George Gier and family, a tract of about two thousand acres constituting the ranch property, with a spacious and comfortable house where we were most hospitably entertained over night, with the opportunity of quietly taking notes, and philosophising upon the changes now more deeply realized in this new environment.

The little village of Kearney has its church, post-office, store, amusement hall, and its schoolhouse at the base of Pilot Hill, where the young idea is taught to shoot, and tells a different story from the shooting and signals of 1866,—signs of the times, in verity.

How strange it seemed, that evening, to hear the strains of a piano coming through the parlor windows of this ranch home instead of the bugle note of warning, and crack of rifle; and to sleep undisturbed by howling wolves and Indian alarms as in the days of yore.

The site of the old fort is part of the ranch property, and a luxurious growth of alfalfa covered the entire parade ground. Here also, beautiful flowers were gathered where the tramp of feet once resounded, either for parade, or hurried exit to the relief of comrades fighting without the gates.

A few relics were discovered, a piece of the powder magazine was presented by an earlier visitor. One look at this relic awakens the memory of that day when we watched its preparation, as our last refuge, if the fort should be taken by the Indians.

The monument was erected by the government through the efforts of Congressman Frank Mondell of Wyoming, whom the people delight to honor as one who holds their interests dear to heart. Just across the crest of Massacre Hill runs a large irrigating ditch watering the alfalfa field,—once the field of blood, and well graded roads are gradually taking the place of the old buffalo and Indian trails. Where once was but the wild native grasses and undergrowth are now irrigated fields of waving grain; once again suggesting Isaiah and the wilderness,—and this irrigating ditch has its parentage in the beautiful and bountiful Goose Creek, that makes its debut from the Big Horn Mountains near Fort Phil. Kearney, and its twin fork, so familiar to the garrison in 1866, as the special locality for the lodges of hostile Indians, now unites or joins in the very centre of Sheridan to irrigate its gardens and streets as well as give water power for various uses.

CHAPTER XXXII.

THIRD OF JULY—ATTENDING VETERANS ACCOMPANY
REVIEWING OFFICER—MASSACRE HILL AND THE OLD
FORT—ADDRESS BY GENERAL CARRINGTON.

THE ceremonies of the morning of July 3rd were to be held at the monument, and thither we retraced our steps accompanied by the Kearney band, under the leadership of Mr. Siesler, in thin shirt-sleeves, but with a true patriotism tingling to their finger-tips, augmented on the way by several hundred people from Buffalo, Clearmont, Big Horn City, and elsewhere in gaily-bedecked vehicles, others on horse-back appropriately adorned with the national colors, to be joined by the crowd from Sheridan twenty miles away, a peaceful gathering at the historic spot of two thousand people to do honor to the memory of the dead.

Around the monument enclosure old acquaintances were renewed, and among the number, and not the least interesting, was the meeting with General Henry B. Freeman and wife, who had come from Douglas, their present home, and whom we had not seen since leaving Fort Casper, forty-two years ago, and Mrs. Freeman's special kindness at that time was a pleasant memory recalled with the grasp of friendly hands.

The leader of the band, interpreting the spirit of the hour, gave the signal and the band rendered most touchingly "Should Old Acquaintance be forgot," accompanied with hand-shaking and tears by the veterans who had shared our common dangers, and sympathetically by those around "who did pity them."

"Assembly" was sounded by bugler Pobloskie of the Nineteenth Infantry from Fort Mackenzie, and Lieutenant Wheeler of the same regiment, Congressman Mondell, and the veterans took their places within the immediate enclosure of the monument. General Carrington's memorial address, delivered at the monument on Massacre Hill, is given in full:

MEMORIAL ADDRESS OF GENERAL H. B. CARRINGTON, DELIVERED AT THE MONUMENT ON MASSACRE HILL, SHERIDAN COUNTY, WYOMING, JULY 3, 1908.

EQUAL JUSTICE TO BOTH LIVING AND DEAD.

MY countrymen and friends, for such indeed you are in its profoundest sense;—and although you came to this country later than myself, I know that you cannot regret that the Eighteenth United States Infantry, through their arrival in 1866, made it possible for your later enjoyment in the largest fruition of its rich soil, its fertile valleys, its magnificent mountains, abundant timber, adequate streams, and indeed of all other blessings on or beneath the surface, within the power of nature to place at your disposal.

Forty-two years ago to-day, having just crossed Powder River, the sutler at little Fort Reno hurriedly advised me that his stock, just across the stream in my rear, had been run off by Indians who had been creeping along on our trail. In five minutes fifty mounted men were in pursuit. One of those brave men is here to-day. A pursuit of nearly fifty miles toward Pumpkin Buttes failed to recover the stock, but did overtake one Indian squaw and her pony, which was loaded with presents just received at Fort Laramie, including powder, which had been given on the supposition that the Indians would be honestly friendly.

War had indeed begun!

On the day following we fired a National salute, the first ever heard in present Wyoming, and started westward. So intense was the heat that we halted at Crazy Woman's Fork to burn charcoal and weld tires before we could advance with our heavy teams.

Do you wonder that, even to-day, I almost tremble with emotion as I recall the faces of many of those who left Kentucky with me and marched even from Fort Leavenworth, Kansas, to this wild region, anticipating, as did the Peace Commission, that we were to find only the usual occupation of road-building, bridge-building, and peace?

Those men are honored by this shaft, just before me. Am I not, indeed, addressing them also, as well as yourselves, through that infinite conception, the wireless telegraphy of the soul? Do not they know that I am speaking of them to-day to honor their virtue and their valor? I mean those dear men who fought with me day and night, and who are memorialized on the bronze tablet to their memory!

Friends! The Grand Army is gathering above! Yes, the sanctified Grand Army of the Cross! Those who rallied for their country, for God and Country, are gathering and regathering all the time, one by one, score by score, battalion by battalion, regiment by regiment, until to-day less than ten per cent. of any regiment that fought in the Civil War can answer to the bugle call on earth. Welcomed with such effulgent affection as these veterans have manifested in coming hundreds of miles, and from distant States, to offer tribute at this Memorial Battle Shrine, can you wonder that I seem lost, not so much in the development of your beautiful land as in the evidence that you, people of Wyoming, have proved yourselves so worthy of all the sacrifices made in your behalf in the tragic scenes of the years gone by. Thank God, who gave us such men, so loyal to their commander!

To-morrow will be repeated the National salute of forty-two years ago.

"If the three battalions of my regiment had been given me for the expedition to this country, the Indian War would have been of short duration." Ex-Senator General Manderson so stated

AFTER MANY DAYS

at the Coliseum last week in Omaha before the Knights of Ak-Sar-
Ben. At the end of the Civil War the few surviving veterans
of the Regular Army were hastened to the frontier. The few
that I brought with me from Kentucky and Tennessee were joined
by 1900 recruits; but when I came to Fort Kearney, Nebraska,
there was not a white family between Fort Leavenworth and that
fort and Grand Island, except the few in little clusters of houses
near the fort, and when ordered to advance westward and open
this country to travel and settlement I was allowed to retain
but eight companies of my rightful command. Upon reaching
Laramie I was given only one thousand rounds of ammunition
instead of twenty thousand promised me. Upon reaching Powder
River, where the little post of Reno had been held for a time,
I found awaiting my arrival only 7000 rounds of ammunition,
although I was informed at Laramie that I "would find there
all I could use."

I have said enough of the days that were succeeded by the
more tragic experiences that bring us about this funeral shaft
to-day. It stands about five miles from where the first flag floated
over your soil, on the 31st day of October, 1866; and at the
outset I must take notice of one fact ignorance of which has
given wrong impressions for nearly a third of a century. It
took us this morning forty-nine minutes to ride to this hill from
the site of old Phil. Kearney. We left at nine and arrived a few
minutes before ten, and none of you would deem it practicable,
to-day, to move on foot, with heavy ammunition wagons in a
shorter period of time.

Now my good friends of Wyoming, and you gentlemen of the
Sheridan Chamber of Commerce, and you, Mr. Congressman,
and you, men and women, one and all, who hear my voice, I did
not come here after a journey of twenty-five hundred miles, and
at my advanced age, entirely for my own gratification. Although
Mrs. Carrington and myself had long hoped and prayed that we
might live to see this country once more, under powerfully contrasting conditions, I came deliberately, and under the spur of
a most solemn and sacred duty, and your generosity and welcome
show that duty conscientiously done never fails to find friends.
It was not simply because so many years passed before Congress

recognized the service rendered in 1866, but pitiful appeals from the family of brave Captain Ten Eyck were irresistible in their claim that I vindicate his good name at whatever risk of travel.

I therefore, before this assemblage of sturdy men, noble women, and these many youths and little ones, will tell you in simple words just how this monument happened to be erected on this very hill, and why I am standing, as I am, on the largest of these three-stones, which enclose this little triangle of ground before me, in which space I gathered the bodies of two officers and three dead comrades, for honorable burial at the Fort.

Fort Phil. Kearney had been finished, with a strong stockade enclosure, winter had set in, and we still needed logs from the head of Piney Creek for our saw-mills, and to finish our hospital, the roof of which had not been closed.

My Official Report shows that on the 19th I sent Captain Powell, who had recently arrived at the Fort, to relieve a threatened wood-train. He reported that " he saw two or three hundred Indians," as he estimated the number, but " declined to force an engagement because of my positive orders to the contrary." It is just to him that I repeat the record made so public on the 3rd of January, 1867, to his credit, as it was the first and only case in which he was out of the stockade after his arrival, and my Report also shows that on the 20th of December, the day before the great disaster, now celebrated, I went in person, with a large force, to feel the position he had reported as dangerous, and brought in a full wood-train, although delayed to build a bridge to the island where the timber was cut. But on that day no Indians appeared.

On the 21st of December the wood-train, as usual, took the trail just south of Sullivant Hill, as late as ten o'clock. The signal was soon given from Pilot Hill that the party was threatened by Indians. I started Captain Brevet Lieutenant Colonel Fetterman with a strong detachment of troops to the relief of the train with positive orders, twice repeated, to "relieve the wood-train, escort it back in safety, but not to pursue Indians, under any conditions, and especially, not to cross Lodge Trail Ridge, north of the Fort." He disappeared from sight, apparently having taken the right direction around Sullivant Hill to the north, so as to cut the Indians off from retreat over Lodge Trail Ridge.

The wood party went on unmolested, brought home forty wagon-loads of logs, two on each wagon, and some of them eighteen inches to two feet in thickness, without having had a fight, or having heard a shot, or having knowledge that there had been a fight.

Fetterman, gallant through the entire Civil War from the time he joined my regiment in 1861, was impatient, and wanted to fight. He said, "I can take eighty men and go to Tongue River." To this boast my Chief Guide, the veteran James Bridger, replied in my presence, "Your men who fought down South are crazy! They don't know anything about fighting Indians."

I had supposed that Fetterman was with the wood-train. All at once I heard two or three successive shots, but in the wrong direction, far over Lodge Trail Ridge. Hardly a minute passed when a few scattering shots were succeeded, three times, by something like a volley.

In sixteen minutes shots began to *drop, drop, drop, drop,* and then came dead silence. At the first shot I went to the balcony lookout, on my building, and instantly ordered the sentry in front to fire his piece, and had the "assembly" sounded. I inspected every man and his piece, and in seventeen minutes both the infantry and a few mounted men to guard their wagons were out of the Fort and moving at a double-quick pace for the crossing, toward the scene of conflict. Just as they crossed the creek the firing ceased. I said to my orderly and officers by my side, "that means that Fetterman has killed or repulsed them all, or they are accumulating for a rush." We could not imagine the real facts; but the surprise was simply stunning!

Ten Eyck, after crossing the creek, had gone to the nearest high hill, and in sight from the Fort, to get the bearing of the Fetterman party, and sent back my Orderly, Sample, who went with him, to tell me that "the Valley was full of Indians, challenging him to come down, but he could see nothing of Fetterman. I sent the Orderly back, followed by reinforcements, with this written order, "I send you forty men and ten thousand rounds of ammunition. Join Fetterman at all hazards! Keep cool! You would have saved two miles to-day if you had gone as I directed over Lodge Trail Ridge." This was not a reprimand at all, but suggestive as to location of the enemy, as he could not otherwise know after the firing had ceased, and he could not judge as I could, on my lookout, of the locality in peril.

As a fact, Ten Eyck obeyed my order. He pressed on, kept his men in hand, rescued forty-nine dead bodies, brought them home in safety without the loss of a man. The whole firing was over and the last man was killed inside of twenty-one minutes, and, as already stated, it took me fifty minutes to come from the site of the Fort to-day.

Before noticing the errors of record that have confused popular history, there is some correlative history that has great value to illustrate both the Indian plans of that Campaign and to indicate the wisdom of obeying General Sherman's orders, " To avoid a general war, hold my own at all hazards, without any attempt to compete with the Indians of that great region until the army could be recruited in strength."

The incident I refer to is this:

A Sioux chief, named "Two Wounds," claiming to be friendly, had visited the Fort and received, as he states, presents of tobacco, bacon, and flour. Sergeant Gibson may tell you that story to-night. This chief says: "I went to Red Cloud and told him that he never could take the Fort; that there was a block-house at every corner, and that the only way was to cut off wood-parties as they went after wood and so reduce the garrison." "Two Wounds" made this statement also, which I have at my hotel, when I explained to him the use of the mountain howitzer and the distance it would shoot and fire the second time with a shower of balls after it had gone over the heads of the Indians, that "Red Cloud agreed that he would have to pick off the soldiers of the wood-parties and would not try the Fort."*

"Two Wounds" also described the Fetterman fight and stated that "when they saw more soldiers coming out (meaning

---

*"Mountain howitzer." A small, short gun, with chamber, like a mortar, to be borne by mules, for mountain use, the gun itself, on a single saddle.

Ten Eyck's party) they made a rush and killed them all before any fresh soldiers could get there." And yet for years the name of Ten Eyck was counted as a reproach, and the gallant service done was tortured into fear of the Indians, whereas he risked all the fight possible to save his fallen comrades, and it was the highest military art to have done just what he did do.

I knew that with my surveys of the entire ground, my prepared ranges of howitzer fire from the palisade, that only my personal presence here could establish history as it was really enacted. Soldiers could do much, but with compass in hand, and my old notes, as well as Hazen's and Bridger's field-notes, duty called me here, at whatever risks, and here I stand.

But there is another element of duty and obligation, equally as exacting, even if it have its painful element in the recital. " Justice to both living and dead " has to be meted out, while survivors live who are the sole repositories of events and facts.

On the night of the massacre, a Portugese by the name of John Phillips came to my house and presented to our guest, Mrs. Grummond, now Mrs. Carrington, his handsome wolf-robe, while overwhelmed with sympathy, and pledged himself to go to Fort Laramie with the news and call for troops, " if it cost him his life." He accomplished his mission, being just able to get a telegram off from Horse-Shoe Station, between Laramie and Casper, before the hut was wrecked by Indians.

The shock at Laramie, of course, was great. Some misconduct of the Commanding Officer was *assumed,* as Fetterman's old comrades never supposed he could be whipped by Indians, and the loss itself was so serious and unlooked for that it seemed utterly inexplicable. Hence, concurrent despatches flooded the eastern press and even mutilations of the original were current, by sending supposititious hints of how it must have occurred. Many were absurd, as no details could be had, and officials at Washington, Bogy, Indian Commissioner, for example, were intensely ridiculous. In fact, nearly all the casualities from that country had been treated with a sort of contempt, at Laramie, where the idle companies could not be made to realize that their comrades of the Eighteenth Infantry were constantly in a life-or-death struggle. If the original telegrams sent to Washington had been treated with decent respect by the aged Department Commander, General Philip St. George Cooke, their solemn dignity of demand for reinforcements would have commanded respect, instead of being used as a scapegoat to falsify the true record.

A mixed military and civil commission of nine persons was ordered to meet at Colonel Carrington's Headquarters at Fort McPherson. The meetings were held at my house (as I still used crutches on account of wound received in closing up a train), for thirty successive days. All his letter books, order books, itineraries, and despatches, covering the entire history of his march from Fort Kearney, were fully discussed and compared, and, as the result, a complete vindication of his conduct of the entire Campaign was forwarded to Washington, with the following closing conclusion:

" Of those who have been more remotely connected with the events that led to the massacre, we have endeavored to report so specifically as to enable yourself and the President, who have much official information that we cannot have, to determine where the censure must fall. The difficulty, in a nutshell, was that the commanding officer of the district was furnished no more troops or supplies for this state of war than had been provided and furnished him for a state of profound peace.

" In regions where all was peace, as at Laramie in November, twelve companies were stationed; while in regions where all was war, as at Phil. Kearney, there were only five companies allowed."

The commission immediately adjourned, *Sine Die;* subcommittees visiting various posts, citizen Kinney going to Fort Phil. Kearney to advise with Crow Indians as to the plans of the still hostile Sioux, in that region.

President Johnson, who on December 8, just before, had advised that satisfactory peace had been secured through that whole region, ordered a strictly military court, made up of officers of the new regiments formed from the large Eighteenth, with General John Gibbon as President, to report " who, if any, were to be punished for the Fetterman tragedy."

Their finding confirmed that of the mixed commission, closing with these determining categories and conclusive replies.

QUESTION: " Are these the orders given to Colonel Fetterman ? "

ANSWER: " They are."

QUESTION: " Did Colonel Fetterman obey your orders ? "

ANSWER: " He did not."

QUESTION: " If Captain Ten Eyck had obeyed your orders and taken Lodge Trail Ridge, would he have saved Colonel Fetterman ? "

ANSWER: " He would not. The whole firing was over and the last man killed in about twenty minutes."

The official report of the special commission, as found in Senate Document No. 33, 1st Session of the Fiftieth Congress, covered one hundred and fifty-five pages of typewritten foolscap paper, and after twenty years of neglect and suppression was found upon the third demand of the United States Senate, " in a mass of waste-paper in the cellar of the Interior Department," with no possible intent to have the same published. I am here to do justice both to the living and the dead, and in justice to General Grant, who withheld the publication of my official report of the massacre, dated January 3, 1867, although I demanded it both of himself and Secretary Stanton, give the conditions that induced him thus to disregard the peremptory call of the Senate. That official report was in Washington, as the official files show, and so was the full report of the special commission. General Grant had been placed in possession of documents that impeached the facts and whole tenor of my report and of my entire administration of the whole campaign of 1866, and that is the simple, solemn truth.

But when that commission met at my headquarters at Fort McPherson,—I want to make it clearly understood that sometimes very queer things occur in army life. On that commission was John Bullock, merchant, sutler, of Fort Laramie, and John Kinney, post sutler of Fort Phil. Kearney. He bought out the original sutler by paying gold for the same, and had presented to me for approval, some time before the date of the massacre, a large claim of over $1300 for goods alleged to have been stolen from his sutler's stock by my soldiers. When his claim was compared with his sworn invoices of stock, required by

MY ARMY LIFE

military law, the whole invoice was less than one-third of the value for which he claimed payment and the account was rejected.

What did he do, on coming to Fort Kearney to meet some Crow Indians, but make record of the occasion as "a special meeting of the original special commission," with its official heading, and proceed to fortify his claim by inducing Captain James Powell to not only approve his claim but to assert under oath that the soldiers also freely robbed the commissary supplies without notice or disapproval of the commanding officer; that the chief duty of the mounted infantry was horseracing, gambling, and drinking; that on the day of the massacre the Colonel requested him to take executive charge of the Fort because when a private soldier in the old army before the war he had fought Indians on the Pacific Coast; that he organized and armed the civil employees on the day of the massacre and organized the force sent out to relieve Fetterman, and that, on the nineteenth day of December, when he went out to relieve the wood-party that had been threatened by, as he had officially reported at the time as two or three hundred Indians, there were in fact two or three thousand in sight; that "discipline was chaotic and the mounted men went out when they chose; and the soldiers, at will, climbed over the stockade, etc., etc., etc." All these original documents are at my hotel.

John M. Kinney, in reporting to the Interior Department as to the Crow Indians, whom he was delegated to consult, took no notice of this visit to Fort Phil. Kearney, but sent Powell's affidavit privately to Washington and had it placed in the hands of General Grant. The whole affidavit was not the act of a sane man, so transparent were its absurdities, and a copy was sent at once by Secretary Browning to myself, and regarded as not to be noticed other than for my response explanatory of the strange paper. That response is also at my hotel, as approved by the Interior Department, and a complete set of these official papers will be left with your Chamber of Commerce. This was immediately after the adjournment of the original commission of nine members, and the affidavit was forwarded to Washington *purposely,* in this secret way, to undermine and

258

defeat the official report of the commission, of which he (Kinney) was a sworn member, before General Grant could see the official vindication itself. It had its effect. It reached General Grant, and when the tiding of the Wagon Bed Fight afterwards reached his headquarters, its contrast with the fight of December 21st of the previous year was so great that the publication of my own official report as Commanding Military District and *prima facie* authoritative was suspended. I called upon Secretary Stanton, who referred me to General Grant, and I gave to General Grant the facts as to that affidavit, claiming that as Commanding Officer I had a right to have my report made public. When I made my statement and he answered that I was making a very grave charge against a brother officer, I stated that " I was risking my commission as Colonel in the Army and would prefer charges if he so wished; " but upon the advice of General Sherman it was allowed to drop as unworthy of notice; still, it was the document that had originally influenced General Grant, resulting in twenty years of silence as to the whole history of that campaign. At the very date of that interview, of which I was ignorant, the nomination of Captain Powell to a Brevet as Lieutenant Colonel, for bravery in the Wagon Bed Fight, had been sent to the Senate. Powell did well in that fight, and his later broken health testified of the strain of frontier service. I, therefore, endeavored to spare him, and did not oppose his brevet. But justice to both living and dead comrades is simply right. Several years after the event General Grant acknowledged to me that the affidavit of Powell was that of a man bewildered, wrongly influenced, or otherwise deficient. General Grant's action was supposed by him to be the wise course for him under the pressure of that affidavit, and General Cooke's unwarranted endorsement upon my report he had sent to Washington.

When, in 1887, General Cooke's transmissal of my original report (then first brought to light) was found to be endorsed with extracts from a private letter of Captain Powell to a member of the Department Staff, which had been sent in the same mail with my report, in January, 1867, of the same tenor as the affidavit, and of which I had no knowledge at the interview with General Grant, there arose the necessity of perfecting the historic record for future students of Wyoming history, as well as my own, distasteful as it may be, and it is my right and duty, thus publicly, and here, in the presence of the veterans who were with me during those weeks of fearful ordeal, including the survivors both of the Crazy Woman's Fight and the Wagon Bed Fight, of whom there are several here to-day, who know the whole truth as I state it. So many writers have magnified the Wagon Bed Fight as a distinct contrast with service in Wyoming that this brief record of the failure of my report to be published for twenty years is duty to myself and the Eighteenth Infantry as well as to General Grant.

General Sherman wrote to Mrs. Carrington that she might publish my report, and it appeared, with the official report of the commission, in " Absaraka " as soon as practicable.

My men were not drinking men. They were not gambling men. They were not deserting men. Don't you know that I rightly feel proud to have so many, few as they are, with me here to-day? During my whole term of command I never heard, more than three or four times, of soldiers swearing in my presence, and my order, No. 38, read on parade, rebuking officers for the habit, though grumbled over, was the type of my discipline in contrast with that of the old army, before the Civil War. Those men worked themselves almost to death. Gibson and Peters will tell you at the Camp Fire some of the details of their loyal, loving, and patient service. They were always ready for duty by day or night, regardless of hours for sleep or rest. And such was the style of men that so rapidly, from time to time, enlisted in the Eighteenth U. S. Infantry, which during the Civil War numbered in the aggregate 4773 men, in its three battalions. General Manderson in his speech at Omaha, already noticed, stated "To this three battalion regiment was left to open the whole territory west of the Missouri, and the Eighteenth Infantry saved Nebraska as well as Wyoming, in opening to civilization the West."

I am glad to have this opportunity, for I was bound to say what I have said should I ever live to reach this sacred resting place of the dead. I wished to show that General Grant's action in suspending the publication of my report was from what he supposed to be sufficient data, for the time being. I also was determined that even the grave itself should not be silent as to the gallantry of brave Ten Eyck, whose widow and children have been agonized almost to death by my silence. Right here is the place and this the hour for justice to historic truth.

This monument, so simple, fashioned from the gathered stone near by, is a very poor testimony of the valor of those it honors. The Nation, and even this grand Commonwealth might yet do something more enduring, to their honor, and yet it is in its very roughness an exponent of their career and their struggles for you and the west still beyond you.

We go from here to the site of the old Fort, and for social reunion along the waters of Piney Creek near by.

My tribute is done and the hour for leaving for other ceremonies has arrived.

NOTE: In cases where the reporter, taking notes in the hot sun and under difficulties, was compelled to lose or note disconnectedly certain data that he found among the documents in the hands of the Chamber of Commerce I have supplied omitted material.

In justice to Captain Powell and to General Cooke, I add in connection with copy of the address the following:

When after my retirement I was on duty as Military Professor at Wabash College, Indiana, I learned that Powell, also retired, was in poor health. I visited him near Peoria, Ill., was kindly received, and the following is his response, in part, to my reference to the Kinney affidavit.

" It has been so long since that I remember nothing, more than the fact that Kinney wanted some backing up of a sutler's claim which had been disallowed by the Council of Administration at Phil. Kearney. I had the time of my life afterwards in fighting with Red Cloud and his red devils when they attacked a wood-train which was in my charge and have always wondered we were not all butchered before Fetterman himself was surprised and killed with his whole command." He added, " It was enough to craze anybody to hold that Fort, when there was everlasting danger with neither men nor ammunition enough to hold our own and save the Fort."

Sergeant Gibson, now present with me, and of Captain Powell's own Company, a survivor of the Wagon Bed Fight, in giving me his written report of Captain Powell's mental condition at the time of the Phil. Kearney massacre, as well as the Wagon Bed Fight, and who loved his Captain with intense ardor and devotion, was as deeply pained as I myself to learn of his private letter of January 4, 1867, to a brother officer on General Cooke's staff, whose name I have purposely omitted, and of the affidavit procured by Major Kinney, already sufficiently noticed.

I also visited General Philip St. George Cooke at his home in Detroit, taking with me copy of my official report of January 3, 1867, as furnished the U. S. Senate in 1887 (twenty years after the massacre), and called his attention to the endorsement.

In very strong terms he deplored the incident, and giving me a warm congratulation that the true version of that whole campaign had been a complete vindication, added: "I have no recollection at this date of any such endorsement, but must have signed the same, as I often did formal endorsements prepared by my staff, assuming, even when I did not read them, that they were correct. It is certainly evident that the endorsement was improper, when quoted from a private letter, as well as untrue in fact."

Among the documents before referred to, that I leave behind, are authentic copies of the official statements of all officers who with myself survived the massacre, as to the subject-matter which I have so reluctantly, but impartially and justly, made of record.

The closing scene at the monument was one of intensely dramatic interest. "Attention" was sounded, the band playing "Auld Lang Syne." "Retreat" was sounded, the band rendering "Nearer my God to Thee." Then came the final call that melted many to tears; "Sound Taps," the usual military order closing the exercises at burial of a soldier.

Emerging from the shadow of the monument we came into the light, life, and interest of the remaining hours of the day.

The band led the procession, playing "Hail Columbia," hardly less inspiring than when sung on the stage of the Philadelphia Theatre a hundred years ago, augmented by the associations of years. The crowd fell in line of march for Piney Grove, through which the merry little mountain stream flowed as of old, furnishing refreshing draughts to man and beast, and there resolved themselves into picnic groups in vivid contrast to the time when only strongly guarded parties could venture from the Fort for wood and water, by no means suggesting a picnic excursion.

Our party was regaled with delicious edibles of every attainable variety, with snowy linen spread upon the grass, reminding one at least of old time barbecues in the South in ante-bellum days. As Mr. Fred. F. Newcomber and his estimable wife dispensed their bounty, they could not know that with retrospective glance I was thinking of a less remote experience since barbecue days, when we cooked our dinner, too insignificant as to menu, in a camp-kettle with sage brush, sometimes with buffalo chips, when other fuel was unattainable. One other feature was described, perhaps more novel and expressive of later day development. Some of the ladies partook of the repast seated in automobiles immediately beyond the table linen environment, and all were quite disposed to eat heartily and laugh at everything, as did the poor relatives at Mr. Wardle's banquet described in Pickwick Papers.

It was in reality a "moving picture," this rural festive scene, worthy description by pen, or portraiture by brush, in lieu of which the omnipresent kodak artist exercised the particular functions of the profession by a frequent "just one more, please," a request not unheeded, for the interests of the hour found people ready to give and take in a spirit of whole-hearted responsiveness.

Dinners do not go on forever, or even a day, and in due time as "assembly" was sounded by our alert bugler, all faces were turned toward a platform that had been erected on the outskirts of the grove, as eager, apparently, "for the feast of reason as the flow of soul."

CHAPTER XXXIII.

MASSACRE HILL—ADDRESSES BY CONGRESSMAN MONDELL AND SERGEANT GIBSON—FLAG-RAISING BY MR. DALEY.

THE program began with music and a flag drill given by fourteen young ladies under the direction of Mrs. Siesler, wife of the leader of the band, some of whom had ridden twenty miles for preliminary practice for the present occasion.

The address of welcome was delivered by Mr. Charles E. Bull of Johnson County (just south of the county boundary lines), and Mr. George Gier as master of ceremonies introduced the speakers in appropriate and felicitous speech, to which the chief guest responded in like vein.

Mr Mondell gave the principal address, which reads as follows:

We stand on historic ground. On yonder hills was fought one of the three battles in all history from whose field of carnage came no survivor of the vanquished to tell the story of defeat.

Yonder on the Piney in the shadow of the Big Horn occurred one of the most gallant defences of all time, when thirty-two brave and determined men drove back with fearful slaughter the successive and desperate charges of three thousand of the best warriors of the Sioux Nation under the famous Chieftain Red Cloud.

Here on the banks of the Piney stood a post unique in all the annals of American border warfare. From that July day in 1866 when the gallant little band of troopers under their intrepid commander, our honored guest to-day, began the construction of Fort Phil. Kearney, down to the time about two years later when, in pursuance of a mistaken policy, it was abandoned, it was never for a single day free from investment and surveillance by a savage foe.

The first six months of its history witnessed more than fifty distinct attacks in its immediate vicinity, nearly every one of which had its victims, and in that period the lives of over one hundred and fifty soldiers and civilians were lost, while no man knows the loss of the savage foe.

Of all the heroic men who first and last made glorious the history of old Fort Phil. Kearney, and its locality, the one whose courage and genius, loyalty and devotion, most commands our admiration and respect, who planned and built the post and commanded it during the most stirring and terrible period of its existence is he who returns to-day, after an absence of forty-two years, as our honored guest.

It affords us extreme pleasure to welcome in triumph to the scenes of his early and gallant struggles one who has been fitly described by a celebrated writer as " a high minded Christian gentleman, a soldier of large experience and proven courage, an administrator of vigor and capacity, and a man of fine literary talents,"—our guest, General Carrington.

We have also as our guests, General Freeman, now a resident of Douglas, who served gallantly during 1867, and Mrs. Freeman, who shared in her husband's life on the frontier; and Sergeants Murphy, Gibson, and Strawn, who have come hundreds of miles to view the scenes of their former service, and our own Dennis Driscoll, all of whom participated in the struggles hereabout, and Hon. Wm. Daley, of Rawlins, who raised the first flag over old Fort Phil. Kearney, and who will to-day raise the flag on the new flag-staff on the site of the old one.

Nothing would please me better, did time suffice, than to recall to your minds some of the stirring scenes enacted hereabouts in 1866–7, when the entire force of the great Sioux Nation under one of its most intrepid and courageous leaders, was exerted in a ceaseless effort to close this gateway to the on-coming white man, to reserve as the hunting ground of the red man the fairest and most desirable portion of the territory then claimed by the great Sioux Nation.

AFTER MANY DAYS

History contains no more thrilling pages than those which tell of the struggles here, and early in my service in Congress I became so impressed with the character of these struggles that I determined to secure a monument or marker of the spot on Massacre Hill where occurred the awful and fatal conflict which peculiarly distinguished the struggles about old Fort Phil. Kearney.

But there is neither time nor need to relate the story of those early conflicts. It is familiar to you all. It is a part of the inspiring history of the region, and my thoughts and purpose is to talk to you briefly of some lessons these struggles teach.

To me this celebration and the incidents which it commemorates suggest two thoughts. The first is that earnest, faithful and courageous effort and service will be recognized eventually, and whatever may be the injustice of the moment, in the running of the years truth will triumph and justice will prevail.

Forty-one years ago last February, in soldierly obedience to a cruel order founded on a misapprehension of facts and conditions, General Carrington with his wife and children, the members of his staff and their families, including the heroic lady who is now Mrs. Carrington, then mourning the awful death of her husband on yonder hill, left Fort Phil. Kearney on their fearful march to Fort Casper in the face of the bitter winter and the relentless foe. No greater injustice was ever done. To the bitterness of defeat and personal loss was added the humiliation of implied lack of confidence, and those who most deserved the thanks of their country were condemned to criticism, to discredit, to humiliation, and to physical suffering. But time has righted it all.

Long since the country came to recognize the splendid service of General Carrington to his country, and the wisdom, sagacity and courage with which he planned and executed, and he returns in triumph to find an enthusiastic welcome, and in welcoming Mrs. Carrington and Mrs. Freeman, we pay a heartfelt and deserved tribute to all those loyal, devoted and courageous women in army and civil life who like her faced the trials, the dangers, and the sufferings and the anguish of frontier life.

MY ARMY LIFE

The other thought that comes to me in connection with this celebration is this, that we shall best honor those who fought the good fight on these bloody fields by here resolving that with God's help we shall perform the duties of citizenship as well and as truly as they performed their duties, both as soldiers and as citizens.

The blood-curdling war-cry of the savage no longer rings through these hills. Torture and death no longer haunt the trails. " Our ways are ways of pleasantness and all our paths are peace," and yet we have our duties to perform no less important in their influence on the present and future than those who faced these men and women on the frontier.

As citizens of the commonwealth and the republic, as sovereigns of our country the duty devolves upon us to do our full share in preserving our free institutions, in assisting to the best of our ability in solving the manifold problems which are constantly arising in the development of our country and its resources.

We are not called upon as were these men and women to accept the chances of suffering, torture and death, and yet we must remember that as eternal vigilance is the price of liberty, so eternal attention to all the duties of citizenship is the price of good government.

Every man and woman owes it to themselves, their children, and their country to keep informed upon the questions of the day and without prejudice or passion to exert their influence in behalf of those policies which best serve the interests of all our people; to give aid and support to those who serve the peoples' interests; to take a helpful part in the affairs of their community; to perform cheerfully their share of all the duties of citizenship, and to do all this with as little thought of the personal inconvenience or discomfort involved as did the brave hearts that consecrated this ground.

Thanks to the wisdom of the founders of this Republic, to the courage and self-sacrifice of those heroic souls who preserved it, and of those who on the frontier, as soldiers or settlers, met the savage foe or performed faithfully the hard and trying tasks of a new country, we are enjoying the blessings of liberty, of peace and of prosperity We are the heirs, the beneficiaries and guardians of these happy conditions and it is our sacred duty to continue and transmit them to posterity by doing our full duty as citizens of the grandest and most glorious country the sun has ever shone upon.

At the close of Mr. Mondell's address, Sergeant Samuel Gibson, U. S. A., Retired, who with his comrade, S. S. Peters, had accompanied their old commander from Omaha to Sheridan as personal orderlies and alike guests of the city, responded to the cordial welcome given him, as he said, "right on the Banks of Piney Creek and within 'Bugle Sound' of the old Phil. Kearney flag-staff itself."

The official program announced camp-fire addresses by surviving veterans for the evening so that the reporter failed to secure his. The evening camp-fire was abandoned for other exercises but it was afterwards written out in full for his old commander to condense for this narrative. It certainly describes the "most sanguinary engagement between the white man and the Indian ever fought," wherein, with only twenty-six comrades under Captain Powell and Lieutenant Jenness, Red Cloud himself, the famous Sioux Chief paid the full penalty for that fearful tragedy of December 21, 1866, whose noble victims are now honored by the monument on Massacre Hill.

His thrilling story of more than 12,000 words deserves separate publication as an example of Indian warfare where every soldier was a hero and the battle itself was in fact an "individual soldier's fight of marvellous daring and execution."

MY ARMY LIFE

SERGEANT GIBSON'S ADDRESS.

I came out with the regiment from Fort Kearney, Nebraska, in May, 1866, the youngest boy in the company, ardent to follow the destinies of the company at whatever cost. I accompanied General Carrington in the rescue of Fetterman's heroes from the field of battle, little dreaming in the anguish of that fateful hour, that it would be *my fate,* while guarding a similar wood-train some months later, to aid in avenging that massacre, by retribution so signal, just and complete. General Carrington himself, my dear old commander, sufficiently detailed that campaign in his address this morning, as we gathered about the monument itself. It was supported by infallible official documents, and though it had some phases that were saddening to myself, all of us survivors, five in number with "Big Bill Daley," of Rawlins, Wyoming, realized that it perfected history never before explanatory of the twenty years of delay, until the official report of the massacre of December 21, 1866, itself was made public.

On the 31st of July, following, after the Second Battalion had become the Twenty-seventh Infantry under Colonel John E. Smith, and the usual inspection had taken place, we doffed our dress uniforms, packed our fourteen wagons with a month's rations and 7000 rounds of ammunition and marched to the lower pinery to relieve Company A which guarded the wood-choppers during the month of July. Our new arms, the breech-loading rifles, had taken the place of the old muzzle loader. We pitched our tents outside of a corral, about 120 feet by 70. At each end was one covered wagon, one for the wood-choppers' rations and the other for our own stores and rations. A smaller camp was that of the wood-choppers themselves.

Not a wagon was shod with any metal, and all such stories are absolutely false.

On the 1st of August I was with the detail guarding the choppers at the lower pinery and on picket duty all day. The night was clear and other than a suspicious silence, there was no signs of Indians. I had my own convictions and "Rain-in-the-Face" afterwards told me that they had watched our every

270

movement, expecting an exterminating victory. The wood-chop-pers had a camp of about eight or ten wagons some 1300 yards from our camp. One loaded train guarded by twenty men under Lieutenant Francis McCarthy and Corporal Conley started for the Fort and the other with an escort of thirteen men under Corporal Porter, afterwards Color Sergeant of the Seventh Infantry, started for the lower pinery. With this party was John Phillips, bearer of dispatches to Laramie in January, who had been hired by contractors who owned the cattle teams.

Soon after 6.45 and when breakfast was over, while relieving private Grady, on guard, comrade Garrett, then on the lookout, suddenly yelled, "Indians!" Demming and I jumped to our feet. Sure enough they were coming in single file down toward Little Piney chanting their war songs for immediate charge. I risked one shot at 700 yards, dismounting one Indian. Demming then looked to the north and cried, "Look! Look at the Indians! My God! there are thousands of them. We have got to fight like H—— to-day for our lives."

No recall had been sounded but we were forced to run for our camp. The wood-choppers' camp was instantly burned by the Indians and its guard and axemen had taken to the hills. From 7 o'clock till 3 o'clock each moment of the seven hours seemed an eternity, but the "life or death battle" went fiercely on.

The following brief abstracts feebly shadow forth the inten-sity and heroic devotion of the brave handful. It thus gives to the Second Battalion, as the new Twenty-seventh Infantry, fresh honors to be added to those earned by them as part of the Eighteenth Infantry from 1861 throughout the entire Civil War.

All at once yelling Indians with waving feathers, hideously painted, came from over the hills like a swarm of bees and seemed to rise out of the ground as they emerged from the ravines in every direction. Fighting as best we could at every step, we made for the corral, met by Sergeant Littlemen, and reached it at last in an exhausted condition. Upon reporting to Captain Powell, he looked me straight into the eyes and said, "You did nobly, my boy!" "Men! Find a place in the wagon beds! You will have to fight for your lives, to-day."

271

I shall never forget the fierce, determined "do or die look" in his eyes, as he looked at me when I reported to him that terrible morning. The eyes of all our men were not those of desperation, but of resolution, as much as to say, "We are lost; death is certain; we are doomed to the terrible torture, mutilation and scalping like Fetterman's men, but the Indians shall pay a terrible toll of death before getting us in the end." One old soldier made a loop of his shoe strings, fitting it to his right foot and a small loop at the other end to fit the trigger of his rifle, meaning: "*the red devils will not get old Frank Robertson alive.*" All at once the Indians, singing and chanting their war and death songs gathered from all directions, and with Red Cloud distinct upon the top of the opposite hill. Then came the order: "Take your places men! Here they come! Shoot to kill!" These were the only words of command given us during the whole day's fight. They circled around us in every direction, amazed but undaunted by the intensity of our marvellous fire. We had not forgotten Massacre Hill; we were not fiends, but avengers. It was our lives or theirs. Our men crawled out to cut the tent ropes a little outside the corral that covered the Indians from our aim. "Water! Water!" was the constant cry. There were some camp-kettles a short distance outside and in getting them several kettles were pierced with bullets. Fire arrows came down and set fire to the dry dung from the animals enclosed in the corral with us, and the smoke became dense and sickening. Once there was a lull and we had time to open the breech locks of our rifles to let the barrels cool. Haggerty, shot through the left shoulder, still fought on, and Lieutenant Jenness was fatally shot at a moment of partial exposure. The Indians rushed here and there in advanced groups, while others came more closely, swinging lariats around their fallen dead to drag their bodies away. One giant Indian, magnificently built, seemed to dare danger, but we centred our fire and he fell from his horse. Then death chants filled the air and he was borne away by those who seemed to have lost a leader that appeared to have a charmed life. Five separate attacks that threatened our extermination were repulsed, while screaming squaws on the overlooking hills rent the air with their wild laments.

About three o'clock they had drawn nearly out of range. We could hear Red Cloud and another chief addressing them and a great number rode towards Big Piney and out of sight.

Only two of the men had fallen and we had plenty of ammunition and we waited for the awful moment to come. It might be death; it might be rescue. What did the retiring of the main force mean? A humming sound in the valley grew louder and louder. The strain on our nerves of their awful chanting was terrible. All at once there came a large body on foot about 90 yards east of the corral in a wedge shape like the letter V led by Red Cloud's nephew, wearing a gorgeous head-dress. In this last attack they came so near we could see the whites of their eyes but it was over in a few minutes.

Suddenly, the Indians on the Big Hill moved swiftly down into the Valley of Big Piney. The boom of the big gun was heard, and again, and again, and towards the east we could see the glorious caps on the heads of our comrades in the long skirmish line. We jumped to our feet; we yelled; we threw our caps into the air and hugged each other and some of us cried. The strain was over! Again came the boom and another. They were throwing shell from the hill into the Indians in the Big Piney Valley.

Major Smith came with the rescuing party and our genial post surgeon, Dr. S. M. Horton, God bless him!

We reached the Fort shortly before six o'clock through the west gate. As we halted before the headquarters' building that Colonel Carrington had built and occupied the year before and on the same steps where he welcomed Captain Ten Eyck and his brave command after their return as a rescue party in 1866,— our new Colonel, Brevet Brigadier General John E. Smith, gave us a welcome in words thrilling as well as jubilant, to congratulate us as " deserving, every one of us, of a gold medal from Congress, for valor unequalled in any other fight by so few against the overwhelming multitude of savage foes."

The only woman survivor of the experience of those early days, except the wife of Dr. S. M. Horton, who was not present, was myself, and there was no alternative but to respond to a call. To simply bow my acknowledgments, while a guest, with my husband, of the Chamber of Commerce, would not have graciously met the wish of the people, and only an impromptu response was befitting the occasion. The ever-present reporter caught the general trend of my few words, and as legitimate features of the occasion, they are quoted, in part, as follows:

" Mrs. Carrington first dwelt upon the pleasanter features of the occasion, as she stood before so large a gathering of men, women, and children who had come from a range of nearly fifty miles to help celebrate the delivery of their beautiful country from the savage redman, and then took a more serious attitude as she called vividly to mind her experiences of long ago, and suggested that a Scripture text was suited most fitly to the occasion, viz.:

" ' Thou shalt forget thy misery and remember it as waters that have passed away.'

" As an appropriate text and comprehending fully the relations of all present to their chief guest, she wished to bear witness to the kind Providence of God, through the by-gone years, in the words, ' Surely goodness and mercy have followed me all the days of my life,' and she felt the present moment itself to be the supreme import, since she could personally testify in the presence of so immense an audience the force of those words.

" She recalled the time forty-two years ago, when, on the march homeward from the land of slaughter, almost in that very locality, she passed through dangers, many deep snows and intense cold, and upon reaching a hasty camp, one night, some of the men were so badly frozen that when they reached Fort Reno several amputations were necessary.

" Such were the grave conditions on that terrible winter's forced march, ' that even the mules were so hungry that they ate wagon-covers and even gnawed wagon-tongues and spokes of wheels before forage could be made ready for them.'

" She also recalled the fact that after being helped from an ambulance at Fort Reno and refreshed by a bountiful repast provided by the officers of the Eighteenth at that post, and opening her Bible, the first words that met her eyes were these:

" ' The Angel of the Lord encamped around them that fear Him, and delivereth these.' (See 34th Psalm.)

" She added that she marked that Bible verse and that every Bible she had since owned bore the same characteristic mark. She closed with the most earnest assurance that, ' This is no historical flourish, from present inspiration, but a statement from real experience, yesterday, to-day, and forever.' "

The punctuation of cheers and the parenthesis of tears, are better imagined, as not transferable to a written record. A simple reference to a few leaves back in the narrative will produce the scene described, then and now.

"Assembly" was then sounded for all to gather at the next point of interest, and the crowd moved to the site of the old fort, at present a luxurious field of alfalfa, where a flag-staff had been erected at the identical spot where, forty-two years ago, the first flag was unfurled in Wyoming.

As I saw the first flag raising, in 1866, so again I could stand in the shadow of its folds and while the band played "The Star Spangled Banner," "Old Glory" was pulled to the staff masthead by the same man, Hon. Wm. Daley of Rawlins, who officiated in the same capacity on the first occasion, October 31, 1866. The few survivors, with bugler Pobloski, and Lieutenant Wheeler of the Nineteenth U. S. Infantry detailed as a special aid on the staff of the General that day, forming a group around the base of the flag-staff presented a scene never to be forgotten by the participants. While the flag remained hoisted the General again addressed the people, pointing out the boundaries of the stockade; where the gates were located; how and where the Fetterman party left the Fort with orders to succor the wood-train; the direction they took to Sullivant Hill, and where they did go instead of obeying orders.

The flag was then lowered and presented to the General by Wm. Daley on behalf of the Chamber of Commerce and the people of Sheridan as a souvenir of the occasion, so that any day we can touch its folds; and, lo! what associations arise!

The flag episode was a genuine surprise, not having had notice in the program.

Chief Red Cloud himself had been advertised to be present, but was too feeble and too nearly blind to attempt the feat, but his mourning over his braves who had passed away did not prevent his sending a message that if he could he would like to meet the "White Chief."

A mimic fight, or sham battle, had been announced as a sort of sensational incident to represent the fight of December 21, 1866, more as a drawing card, of course, when nothing of the kind could lack the elements of a painful burlesque entirely out of harmony with the feelings of the guests as well as the dignified memorial honors of the celebration itself.

The formal exercises of the day closed with varied field sports on the level plain before the *glacis* of the old fort and along the Big Piney Creek, including bronco riding, roping and straddling steers, base-ball, and other out-of-door sports, foot races included.

Locally the day was rounded out by a grand ball at Sturgess Hall, which would accommodate at least four hundred people, and this was attended by young men and maidens from far distant homes who had anticipated the entertainment for weeks, and July 3, 1909, passed into the history of Wyoming, once the wild land of the redman, as an occasion of enduring interest. It had been made possible only by the presence of those witnesses of its early past who had come to share their own pioneer experiences with those of the living present.

Our trip outward on the previous day had been full of curious speculation as to how soon we would reach familiar scenes, and whether Cloud Peak itself, with its snowy crests, would still loom up with the supernal grandeur of old time remembrance!

Every gleaming stream of irrigating supplies led us to challenge our genial guide, Judge Foster, as to its relations with old time memories of survey or skirmish. Redundant crops, orchards, gardens, groves, and hedges amazed us by their reflection of Eastern enterprise and skill that had so deftly and luxuriously converted savage wilds into fitting home surroundings, worthy of New England's best colonial record. All of these groves and hedges, so rapidly springing up along our journey, had been the product of the wise and intelligent industry of pioneer men and women who had faith in the future of their chosen homes at the west.

Domestic animals were everywhere abundant and six school houses, well painted and well protected for the summer vacation, were noticed during that short morning ride. Even the sight of an old fruit can, an old coal bucket, and an empty cracker box for reception of the rural mail delivery was typical of the progress of civilization and intelligent industry as well as of the ingenuity by which the occupants of ranches or farm-houses at a distance could catch the carrier's indication that there was something deposited for a prompt delivery.

Stacks of old straw and monstrous ricks of well-preserved hay were abundant, and our eagerness to catch the earliest possible view of our old-time camping-grounds was only intensified by all these signs of swift development and abounding prosperity and peace.

Our return to Sheridan in the afternoon was of a different order of excitement. The outward ride, to all but ourselves, would have seemed dull and prosaic, because no past would have a place in the mind of the traveller. Our return was full of quickening sensations of realized advance in the people, more than in the country itself. Automobiles raced for quicker return to the city. Girls on ponies, gaily caparisoned, vied with each other in passing automobiles, in leaping irrigating ducts, or small ravines. Once, two of these, mounted on fiery ponies, took a jump so clumsily that sharp whip strokes forced their horses back to try it over, in better shape, and the ditch was at least four feet in width.

General Freeman, himself, the first recruit as

elsewhere noticed, for the Eighteenth Infantry in 1861, who came from a long distance to attend these memorial exercises, passed us in an automobile, only to find when we overtook him repairing his conveyance, that the race was not always to the swift, and that gasoline for speeding uses was not at constant reach among Wyoming highways of country travel.

One single incident marred the pleasure of this return to the city, and that was an accident to our esteemed friend, Dr. H. P. Holmes, by the overturn of his automobile, from which, to the regret of all his friends, a quite lasting disability ensued.

We reached the outskirts of the city just in time to halt on its hillside summit and view the wonderful panorama, about and below, when thousands of electric lights illuminated the magic compass of this rare vision of natural and cultivated beauty of scenery and home delights.

CHAPTER XXXIV.

THE 4th of July was ushered in by a sunrise salute from a hilltop east of the city, as well as from Fort Mackenzie. The eagle screamed and cannon (crackers) roared!

In writing of this celebrated 4th, for a more permanent record, I realize it is beyond mental range to suggest adequate expression for emotions experienced, the blending of the solemn and serious, with the hilarious, under present excitement; in some features rehabilitating old-time scenes of antebellum days; from another view-point, recalling the scenes of yesterday, July 3rd, that day of itself reviving historic scenes and personal memories extending back over forty years, yes, and still further back to the national record and the prolific associations of one hundred and thirty years, until we seemed to be living, all of it, in that one brief day. Surely, "our thoughts were linked by many a hidden chain."

But, to the record.

The citizens were alert to commemorate this day, with its old time significance, interspersed with some later day interests emphasized doubtless by the exercises of the previous day.

Spirits, of whatever kind, were not exhausted. The celebration was sane and orderly, and possessed unique features, moving pictures in real life, especially during the morning parade which began at ten o'clock in the morning under command of Colonel C. Z. A. Zander, of the State Militia, Chief Marshal.

The various organizations led by bands discoursing appropriate music marched in review before General Carrington and his staff, seated in gaily decked automobiles, which halted as the procession passed.

They included a company of the National Guard of the State; a battalion of the Nineteenth U. S. Infantry from Fort Mackenzie; Grand Army Veterans; Odd Fellows; Modern Woodmen; the Fire Department; National Order of Eagles; Improved Order of Red Men (not Indians); Japanese Citizens, in uniforms of red, white and blue; a contingent of Crow Indians, a few in war-paint and feathers; other Indians preferring to ride in their own conveyances; private citizens in carriages and automobiles with flags dispersed in every available space; a sprinkling of cowboys and cowgirls, mounted on appropriately caparisoned steeds, all passing the point of review on Grinell Avenue.

Opposite this point a stand had been erected for the speakers and other guests, among these General Henry B. Freeman, who joined the Eighteenth Infantry at its first organization, in July, 1861, and Mrs. Freeman, who had shared in the exercises of the previous day.

Rev. M. DeWitt Long, the Presbyterian Minister, invoked the divine blessing.

The Declaration of Independence was read clearly and impressively by Mr. Charles A. Kutcher to the crowds rallying around this coigne of vantage. Mr. M. B. Camplin, the Master of Ceremonies, introduced the Hon. Frank Mondell, who delivered a brief but stirring address. The Sheridan Band interspersed fine music, enlivening every occasion by their presence, and the morning exercises closed with adjournment for dinner.

At two o'clock "assembly" was sounded from Kendrick Park, the next rallying place for the afternoon exercises, where an enthusiastic and tireless audience of several thousands greeted the speakers. All kinds of vehicles were present, and large families with children of all ages filled the grove, enjoying their picnic lunches along Goose Creek, which flows through the beautiful grove, until speaking began.

The address of welcome was delivered by the Hon. Fred H. Blume, as well as the presentation of the key of the city, with the familiar interpretation thereof, to the principal guest, General Carrington, who responded with appropriate words, in part as follows, having first requested the great crowd that surrounded the platform to come to the front that all might come within reach of his voice and he could see them, face to face:

My dear Sir, and friends of Wyoming:

I accept this key of your beautiful city, as well as the bright welcome of this great concourse of your people, with sincere thanks, and there instantly comes this thought to mind, something like that laconic query of a certain Texas Congressman not long ago: "Where am I at?"

AFTER MANY DAYS

Having been classed by your press as one of the venerable original pioneers of Wyoming, this assembled progeny of various ages, bountifully fruitful in your development since forty-two years ago, suggests as a spontaneous answer to my own internal curiosity that " I am indeed at home " and somehow related to all of you.

The key itself is so typical of your unbounded generosity that I shall ever preserve and use it to lock up within the inner chambers of my heart these treasures of your regard.

And now to all of you as we assemble like one great household, a word as to just " Where we are at." This beautiful and plentiful stream that glistens in the sunlight and is as wholesome and priceless in its flow as it is beautiful, is the same Goose Creek that escaped from Big Horn Cañon, only a few miles from my own headquarters at Fort Phil. Kearney, forty-two years ago, until you utilized its precious waters for your own delectation and profitable service, both civil and domestic. Its whole border then lined by cottonwood trees was in the possession of more than 3000 savage and hostile red men. Every detachment that went forth from our impregnable stockade to Tongue River and its tributaries was checked by their flanking bands along this creek as they invariably threatened our rear when we ventured more than a few miles from the Fort for wood or the rescue of threatened emigrants or stolen stock. Now how beautiful is the stream with all its surroundings. Every promise then recorded of your future growth, development, wealth, and civilization has been verified not only in twenty but even a hundred fold of glorious and abounding fruition.

Yes, I am at home! Even as in my own New England, every choice type of culture, refinement, and religion, as well as education, is abundant, progressive, and fruitful. All the blessings of wholesome peace, prosperity, and happiness abound, as if they already had become indigenous to the soil.

In social customs, graces, habitudes, and adornments, as well as in architecture, avenues, school-houses, and churches, and no less in gardens, groves, and pleasure resorts, as well as in redundant crops, and both commercial and manufacturing lines of mental and physical activity, there has been the incubating force of a certain intelligent, charitable, and fraternal combined harmony of effort.

Add to this brief epitome the surface irrigation of your upper soil and the magical unearthing of subsoil treasures and how can even the most unsophisticated American in search of the health, happiness, and domestic peace that attach to the magic of the word "home," ever fail to realize all that human life can expect or even hope for in this brief life of change here below.

Everything I see of your accomplished endeavor commends solemn thought as well as recognition and profound respect. Peace, so orderly, safe, and progressive to be permanent and undisturbed by national gusts of partisan or other disturbing antagonisms, or jealousies, must ever retain the same high moral as well as intellectual, social, and industrial merit. In brief, the citizen, by day and night and in all relations or functions, must not only be in accord with nature in her best agencies and resources but in allegiance to those higher laws upon which individual, family, and society life must predicate all their real and enduring value, namely, the Code Divine! Honesty, industry, and thrift will then be in supreme accord. Purity in thought and purpose in the household will then become the basis of all external, political, as well as social endeavor.

A great national election is at hand. Greed and graft have already too often stimulated a natural and otherwise laudable ambition by fictitious promises of fancied good in which the combined faculties of "mind, heart, soul, and strength," could never find their highest fruition.

Our visit to you was not alone from an earnest desire to see what had been wrought in the development of a wilderness into a realized land of promise; but to give more exact definition to dates, localities, incidents, and persons, concerning which we alone, while living, could resolve all ambiguities and injustice incident to the careless gossip and baseless legends of the long ago.

And now, in closing, I may say to all you men, women, and the boys and girls as well, who came out of curiosity to see Red Cloud's old enemy and your own friend, of the long ago,

AFTER MANY DAYS

we leave you our best wishes, knowing that these little people here are to be the determining factors in the future of Wyoming. I now leave to my surviving veterans their words of greeting with the simple reminder that the supreme longing of my inmost soul for you and yours, when the hope of this visit had been fully assured, was, that your exceptional freedom from many evils that had marred the history of some of our later States, might never be realized by you, and I close by challenging you to willing and righteous competition in the national, perhaps world-wide conflict now being waged.

This appeal is not alone to survivors of the various wars which gave America her proud independence as the great Republic, but to the great struggle between right and wrong.

I close with that appeal, already in song:

> Sound, bugle, sound! the fight is on!
> 'Tis life—'tis death, but life beyond!
> Gird tight your belts! be strong, be brave,
> As one, again your country save!
> > Sound, bugle, sound!
> > Sound! sound, bugle, sound!
>
> Not serried ranks of flashing steel,
> Endanger now your country's weal,
> But frenzied self counts gold as God,
> And smites your life with passion's rod!
> > Sound, bugle, sound!
> > Sound! sound, bugle, sound!
>
> Join faith with trust, nor doubt success,
> With these allied, be doubly blest.
> Truth never fails, if boldly urged,
> As gold from dross, is fully purged!
> As gold from dross is fully purged.
>
> Sound, bugle, sound! the cross lift high!
> Of passion purged, bring freedom nigh!

Bind arms of steel with cords of love,
And bring glad peace from heaven above!
Sound, bugle, sound!
Sound! sound, bugle, sound!

The closing verses which thus emphasized the
burden of General Carrington's address had been
set to music by Mr. L. O. Emerson, the noted musical
composer, of Hyde Park, Mass. When silence
ensued, the Apollo Quartette, consisting of Messrs.
Little, Long, Stuby, and Decker, immediately came
forward and rendered the music, which came in the
nature of a surprise, though none the less a touching
tribute to the authors of both music and verse.

When the chairman of the morning exercises
announced the names of the speakers for the afternoon program, I was quite startled to hear *my own
name called.* "A Fourth of July Speech" to a promiscuous audience, or any audience, for that matter,
was something unprecedented in my history.

I had been resting in the thought that the ordeal
of the day before was all-sufficient for me in that line
of effort.

In my perturbation a resourceful friend whispered in my ear "say the same things you said yesterday." "But new occasions teach new duties."
It was no time or occasion to "hang the harp on the
willows."

A reprieve was thoroughly enjoyed at luncheon
and a delightful drive around the city, which however did not include any preparation for a speech,
when we drove up to the entrance of the grand-
stand, and execution was delayed by other exercises

already noticed. But after the song and a National rendering by the band the regular program was to be followed of course.

My time had come!

I had absorbed so much of kindness and pleasure from association with the generous people that subconsciously this thought was stimulating.

I girded myself for the execution, trusting at the same time that the audience might "not view me with a critic's eye, but pass my imperfections by."

The suggestion of my friend was not followed in detail. Recalling to mind that I was in Wyoming, where women stood on the same footing as men, literally true that day, and though the only representative of my sex set down for a speech, I rose to the occasion somewhat fortified in my position.

The story of the old woman who lived in a shoe was chosen as a suggestive theme for a beginning, taking the cue from a scene in the morning parade, when a vehicle was driven by the point of review so packed with children that for the moment they could not be counted, and on being informed that they were all of the same family the needless fear of race suicide was emphasized.

Further localizing the interests of the day, certain events in their State's history were noted as having come to pass within my own knowledge.

The month of July was the month of all others for commemorating these events.

The establishment of Fort Phil. Kearney in July, forty-two years ago, the fortieth anniversary of being given territorial existence under the name of

Wyoming, the eighteenth of Wyoming as a State, and the forty-first of the commencement of the first house in the first town, and though as the old song goes, "Come along, Uncle Sam is rich enough to give us all a farm," meant for them an uphill fight with nature, as well as conflict with a hostile foe, they had erased from the map the name "The Great American Desert."

"It is not with heathen pride that you can point out results and say behold Great Babylon that I have built, but under the providence of God through personal effort and co-operation, patient toil, endurance of isolation and a hundred other disadvantages, by a splendid system of irrigation, behold the evidences of how faithfully and well your work has been done, smiling fields on every side and prosperous cities and towns have grown up even within my personal knowledge."

There were many women and children present, and as the children suggested the initial remarks, the closing appeal was made charging them to be faithful to their country, the land, and the opportunities bequeathed them through the privation, suffering and sacrifices of those whose deeds they were there to commemorate. Surely, "there is no epic like the making of a State."

On the capacious platform were seated many invited guests, prominent citizens and pioneers, notably among the latter were Colonel Foote and wife. The Colonel himself had lived in Wyoming and the West almost a half century and was thoroughly identified with Western life, yet not altogether forgetting Scotland and "Bobby Burns" when occasion offered for early reminiscences of his native land.

Mr. S. S. Peters followed on the program, and in his address paid tribute to the heroism and suffering of the women at Fort Phil. Kearney during the summer, fall, and winter of 1866, and the spring and summer of 1867 as follows:

Weary indeed would have been our lives as soldiers in those trying days but for the inspiration of the presence, patience, and gentle devotion of the women of the command, who dared, with a devotion more than heroic, to accompany their husbands to this land of desolation, wilderness, and savagery.

No privation was too great for these women to brave, and brave it they did, without a murmur. They were angels of mercy in truth. They were constantly seeking to alleviate the discomfort of the men by kindly act and patient example.

At Fort Phil. Kearney, the first Mrs. Carrington was our good angel. Her every purpose was for the betterment of the condition of the command, morally and socially. She was more than the Colonel's wife, she was the mother of the regiment, loved and revered by every man, woman, and child at the Fort. She was a woman gently nurtured in her youth, broad, kind, sympathetic and of distinct force of character, a true Christian, a devoted mother, and above all a woman who knew how to suffer, how to sympathize, how to comfort.

Nor was the Mrs. Carrington who is with us to-day less kind, less true, less Christian, or less sympathetic. Coming to us as the bride of Lieutenant Grummond, reaching us in September, it was but a few short weeks until she was made a widow by that awful tragedy of December 21st, and we shared our tears and anguish over the loss of our comrades, with her bereavement, feeling that her grief was our own. Thus was she knit to us with a tie of comradeship and sorrow that shall endure with increasing love as long as the memory of that December day tragedy shall endure.

But from the shadowy gloom of the tragic past, I must come to a demand of the present.

I have a letter just handed me since on the platform. I have not yet read it, but the name attached to it suggests that Providence has had a hand in it. It is written by Miss Florence Ten Eyck, the daughter of my dead Captain, Tenodore Ten Eyck, who led scarcely fifty men from the gates of Fort Phil. Kearney to the relief of Colonel Fetterman on that fated December day of forty-two years ago. This devoted daughter has for years sought to secure justice for her dead father from the cruel and untruthful aspersion cast upon his name by writers who, not having secured true data from the General, himself, adopted current reports, charging Captain Ten Eyck with the loss of Fetterman's command, because of falsely alleged delay, by him, in going to the relief of Fetterman. I have come nearly a thousand miles to give the lie to all such statements. General Carrington has come over half the continent with his weight of eighty-five years to tell the people of Wyoming how unkind, how unjust, and how causeless this aspersion was on the name and fame of a gallant soldier who long since has filled a soldier's grave. I have and now call upon *you* William Murphy and *you* John Strawn, who were of that devoted band that marched out of the old stockade at Phil. Kearney, with myself, under the command of Captain Ten Eyck to Fetterman's relief that December day, you who are the living witnesses of and participants of that dash for the lives of our comrades to denounce this blot upon the name and honor of our dead Captain.

You knew, as did I, and General Carrington, that before we had crossed through the ice of Piney Creek that day, Fetterman's men were then either dying or dead, and that no arm but God's could have given them any relief.

The simple truth is this: Fetterman and his men were overwhelmed in almost an instant by a force so overpowering in numbers that their destruction was as complete and sudden as if they had been engulfed in an avalanche without warning, and without hope of escape.

AFTER MANY DAYS

Turning to General Carrington, with much emotion, he said to him as they grasped each others hands:

And I thank God, this day, General Carrington, that you and ourselves were spared, in the passing of years, to meet here and vindicate the honor of Captain Ten Eyck. I too thank God that you were permitted to stand on that rock at Fetterman Monument made sacred by the blood of Fetterman's men and "Baldy Brown," the spot where they gave up their lives, probably self-inflicted, when all hope was gone, while you vindicated the name of Ten Eyck before assembled thousands of the good people of Wyoming. Surely God's hand was in this, and we can both rejoice that he has chosen you and I, and Murphy, Strawn, Driscoll, and Gibson to forever efface that blot from the name and fame of Captain Ten Eyck.

William Murphy, another of the old heroes of Fort Phil. Kearney, told his story. He came from Spokane, Washington, to attend the reunion:

MURPHY'S STORY.

I was a member of Company A of the Eighteenth United States Infantry, Colonel Henry B. Carrington commanding. We were stationed at Fort Kearney in Nebraska in 1866, when we were ordered by General Pope to build a couple of new forts on the historic Bozeman Road beyond Fort Connor, or Fort Reno, as it was subsequently called. Gold had been discovered farther west and the argonauts were hastening towards the land of promise through a country infested by bloodthirsty savages. They must be given protection and we were sent out to erect the forts.

Our command left Fort Kearney on May 19, 1866, and pursued its way up the Platte, following the North Platte route to Fort Laramie. There were nearly 2000 troops in the command, but over 1300 of these were intended to relieve volunteer troops who were guarding the telegraph and mail line in Wyoming.

Our expedition reached Fort Laramie on June 13, in time

for Colonel Carrington to participate in the council being held with Red Cloud, Man-Afraid-of-His-Horses, and other Indian Chiefs to secure the Indians' consent to the construction of a road and the erection of the promised forts, the Indians protesting vigorously against this.

Red Cloud made a dramatic and effective speech. He claimed that the Peace Commissioners were treating the assembled chiefs as children; that they were pretending to negotiate for a country which they had already taken by conquest. He accused the Government of bad faith in all its transactions with Indian tribes.

In his harangue to the Indians he told them that the white men had crowded the Indians back year by year and forced them to live in a small country north of the Platte and now their last hunting ground, the home of their people, was to be taken from them. This meant that they and their women and children were to starve, and for his part he preferred to die fighting rather than by starvation.

Red Cloud promised that if the combined tribes would defend their homes they would be able to drive the soldiers out of the country. He said it might be a long war, but as they were defending their last hunting grounds they must in the end be successful.

The powwow continued for some time, until finally the hostile Sioux under Red Cloud withdrew, refusing to have any further counsel or to accept any presents.

While we waited there at Laramie, Colonel Carrington received subsequent orders directing him to name the proposed posts Fort Phil. Kearney and Fort F. C. Smith. Previous to our departure there was great excitement, not only among the Indians at the post, but among the soldiers. Fair warning was given by Red Cloud and Man-Afraid-of-His-Horses, that the troops could not go beyond Fort Reno, and that if an attempt was made to build new posts beyond that point there would be bitter, cruel, and relentless war. In spite of all this, we had our orders and we went ahead to obey them.

We reached Fort Reno in safety, June 28, although signs of Indians on every hand had been many. We left Fort Reno on July 9. A day or so out a number of the men deserted, being lured by the tales of marvellous riches to be found. Colonel Carrington sent a force out after them, but they met with some of Red Cloud's Indians, who sent an ultimatum back with the troops that if the soldiers would go back there would be peace, but if they remained where they were, went ahead, or built forts, hostilities would begin.

There was nothing to be done but to obey orders, and on July 15, 1866, we located the site of Fort Phil. Kearney, destined to become historical. The next day a detail of wood-choppers was sent out to cut timbers for the necessary buildings. Pow-wows and trouble with the Indians began at once. A mounted force was sent out after them and soon came upon the scene of a massacre, a party of six white men being found dead, the Indians having driven off the cattle belonging to the train and partially plundered the wagons.

The soldiers from the Fort attacked the Indians, but finding them in great force retreated to the Post, two soldiers being killed and three wounded.

From then, on throughout the summer, things were lively around the Post. The plan of the Indians was to constantly harass the forts by running off stock and cutting off soldiers or citizens who ventured any distance beyond the stockade. All Government or immigrant trains were threatened and attacked if possible. From the 15th of July to the 29th there were no less than eight attacks on trains between Reno and Phil. Kearney. On the 29th nine men were killed and two dangerously wounded. The separate killings during these fourteen days amounted to twenty more.

Twenty mules belonging to citizens at our Post were cut off from a herd a short distance from the Fort early in September. Two other demonstrations were made that day. Ten herders were attacked within a mile of us and thirty-three horses and seventy mules were driven off. Practically every day after that there were encounters; stock were run off; soldiers and herders were killed. We were constantly harassed. The Indians succeeded in driving off twenty-four head of cattle feeding near the Fort September 23. Quartermaster Brown with twenty-three soldiers and several citizens dashed in among the Indians and killed thirteen of them and recaptured the stock.

Notwithstanding all these encounters, work on the Fort was pushed ahead and the Post completed on October 31. Colonel Carrington allowed us a half holiday in honor of the completion. The Fort itself was very strong. It was 600 feet by 800 feet, located on rising ground. The stockade was of pine logs, hewed to a touching surface, and set in the ground four feet but projecting upward for eight feet. There was a block-house at the two diagonal corners, from which the four sides of the stockade could be swept.

December 6 was an eventful day at the Fort. There was an attack on the wood-train early in the morning, and Lieutenant Colonel Fetterman, commander of the company I served in, was sent out to rout some Indians, while Colonel Carrington and Lieutenant Grummond, with thirty mounted men, went to intercept the Indians when they were driven back by Fetterman. Our men under Lieutenant Colonel Fetterman met 200 Indians, who made a determined stand. Colonel Carrington and his force came galloping up and there was a general engagement, fierce and bloody. One of our men fought single handed and killed three Indians before he received his own death blow.

From that day on, we were in the attitude of strict defense. The wood-train went out each morning, but the greatest caution was observed. The train went out as usual December 21, and proceeded about two miles when it was attacked by a great band of Indians.

Colonel Carrington immediately dispatched Lieutenant Fetterman with seventy-six men to the relief of the train. Fetterman was my commander but I was not in that first party sent out. From the Fort we could see Fetterman's command proceed to the relief. Then came the sound of rapid discharge of muskets. Fetterman had engaged the Indians, and was in mortal combat with the red foes.

All was excitement about the Post at once. Colonel Carrington dispatched forty-five additional soldiers to the relief of Fetterman. I was one of the number. As soon as he could, he sent forty more. We had but little ammunition. We had to make a detour to cross a mountain stream which was very difficult to ford. We reached the battlefield too late. All had in fact been killed just after we crossed the Piney.

The entire Fetterman command had been massacred. The horses of the men lay with their heads toward Fort Phil. Kearney. The men had been retreating when they were surrounded. There on the ground they lay, dead every man of them. But they had made the Indians pay dearly for their victory, as the numerous empty Henry rifle shells testified. In one place lay the Indian ponies dead and not far away there were sixty-five pools of dark clotted blood. The men had died like heroes; they had sold their lives dearly.

We buried the dead as best we could. Pine coffins and cases were made and a trench fifty feet long and seven feet deep was dug, and the bodies buried there. It was found that eighty-one had been killed altogether. The remains of Lieutenant Grummond and those of three or four others whose families desired to send the bodies east for burial were kept out and the rest buried in the long trench.*

Red Cloud, in after years, talked of the heroism of the massacred band. One man, he said, killed seven Indians and wounded nine more before he was overpowered.

Following the massacre things were in a hard way at Fort Phil. Kearney. The winter was one of intense cold. Men were frozen severely, suffering intensely. To make matters worse, they began to suffer from scurvy.

After the massacre there were hardly more than one hundred men left in the Fort, including two citizens. Many died from scurvy. There were possibly seventy-five survivors forty-two years ago. How many are left to-day?

General Freeman moved all hearts by his eloquent words, recalling the past of which he was a

---

* Murphy is in error as to non-burials, of *several,* and of the " four citizens " given on the monument, itself, as victims of the massacre; two were miners, who were killed outside, and brought to the fort for burial, as noticed in the Narrative.

part, and the present, so promising, which he also shares, having been a citizen of the State since his retirement from active service.

Sergeant Samuel Gibson responded by repeating his story of the ''Wagon Bed Fight'' given in detail the day previous.

The beautiful day was drawing to a close, welcomed indeed, especially as it had been intensely warm, and everybody full of hot air, from one cause or another, and the cooling shade of Mrs. A. W. Perry's veranda was most inviting, as her guests, including Congressman Mondell, Hon. William Daley, Captain Walton and wife, Captain Arnold from Fort Mackenzie, and General and Mrs. Freeman, assembled for relaxation and were later served with a delightful dinner in her characteristic style.

One feature of the day's exercises without the park enclosure was a series of athletic sports on a hill southwest of the city. A prize of $50 in gold had been offered in the wild horse bucking contest which was won by Perry Aber of Wolf Creek, who rode a white mule, and judging from reports he made the rider earn his money.

The entertainment for the evening had for its prominent feature a grand pyrotechnical display from a hill-top near the city, reminding me of one I had once witnessed from Pike's Peak, in an earlier celebration of the 4th, with a difference, however, that the missiles there disclosed immediate snow environment, while at Sheridan the mountain top of green was weird indeed but the rockets were not sufficient to reveal snow-crowned Cloud Peak, always visible during the day hours.

The present exhibition possessed more than ordinary interest from the part taken by the Japanese citizens. They did the work of arranging and touching off the fireworks under the skilful direction of M. S. Imashhaki, an expert, and his assistants, having contributed $150 for this purpose.

The expiring fireworks display concluded the official exercises, and the 4th of July, 1908, also passed into the State's history.

If there were more or fewer in number present in the different houses of worship the following morning to welcome the "day of Sacred rest, within or without the gates of these temples," the sentiment of the majority, from a sense of bodily weariness alone, could "welcome the delightful morn."

CHAPTER XXXV.

THE social festivities were inaugurated on Monday evening, July 6, by a reception at the Kirby Opera House. Winged hand-bills and transparencies of steadier bearing proclaimed a general invitation, and general was the response.

People from all walks of life poured into the Opera House in the best of spirits—and dress as well—intent on making their guests feel welcome, which only supplemented in a strictly social way the more formal receptions of the previous days.

Friendly greetings interspersed with pleasing orchestral music and light refreshments, characteristic of such occasions furnished the order of the evening, until a special musical programme was announced from the stage by Mr. C. B. Holmes, one of the most active of our hosts.

In the receiving line were the Hon. R. H. Walsh, President of the Chamber of Commerce, Mrs. J. J. Bentley, Captain Walton and Mrs. Walton of Fort Mackenzie, General and Mrs. Carrington, Mr. and Mrs. George H. Perry, Samuel Gibson, S. S. Peters, John Strawn, and Dennis Driscoll, the last four veterans donning their white military gloves for the first time in many years.

From the stage Mrs. A. Diefenderfer rendered a fine solo, as did Mrs. Livingston wife of the Congregational Minister, who sang most sweetly and acceptably.

Rev. DeWitt Long, the Presbyterian Minister, and his daughter, Mrs. E. E. Levers, sang the classic duet, "Flow Gently, Sweet Diva," in an artistic manner. Mrs. Decker gave an excellent instrumental number. Mr. L. L. Sherrard also favored the audience with selections, and the Apollo Club, Messrs. Little, Long, Stuby, and Decker, again rendered General Carrington's patriotic song, "Sound, bugle, sound!"

It is well the programme was no longer, or I should run out of expletives in giving due praise to any who might follow their predecessors in the evening's delightful musical entertainment.

The floor was cleared for dancing at the conclusion of the musical programme.

The few days following, allotted to our visit, were signalized by dinner-parties given by Mrs. Edward Gillette, Mrs. Stevenson, and Mrs. Foster in their delightful homes. Mrs. Foster had for guests Major Oliver Perry Hanna, who built the first cabin in Sheridan County, and his accomplished wife, who is President of the Woman's Clubs, Mr. Smyth, and others, who were highly entertaining in their reminiscences of pioneer life. My husband found in Mr. Gillette, himself, after whom the promising town of Gillette is named, and whose profession as Civil Engineer had been so valuable in the construction and management of the C. B. & Q. Railroad, a brother Alumnus of Yale University, as he seems always to meet, either at home or abroad.

He also has charge of the proposed new railroad via Buffalo, as the shorter route to the North Platte River and also of the utilizing of Piney Creek by tunnel, if necessary, as hereinafter suggested, to perfect the Buffalo Water supply as well as to irrigate 85,000 acres of land. His portrait appears, very properly, in a group, together with Messrs. Loucks, Hanna and Coffeen, the original founders.

As the time limit for our absence from home drew too swiftly near, we began to realize more than ever how feebly we had grasped the points of view in this wonderful country to which we had looked forward with most intense interest.

The immediate surroundings of the old fort had indeed been visited, but when, in turn, we were visited by those who now live along the once lonely route of our own tiresome journey in 1866, we more than ever regretted that weeks, rather than days, could not have been given to our visit. During the day and night spent at Kearney, we certainly realized how decidedly modern improvements had taken the place of strategic and military points of vision about the old fort site itself; but when so many wagons, modern vehicles, and even automobiles brought visitors from such places as Clear Creek, Lake De Smedt, and from Buffalo, now the County Seat of Johnson County, only a short ride from Fort Phil. Kearney itself, we felt as if a new country had indeed swallowed up all the landmarks of old, where we had made transient camping spots, and of which the memory was that of a gloomy dream.

Among the most impressive incidents of the visit,

were interviews with Judge Parmelee and the venerable Colonel Foote, listening to their revelations of the changes that had so rapidly succeeded the close of Indian hostilities, and the dawn of peaceful conditions now so fruitfully abundant.

Of Lake De Smedt, whose alkaline water could not be safely touched by man or beast in 1866, and whose rugged surroundings were those of débris, as from former volcanic sources, we learned, that its supply of water for abundant irrigation of the region thereabout would soon be reinforced by connection, perhaps by a tunnel, with Piney Creek itself. Thus, in fancy, we could associate the water supply of our old home at Kearney with the mission of De Smedt, himself, who had given name to the lake, while offering to the savages of the Northwest those living waters of divine truth that would purify all the ills to which that region had long been subjected.

Buffalo, itself, with court-house, high school and common schools, churches, banks and spacious warehouses as well as beautiful residences, was so pleasantly and ideally described as an existing reality that we recognized more fully the treasures of comfort, wealth and prosperity that had so abundantly adorned and blessed these frontier homes, towns and cities.

Photographic views were also furnished, through Judge Parmelee, of Buffalo and its environs, including one of the Main Street during business hours, with spacious stores for all manner of supplies and every indication of thriving business success. All seemed like the work of some magic enchantment, already aspiring to match Sheridan itself in its growth and prosperity. Our kaleidoscopic conceptions, in advance, of reported western enterprise became more than realized through these modern appliances of all the material elements of eastern civilization in the developed West.

Judge Parmelee, also a guest at the Foster' House, stated that on the following Saturday he would hold a special session of his court, to render decisions upon cases submitted for his adjudication, and invited General Carrington to attend by reason of his many years of service as a member of the United States Supreme Court Bar, and to recall some of the antecedents of his early professional life, before entering the regular army. A brief impromptu address, most unexpected by both speaker and his hearers, added another pleasant episode to the visit by contact with both officials and the people in other relations of both social and official life.

Mr. Livingston, the Congregational Minister, invited my husband to address his people, especially the young folks, on the next day (Sunday), upon the value of the Bible, as the Book of books, and the substance of the short address was summed up in this single paragraph:

"The Bible alone differs from all other historic books combined in that it consistently and satisfactorily explains the origin, the struggles, the capacities and the natural destiny of the human soul, as distinguished from the existence and activities of all other created life, and thus confirms the assurance of man in the certainty of a higher and lasting development beyond the grave."

On returning from Church, while seated on the
open piazza of our host, gazing upon Cloud Peak as
it glistened in the bright sunlight, he wrote the following impromptu recognition of the wonderful
panorama in view, dedicating the same to the
People of Sheridan through Mr. R. H. Walsh, President of the Chamber of Commerce, who at once
acknowledged the same with thanks and through
the press.

UNDER THE SHADOW OF CLOUD PEAK.

Piercing the sky with its snow-clad crest,
Pointing to Heaven—the Home of the Blest—
Beautiful Cloud Peak of the Big Horn Range,
Yields tales of the past, both thrilling and strange!

Fauna and Flora, and choicest of game,
Wild beast and red man, in choicest domain,
With purest of water ever at hand,
But waited the white man, all, to command!

He came at great cost of treasure and life,
With blessings for all, at end of the strife,
When wild beast and red man conquered at last,
Sweet peace must atone for pangs of the past!

Among other closing incidents of our Sheridan
visit was a ride accompanied by Judge Foster to the
famous coal mines established by Mr. Gould Dietz,
who was so kind to us at Omaha, and where, known
by his name, quite a town of cottages and gardens
accommodates the miners; and where, more than a
million of dollars has been expended in development
of that great industry.   From the single shaft No. 4,

twenty-five hundred tons of excellent coal, free from both sulphur and slate, were daily developed.

Here, also, we visited the little family of our veteran comrade, Dennis Driscoll, now a widower, who works in the mines, since leaving the army, and is highly respected by all who know of the service he rendered during the battle conflicts of the long ago.

As already noticed, Driscoll was one of the surviving veterans of the 18th U. S. Infantry, who shared with us in the official courtesies extended during the previous week. Unlike comrades Gibson, Peters, Murphy and Freeman, whose experiences were detailed by themselves, Driscoll did not feel able, in like manner, to detail his own self-sacrificing service in his old regiment, and under its colors. That service, however, so commanded the respect of all who knew him and its incidents, that Senator Warren and Congressman Mondell, as well as Captain (afterwards Brigadier-General) A. S. Burt, have already secured by an act of Congress, passed at its recent session, 1909, a comfortable pension in his behalf.

A brief outline of that service, justly his due, is epitomized by his old regimental commander as follows:

Driscoll came as a recruit from the Governor's Island recruiting rendezvous in New York Harbor, and joined the 18th Infantry at Fort Phil. Kearney in time to participate in many Indian skirmishes, being made a corporal in his company, and was one of the detachment which, on the 21st of December, 1866, was sent to support or rescue Fetterman's command.

He served his full term of enlistment in the 18th and, afterwards, in the 9th U. S. Infantry and the 2nd U. S. Cavalry, with credit, and was finally discharged from the service in 1881, at Fort Custer, South Dakota.

The second battalion of the 18th had become the 27th Infantry, and his Company, under Captain E. F. Thompson, was sent from Fort Phil. Kearney to Fort C. F. Smith with supplies.

On its return, along with Company A, they were attacked by a large Indian force which stampeded their mules, while in camp at night, at Trout (Fish) Creek. Immediate relief from Fort C. F. Smith was needed. Driscoll volunteered on the 3rd of June, and started under a heavy downpour of rain on his dangerous mission. Jack Reshaw, a half-breed French-Canadian Indian, loaned him his glasses, and a brace of Colt revolvers. He also carried a new Springfield rifle. The next morning what he supposed to be a herd of Buffalo turned out to be Indians. He brought down two of the Indians and, in return, his mule was shot. Lying down behind the mule and laying his rifle across his body, he again opened fire, which was very effective.

The Indians set fire to the grass and, under cover of its smoke, he crawled upon his stomach to higher ground, and by holding from one pine tree to another, he descended to a small stream but almost ran into an Indian camp-fire, receiving a slight wound in his right foot. He took with him two hundred rounds of ammunition and, behind a protecting rock, he opened fire. The Indians tried to carry off the body of one of their dead, but Driscoll's firing was so hot, and his position so invisible to them, that they rode away.

He struck out for Back Bone Mountain, from which place the fort could be seen, but being after "retreat" and the flag lowered, he could not exactly locate the fort.

Driscoll's own narrative, fully supported by competent testimony, shows that twice, at least, the Indians attempted his capture, and in one instance, an Indian, with a big head-dress, got so near his position that he was able to drop two of his little party, with a revolver.

He says, "I began to lose all sense of fear, and wanted to kill every Indian I could; every shot seemed to tell," "and they could not know that they were fighting only *one* soldier."

He had recognized the locality as at least near the fort and, by circling around, lame as he was, he struck the trail, usually that of wood parties from the fort, where he fainted dead away from exhaustion and loss of blood.

It is officially stated that "shortly afterwards a wood party from Fort C. F. Smith found his apparently lifeless body in the road, and recognized Corporal Driscoll at once. He was searched and his despatches were found, and he was then taken to the hospital. Upon return to consciousness, his first inquiry was, "whether Major Burt, then commanding the Post, had received his despatches;" and then he asked, "Where am I?" "Has the relief party gone?" Being assured that Burt himself had already started, he exclaimed, "Then, I wasn't too late, thank God!" and again relapsed into unconsciousness.

After six weeks in hospital he reached Fort Phil. Kearney, welcomed by the whole command, and borne into the fort itself upon the shoulders of his comrades.

After all the speech-making and use of tongue, literally, tribute should be rendered to the two newspapers of Sheridan, the *Post* and the *Enterprise,* which, metaphorically speaking, as of newspapers in general, are the *tongues* of the city, and nothing I could offer would more express the credit due the newspapers than the following quotation from a writer of another section, but equally applicable in the present instance.

In no other manner has American appreciation of the press as an agency for the promotion of mental, moral, and material prosperity been more clearly shown than in the prominent position given the same in nearly every advance of population and development of the great West. Closely associated with the school-house and church, co-operating therewith, the newspaper has gone as soon and often before the conditions gave reasonable assurance of even meagre support.

Its effectiveness has been recognized by the adventurous

investor of capital in local enterprises, no less than by those seeking any form of benefit from its presence.

These co-operating influences, stimulating the characteristic enterprise of printers, did much toward the early settlement of the West.

The story of this feature of pioneer experience, if fully recorded, would be one to place printers and publishers prominent in the list of sufferers of the early times. The value of the press as an agency led to its employment by the projectors and promoters of cities and towns whose "peculiar advantages" as to locations could not be made known without such a medium; and often the press and type went forward with the first shipment of goods to the chosen site in the new land of promise. In some cases the press was on the ground in advance of the school and the church.

The Sheridan *Post,* in communicating on the celebration while in the midst of it, has this word to say:

Sheridan is in the midst of one of the most important celebrations any section of the West has ever undertaken. The occasion is the visit of General and Mrs. Carrington. The progress of the northern Wyoming country is brought forcibly to the fore by contrasting the conditions that existed when they left this portion of Wyoming forty-two years ago, with the conditions that exist at present. In all these years northern Wyoming has been busy. They left the old fort on the Piney and the vast and fertile country to the mercy of a savage and relentless foe, at the order of the Government when it abandoned the project of establishing military outposts along the Bozeman trail. They return to one of the most magnificent farming and stock-growing sections in the world, where millions of coal are mined, where manufactures are prosecuted and big work of every kind carried on by a progressive, aggressive people.

Forty-two years is a short space of time in which to change a wilderness into a peaceful orderly Christian community, with churches and schools, and all other evidences of civilization at hand. This has all been accomplished. It is all here. It is a different Wyoming from that General and Mrs. Carrington bade farewell to in 1867, and took up their fearful journey through the deep snows to Fort Laramie.

To-day they were whirled to the Fetterman battlefield in automobiles and later viewed the parade ground of the old fort, now a productive alfalfa field.

Great have been the changes marked by the aged hero and heroine.

But not one thing has caused them to marvel so much as the city itself.

The impressions our guests had were of the ancient day, of a vast expanse without the sign of habitation. To be ushered into a modern city, to be driven over its well-kept streets, to view its magnificent buildings and observe its industrious, happy people at their daily toil, engaged in the very occupations that have made the country great and prosperous, both surprised and delighted our distinguished guests.

The message of the *Enterprise,* here transcribed, came in the aftermath of the celebration:

The newspapers of Sheridan are entitled to much credit for the big crowds that came here and participated in the Carrington reunion and Fourth of July Celebration. They did their duty, and more, in giving wide publicity, weeks in advance, to the affair.

The Enterprise not only printed columns and columns about it, but, through its editor, was instrumental in having newspapers of Billings and many other cities devote considerable space to the programme arranged by local citizens, without cost to the Chamber of Commerce or any one else in Sheridan. This work was productive of results, too, and we are not too modest to mention it.

Incidentally, the newspapers are not given credit for many things of a creditable nature due them. While they are not in business for their health altogether, as some people seem to regard them, the fact is that few if any of the various mercantile and industrial institutions of the country give so freely of their valuable assets as do the newspapers, whose principal asset is the space for advertising. "Then why not give newspapers proper credit?"

The closing query "Why not give newspapers proper credit?" is forestalled by the lengthy quotation which expresses appreciation of the work and influence of the press in general, and pointedly of the local press in particular; not precisely parallel with the play of Hamlet, with Hamlet left out, as the old saying goes, but while there would have been a play, possibly, it would have lacked much of value, without its agency.

The conclusion of the matter would resolve itself, in epigrammatic form, as a last analysis, "It pays to advertise."

All these reminiscences of the long ago and of the contrasting conditions in 1908 are mingled with the pathetic story of the rapid disappearance of the red man from his ancestral haunts of domestic experience, both as a huntsman and warrior. With the possible exception of the Delaware, Mohegan, Narragansett, and the Six Nations at the north; the Cherokee, Choctaw, Seminole, and Chickasaw of the south; and the Blackfeet, Arapahoe, Apache, Flathead, and others of the farther west, there has rarely been a more characteristic fatality than among the tribes that so stubbornly resisted the occupation of the Big Horn country by the white man. The controlling masters of this special region, at first, were the Crow Indians; and this tribe, like the Flatheads of Montana, even as far back as the expedition of Lewis and Clarke, under President Jefferson, were always friends of the white man; and this, largely through the early visitations of such enterprising and devoted missionaries as Ravelli, St. Regis, and De Smedt.

The Crows had the vantage ground, in locality, and their wars were almost invariably those of defense against the rapacity and plundering of their more numerous foes, the Northern Sioux.

The Laramie Conference of 1866 had for its purpose to annul the Harney-Sanborne Treaty of 1865, which left the Big Horn region in the control of the Sioux; but it is not to be forgotten that the Sioux themselves had stolen it from the Crow Indians, and the latter were among the most ardent well-wishers of the success of the Carrington Expedition of 1866; and many of the Sioux, themselves, were beginning to realize that their occupation had been one of force, and not of inherent right.

Red Cloud, although invited to join in the Celebration of 1908, declined in kind but most pathetic terms, as to his physical blindness and the fact that ''nearly all his braves had passed away.''

Another character identified with the expedition of 1866 will bear further mention. I refer to the venerable trapper, scout, and pioneer, James Bridger, who had married a Crow woman and had been adopted as one of their chiefs, then quite advanced in age, whom General Carrington had been able to hire as his Chief Guide, and whose experience and advice was always respected, except by those who had contempt for the Indian as an adversary, and counted the old man as behind the times in modern artillery art. To us women, Bridger was always a patient listener, a kind adviser, and sympathetic as if we were children, looking at him as one of our safest champions in hours of danger. He visited the Crows, by orders of General Carrington, and brought back valuable information as to the strength of the hostile Sioux, as "about 3000 in lodges," and "all ready under any trusted leader to wage an exterminating war against the expedition that had been so rapidly protected by a stockade which the Indians regarded impossible to take by storm."

The failure of the Government to support this strong position and its connections with its Laramie base, culminated ten years later in the Custer Massacre. It appears from the Appendix of Brady's "Indian Fights and Fighters," that before that gallant officer started for the west to beg of General Terry that he might command the concentrated battalions of his regiment during the sickness of Colonel Smith, he attended a meeting of the New York Historical Society, in that city, at which General Carrington had delivered an address, and at the close Custer emphatically made this declaration, "It will take another Phil. Kearney massacre before the Government will understand that only an overwhelming force can end this savage frontier war," and added, "if I get leave to go, in spite of Grant's opposition, I will go into it and die, if necessary, to vindicate myself and bring it to an end."

Eventually the two great divisions of the Sioux,

the Brule and the Ogallalla, the former friendly
under Spotted Tail, and the other hostile, under Red
Cloud, were brought into separate Reservations,
and after the final conflict with Sitting Bull, new
conditions had so largely obtained that no general
Indian war was possible.

New railroads, as well as new mining trails and
localities, had so occupied the territory by easy
transit of the whites and mutual support in case of
need that, with the incidental disappearance of game,
the Indians could not travel from north to south and
return without meeting a white civilization that compelled them to fight, retreat, or starve.

The white man had come to stay. The red man
had to leave or submit.

All the contest that survived the Fetterman massacre had its climax through the succeeding Custer
massacre, until an adequate military force, as well
as the causes already mentioned, secured perpetual
freedom from any possible combination of Indians
to impede the white man's secure possession and
peaceful development.

It was not until Sitting Bull and Red Cloud protracted a war that should have been fought to an end
from the first, that we find the Crows once more,
though under constrained conditions, the peaceful
occupants, in part, of their ancestral domain; and
within their immediate surroundings is the National
Cemetery, where the victims of both the Fetterman
and the Custer massacre lie at rest. It is certainly
a peculiar condition that attends their present envi-

ronment. The following recent newspaper clipping
has decided significance:

> A wedding ceremony was one of the most prominent features
> of the Arapahoe Indian festivities given in honor of their
> visiting kinsmen from Oklahoma and other States last Sunday at
> the lodge about three miles below Riverton. The bride was the
> comely daughter of the great warrior Shakespeare, and grand-
> daughter of Scar Face, one of the oldest " Raps " on the Reserva-
> tion, having passed the century mark. The groom was the stalwart
> brave, " Big Tracks," a grand specimen of a once mighty race.

All the peculiar athletic sports and discipline
that once gave vigor to their physical prowess now
find their counterpart in the games and athletics of
their white neighbors; and even their dances, races,
and other characteristic sports are alike enjoyed by
all, the white man also becoming expert in the use
of the lariat in all capture of game or wild horses,
as was the Indian of olden times.

Even with all this, the touching appeals of celebrated warriors, as far back as the days of Logan,
now and then come to our ears with a tender pathos
not unlike that of the ancient Hebrew when in
captivity:

> If I forget thee, O Jerusalem, let my right hand forget her
> cunning. If I do not remember thee, let my tongue cleave to the
> roof of my mouth; if I prefer not Jerusalem above my chief
> joy!

Such an appeal is that of Curley, Reno Crow, one
of Custer's scouts, uttered more than a year ago at
a Council held in October, 1907, in reference to opening the Crow Reservation itself to general sale.

The following is the text of the speech, furnished by the courtesy of Mr. Herbert Coffeen of Sheridan City for our use:

> I am a friend to General Custer.
>
> I was one of his scouts and will say a few words.
>
> The Great Father in Washington sent you here about this land.
>
> The soil you see is not ordinary soil. It is the dust of the blood, the flesh and bones of our ancestors.
>
> We fought and bled and died to keep other Indians from taking it, and we fought and bled and died, helping the whites.
>
> You will have to dig through the surface before you can find Nature's earth, as the upper portion is Crow.
>
> The land as it is, is my blood, and my dead; it is consecrated, and I do not want to give up any portion of it.

And thus it is that the people of Sheridan and the entire Big Horn country, above all other western spheres of original Indian activity, are identified with localities and historic scenes that make their home surroundings almost as classic as those about Concord, Massachusetts, itself.

One Sheridan paper has this patriotic and humane prediction: "The time ought to come before many years, and will come, if the present policy is carried out, when the Indians will have the same rights and duties as other Americans, and will live as they do."

The pictures of the late scenes were as negatives encased in the mind awaiting further development.

Changing the metaphor to that of the stage, on taking up the agreeable task of presenting the little drama, the majestic snow-crowned mountains, dashing mountain streams, smiling fields, flower gardens, and pleasant homes, afforded a unique background for the scenes as the actors appeared on the stage; for the setting was unchanged since late arrival.

In the shifting, some scenes are sombre, others more pleasing; yet the situations were real, and if for the title of the little drama, "Then and Now," be apparently insignificant and not in itself distinctive or suggestive, although dramatized from the story covering a period of many years, its gaps and continuities certainly justify the title.

The curtain descends before those scenes, never again to be uplifted except in grateful memory.

On the "drop curtain" we would see no fanciful or mythological pictures of scenes unrelated to the present, but would as vividly see a large city, perhaps not one of towering buildings, but one of many, conservative in proportion, with larger churches, more commodious school-houses, and one especially attractive building, on which upon closer scrutiny would be seen the cabalistic letters Y. M. C. A., citizens wending their way to the different railroad stations, a city teeming with life, extended in perspective beyond the limit of the canvas.

And yet, amid all the exuberance of our welcome and the characteristic enthusiasm of western people in the midst of Nature's most prolific bounty, beauty and grandeur, there full often comes to mind a very sober as well as tender conviction that our own brief function of solemn and almost heart-rending service during the constrained, forcible opening of the original, historic Bozeman Trail to such a realization

of glad and even redundant fruition, was only that
of simply unlatching a door for an intelligent and
progressive generation to grasp eagerly and firmly,
that it might with something like a fabulous inspiration develop, through the exposed wealth of a new
Promised Land, certain possibilities they had
already discounted; so that, in very fact, their faith
and nerve, more than mere military force, achieved
for Wyoming its brilliant destiny.

Even with such faith and nerve, they could not
have fully realized in advance all the lonely conditions of peopling a strange country, where both
savage man and more savage beast had to be both
faced and fought to subjection, or extermination, before peaceful occupation could be assured.

When the memory of our visit in 1908, as compared with the march in 1866, commingles their experiences, we begin to realize how slow and arduous
must have been the pioneer's advance along lines of
development that have already so glorified their
Christian civilization and commanded the respect of
the world.

Our own trials were indeed many, and they were
not shared by those in authority who sent the expedition of 1866, as on a summer jaunt, expecting
it to fatten upon the treasure of the west without
pain or penalty. But when families made the venture in the belief that they would be fully protected,
and speedily learned, by most bitter experience, that
every home cabin must be a self-protecting fortress,
we can only magnify the energy and courage, as well
as faith of that generation until we largely minimize

our own sad experience, and fain would tender back the laurels so freely given by a generous people, who, by themselves, improved their own opportunities to an extent which no armed force could have so placidly and richly assured, as the deserved guerdon of their protracted struggle.

They had to fight an Alpine climate as well as the brutal savage and wild beast before a single generation could even begin to dwell at peace.

It certainly was a wonderful experience, upon reaching Wyoming, to find catalogued, the first settler; the first cabin; the first merchant; and the first physician. The first school and the first church had proud notice, and even the first horse, the first cow, and the first plow had a history, with the name of its original owner.

In a special edition of the Sheridan *Enterprise,* May 1, 1908 (of which Mr. F. H. Barrow was the champion editor), known as the Sheridan Women's Club Edition, are pictorial and biographical features that fully exemplify Sheridan origin and development. It is certainly pertinent here to notice Mr. J. D. Loucks, President of the Sheridan School Board, born in New York, and in the 6th Iowa Cavalry during the Civil War, who laid out Sheridan, and gave names to its principal streets in 1882; also Hon. Oliver Perry Hanna, the first settler, who built the first cabin, and who was recently elected treasurer, by a combined vote of both political parties; also Henry A. Coffeen, who first settled at Big Horn, and thus became a pioneer merchant, who laid out a great portion of Sheridan itself; also Mr. Lyman M. Brooks, one of the founders of the Bank of Commerce, who made the first real estate deal in Sheridan and donated the site of the present county house to Sheridan County.

These and others incidentally mentioned in our narrative have all held city, county, State or congressional positions, in response to popular choice. Judge Foster who first tilled the old Phil. Kearney parade ground, has been elsewhere mentioned.

Throughout our American Republic, there are societies that treat with reverence and honor those of its founders from whom descent can be traced, but in Wyoming and other recent States of the West the very founders themselves survive, until nearly three generations are participant in a truthful verbal narration of personal struggles and victories that have matured the present abiding peace.

And so, at last, we returned to our New England home, with ever deepening appreciation of the generous western welcome of July, 1908, and the abiding conviction that these latest States, born out of the original Northwest, have been the fruition of local domestic energies, because the germs of these triumphs were of ancestral stock and partook of the heritage which had been divinely vouchsafed to the descendants of those who first planted the American Republic upon the western shores of the mighty Atlantic Sea.